LEAVES OF THE TULIP TREE

To My Sons
Anthony and Francis

There is a legend I heard a long time ago of Eve, joyful in the Garden of Eden, until she was tempted by the Serpent to eat of the Tree of Life. The day came when the Lord expelled Adam and Eve from their Paradise, placing at the east of the Garden Cherubims and a flaming sword to keep them away from the Tree of Life.

With their sword of flame, the angels drove out the unhappy pair and from every bush, every tree, Eve tried to snatch a branch or a flower. She only succeeded in snatching a small piece of the leaf of the tulip tree and you can see for yourself today, the tree never replaced the small tip of its uniquely shaped leaf, although the veins still branch towards the missing tip.

I have always loved the tulip tree and I have tried in this book to search for the tips of the leaves.

LEAVES
OF THE
TULIP TREE

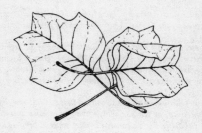

AUTOBIOGRAPHY

Juliette Huxley

Oxford New York
OXFORD UNIVERSITY PRESS
1987

Oxford University Press, Walton Street, Oxford OX2 6DP

Oxford New York Toronto
Delhi Bombay Calcutta Madras Karachi
Petaling Jaya Singapore Hong Kong Tokyo
Nairobi Dar es Salaam Cape Town
Melbourne Auckland
and associated companies in
Beirut Berlin Ibadan Nicosia

Oxford is a trade mark of Oxford University Press

First published 1986 by John Murray (Publishers) Ltd.
First issued as an Oxford University Press paperback 1987

British Library Cataloguing in Publication Data
Huxley, Juliette
Leaves of the tulip tree: autobiography.
1. Huxley, Julian 2. Huxley, Juliette
3. Biologists — Great Britain —
Biography 4. Biologists' wives —
Great Britain — Biography
5. Bloomsbury group
I. Title
942.082'092'4 QH31.H88
ISBN 0-19-282095-8

Printed in Great Britain by
The Guernsey Press Co. Ltd.
Guernsey, Channel Islands

CONTENTS

ILLUSTRATIONS

1 Myself aged about 34

2 T.H. Huxley, his son Leonard and grandson Julian

3 Julian with Anthony and Francis, Oxford 1923

4 Lady Ottoline Morrell at Bedford Square about 1912

5 Mme Baillot, Frieda, D.H. Lawrence and Anthony at Diablerets, 1928–9

6 H.G. Wells, his son Gip and Julian, working on *The Science of Life* at Wells's home, 1927

7 Anthony and Francis on London Zoo postcard

8 Julian and Myself circa 1940

9 Julian and pelicans at the London Zoo

10 The Brains Trust (circa 1942): Julian, Sir Gilbert Murray and Sir William Beveridge

11 Looking for gorilla in Uganda, 1960

12 Julian's first party as Director-General of Unesco, in Paris, 1946; with Walter Laves, Assistant Director-General, and his wife from USA

13 Julian and Aldous, circa 1950 (Photo: W. Suschitzky)

14 Myself (Photo: W. Suschitzky)

AUTHOR'S NOTE

During the slow production of these pages, several kind friends read the script and encouraged me warmly to continue. Among them, Sybille Bedford, Naomi Mitchison, both my sons Anthony and Francis, Selma Huxley Barkham, Julian and Mary Trevelyan, Renée Tickell and Elspeth Huxley. I am deeply grateful for their valued encouragement. Frederick Wolsey and John Moorehead repaired my Franglais with great patience and delicacy. The most precious stimulus, guidance and enduring support all through was given to me by our good friend, Jock Murray, who now publishes the final version. In more ways than one, I can now say that without him, this book would never have been finished.

More thanks are due to Stephen Tennant, who allows me to print a perceptive vision of Ottoline Morrell; to Laura Huxley for permission to quote Aldous; to the executors of Leonard Elmhirst for permission to use his letter to me; to Julian Vinogradov for permission to quote from Ottoline Morrell's journal; to Valerie Eliot for permission to quote a few lines from T.S. Eliot's poems; to Richard Hoggart; to W. Suschitzky for his photographs and to all authors or executors who allowed citations from their books.

⋆   ⋆   ⋆

Many of Julian's papers and scientific books are no longer here at Pond Street; they were bought by Rice University, Texas, where he spent three years as Professor of Biology (1913–1916). In 1984, I attended the opening of the Julian Huxley Archives at the University and found a wonderful documentation of his life's work. With money from the sale of these papers and books and with the generous contributions of individuals and groups, anxious that Julian's achievements and aims should not be forgotten, a Memorial Fellowship was established at Balliol College, Oxford, the Alma Mater of three generations of Huxleys.

I

Swiss Childhood

Each generation must translate for itself
T.S. ELIOT

As a child I often sent myself to sleep thinking of space before the world began – a void of space, an unlimited feeling of an enormous absence devouring my imagination – yet already containing the presage of creation. Then followed a wall of mud, dark, threatening, engulfing, from which I woke afraid and confused, wondering what it was all about, what it really meant. It was a secret experience, born within myself, shared with no one. I never found an answer. To think now, in this context, of my own self seems presumptuous – an infinitesimal point of reference in the vast panorama of human lives. It is my own personal precinct, built of what my memory can recall of my pilgrimage to try and discover what I am – and also what Julian was.

I was born on 6 December 1896, in the small fishing village of Auvernier on Lake Neuchâtel in Switzerland. My father had gone out with two guests who had come to supper, leaving my mother, as they thought, still a few days before her labour. But I jumped the gun and it all happened very suddenly. I was born with no assistance, or need of slapping to make my first complaint about life. In my unseemly hurry, I was also born wearing a caul, a membrane usually split off at birth. Sailors in old days paid large sums to possess these bits of skin, meant to save them from drowning. Special luck was rumoured to await the babe as well.

My brother Alexandre was two and a half years older. Our father was a budding solicitor in Neuchâtel, and rode to his office on a penny-farthing bicycle. His life was pursued by ill luck. An orphan from an early age, he was brought up by Oncle Emile, who became my beloved godfather. Oncle Emile was a vineyard owner and lived at Bôle. He sent my father to school where, among other things, he learnt to write with a beautiful copper-plate script. This led Oncle Emile to suggest to his cousin, the notaire Baillot of Boudry, to take my father into his office and train him.

I cannot resist the Balzacian legend of this man. He was the only notary of the district, depository of many family secrets, and became a very rich man. He had two daughters and a son, Charles – a tall young man, groomed to succeed his father. But Charles developed inoperable cancer of the throat. He had been kind to young Alphonse, my father, during his apprenticeship; it was a hard time for the youth, who was paid five francs a month out of which he had to buy his clothes and some of his food and was always hungry and cold. It was now Alphonse who looked after Charles as the illness progressed; it was also he who ran after and pacified Charles's mother, desperate with anxiety for her son and determined to cut out the growing cancer with a kitchen knife.

Charles made a will in which he left my father enough capital to go to Neuchâtel and study Law. He died and the will disappeared. (I was told by an old friend of my mother's at Boudry that when the notaire died, the undertakers ran away from his corpse which had turned black. They said the devil had a hand in it.) My father was given Charles's shirts which were much too large for him. However, in time he opened his own solicitor's office, having learnt enough of the profession during a long training.

He married Mélanie Antonia Ortlieb, herself a citizen of Boudry, the eldest daughter of a large family; her father, Anton, was Maître-Ferblantier, a title dating back to the age of guilds, conferring a certain prestige. I never knew him, for he died at forty-seven, when the lower part of Boudry was flooded one winter by the Areuse, a turbulent river threading its way through a spectacular gorge. Many people were marooned by this freak flood. My grandfather set out with others in small boats to rescue those in danger. He caught pneumonia and died soon after.

His photograph shows a distinguished long face with a high forehead and dark hair and a pointed beard. His special achievement was that he invented the first washing machine, called a '*couleuse*'. It was a large inverted zinc cone in the centre of which stood a tube ending under a spraying hood. The water heated by a fire at its base rose up into the tube and cascaded over the tubful of clothes, and then rose again in a sort of perpetual motion. The *couleuse* was a great success, and the workshop a busy place. Unfortunately he never applied for a patent and so gained neither fortune nor recognition.

Anton Ortlieb's premature death left his pretty, young and vivacious wife with a heavy burden, for there was the expanding and busy workshop which her four sons were too young to control. My mother, then aged about sixteen, being the eldest, had charge of the two youngest children, Ferdinand (who later became as gifted as an inventor as he was skilled as a tinsmith), and a small sister, Juliette. Deprived of the enjoyment of her youthful years by the family's changed situation, my mother took her responsibilities seriously and, according to her younger sister, became very strict with the small children. Somehow, my grandmother managed to keep going, but it must have been a time of great difficulties.

Tante Juliette, as she became known after many years, adventurously left home at an early age, choosing to learn dressmaking at a famous Paris house. She had a natural gift for her profession and the capacity for hard work. She created her own 'salon' in London, and became a fashionable designer. She was, to my brother and myself, a glamorous figure, descending on our simple home like a fairy godmother, enveloped in delicious scent and impetuous charm. I remember her wearing exquisite white dresses made in her own maison, long flowing with many little lacy flounces, a

Nattier-blue ribbon matching her bright blue eyes, bringing lovely gifts. We cherished her with admiration and gratitude. I was named after her and received from her much loving kindness and understanding.

★   ★   ★

My parents started their married life at Auvernier, in a wisteria-covered old house. Later they moved to Neuchâtel, to be near my father's office. I was perhaps about three when I was put in a waggon carrying our belongings – the horse and the day live in my memory. I also remember bathing in the lake for the first time, carried in my mother's arms. She walked steadily into the water, which rose higher and higher at each step; filled with terror, I scrambled ever further up from her arms, till I found a precarious perch on top of her head, screaming my head off.

In Neuchâtel we lived opposite a small public garden called Le Jardin Anglais. My mother took us there to play and to feed the deer and hinds in their paddock. I was known as '*la p'tite Anglaise*' even though I have not a drop of English blood in my veins. I think it was simply because Tante Juliette sent us pretty clothes from London. She also sent a pair of turquoise stud ear-rings for me which my mother made me wear. One night my hair tangled in the small pin and tore the lobe of my ear. For months afterwards the little tear cracked open when I laughed until my mother took us to stay with her aunt in the Oberland.

This sister of my grandmother was a 'wise woman', famous for her healing powers, blood-letting, laying-on of hands, midwifery and wide herbal knowledge. How I wish I could meet her now and learn her ancient lore. At that time I only saw a short, kind person who seemed very old (she was then between forty and fifty). She noticed that I had a recurring stye, so when the moon was full she took me on her knee on three successive nights, said something incomprehensible to an awed child of five, and stroked my eyes with a gold ring. I have never had a stye since. Then she decided that I should have the lobe of my ear sewn up and took me to the doctor to have a stitch put in. My brother Alex was watching from the gallery, which ran round the chalet, and fainted when he saw the 'operation'. I had been promised a local headkerchief if I was good, and he got one as well, for fainting. I remember feeling very sore about this.

My mother, Alex and I slept in the attic of my great-aunt's chalet. Drying herbs hung from the beams and we slept on the floor. To reach it we had to climb a ladder and push open a trap door. Alex and I discovered we could hide up there during the patients' consultations and watch the ever fascinating process of 'cupping' which the 'wise woman' practised on naked backs: the blood was sucked up into small glass hoods heated with the light of a candle and taken off when cool, leaving a pattern of red discs on the skin.

There was a lot of coming and going round the chalet, presents of eggs and fowl and vegetables were brought by grateful patients, for my great-aunt never took money for her work. All sorts of people came to her. She was well known, far and wide. Years later, when my first child was to be born, my mother came to Oxford to give a hand and brought me a small tin of white powder sent specially by my great-aunt. This powder, she said, would make childbirth easy and painless. I never did take it, as between the doctor and the monthly nurse I felt it might create complications. Therefore, in due time, as it was apparently very precious, my mother took it back to the Oberland. And so, alas, I shall never know what the magic was. Nor, I fear, will I ever find out more about the 'wise woman' who was my grandmother's sister; I did go back there between the wars, climbing the rugged path to a chalet they told me had been hers. It looked small at the foot of the high mountain within a green valley. Nothing was left of my childish vision, my private legend. But I have always felt that something of her faith in herbs, her link with the moon, her knowledge and interest in healing ways had descended to me from her blessed hands. And curiously and more actively to my son Francis.

*　　　*　　　*

My father had a partner, a man called Henrioux. All went well with the office up to the time of military service, a few weeks a year, when my father rejoined his regiment as is customary in Switzerland. All responsibility was left in the hands of the partner. This man absconded with all the available moneys, rents, negotiable securities, etc. owned by clients. A great disaster: Henrioux disappeared into France. My father promised the clients that every penny would be repaid, and so it was, over many years, except for the last £40, owed to Tante Juliette. This debt was 'bequeathed' to me to settle when I should come to earn my living.

We moved to a cheaper place, a garden flat at l'Evole, where my gallant mother took *pensionnaires*, taught various handicrafts at which she was excellent, as well as devoting herself to the German-Swiss teenagers who came to learn French. These, to me, were tiresome and stupid girls who absorbed all my mother's attention and time. The disaster brought out in her a fighting spirit, a magnificent practical fortitude and, inevitably, divided loyalties.

My father became remote, unapproachable and rather frightening. He found a job in the *Compagnie des Tramways* and spent all his evenings at his club. He rarely talked to us children, and his sole parental duties consisted in dealing out punishment for bad marks at school; Alex and I had plenty: mine especially for impertinence, his mostly for bad work. My mother often told me I was tactless but she never explained what the word really meant. I did, I know, say what came into my head, never stopping to think beforehand. The *pensionnaires* were very touchy, and did not like being laughed at.

I secretly adored my father and longed to be able to show him my love. One day, I had the marvellous joy of being asked by him to fetch the keys he thought he might have left in the lock of the garden gate. I rushed off full of hope and searched, desperately, feeling so much depended on my being successful in this errand. I hunted in vain, and at last went slowly back to report my failure. 'Poisson d'Avril!' he laughed.

This part of my childhood was odd. We were very poor because every centime had to be saved to pay The Debt. We never went out, we never had any guests or parties. My mother's Calvinistic streak ruled the house; the very armchairs were never to be sat in, but stood in silent conspiracy to give the place a feeble prestige. We were allowed one book from the school library and, if caught reading it out of time, ran the risk of having it confiscated. Food had to be good for the *pensionnaires*, but we were often warned not to ask for a second helping in case *they* did not get enough. My mother practised prodigious economies, making, mending and using every scrap of anything with a masochistic expediency.

I remember that apartment in every detail; the very thick bare limestone walls; the wide hall between the rooms opening on either side; the dark passage at the bottom, leading on one side to a lavatory and, opposite, to a bedroom which in turn opened into a sort of box-room with a small window. Usually Alex and I slept in this bedroom, but I remember one night when I was there alone and heard in the dark silence a sort of heavy groan, repeated three times. I leapt out of bed and ran, shaking, to the front room where my mother was sitting. And this is where she gave me the best lesson I ever had: 'Let us go and see,' she said, and took me by the hand. With a candle flickering in the draught, we opened the little box-room and peered in. Of course there was nothing, just a few valises and packing cases. 'Always go and see' – this has been a valuable guide-line all through my life, against the night-terrors to which I was prone.

My mother had transformed the hall, once stark with its flagged stone floor and doorways, into a warm living place of moderate comfort with a glowing stove, carpets, hangings and lamps. It opened on to a large verandah and steps went down into a garden of two quite separate parts: the first had flower-beds, a great lime-tree, a grass pelouse. A stone wall and three steps separated that from the lower part, where apples, pears and even figs ripened, enclosing a patch of rank grass; at the very end grew an old poplar tree near the garden gate by the edge of the lake road. My mother contrived to keep rabbits in one of the wood-sheds, and trimmed my winter coats with their fur. We ate the rabbits without compunction.

The lane leading to the wood-sheds ended in the dark opening of a real tunnel, rightly called '*le souterrain*'. This had become the repository for all the junk of the inmates of the house. We children decided one holiday afternoon to excavate it and to reach the Château of Valangin rumoured to be connected with it. Piling up the rusty prams, mattresses, and unclassified rubbish, we reached a brick wall about thirty metres on, blocking further exploration. My father arrived at this point, made us put everything back, and handed us to his wife for a good spanking. But what was this *souterrain*? It haunted our thoughts, but never revealed its secret.

In summer we lived mostly out of doors, using the verandah as an extension to the hall. We children had a tree-house in the bee-singing lime-tree, and the branches were hung with bird-cages where my mother nursed fledglings fallen from nests, brought to her by friends. She had a magic touch with them, and they flew happily as soon as their wings could carry them.

On the tussocky grass a croquet set had been planted. No sooner had we gobbled our meal than Alex and I, together with the children who lived in the flat above us, rushed out to a fierce game of croquet. The hoops were arched invitations to the wildest shots and cheats. We fought each game with rapturous animosity, and only stopped within seconds of having to leave for school or bedtime. The worst punishment we could suffer was to be forbidden to play.

Yet above all, I loved the lake possessively. I watched its every mood, its turbulence, its white horses, its satiny pale-blue peace, reflecting the gambolling clouds. As soon as the bathing season started I was in the water every day – learning to swim. The Swiss lakes are now so polluted that one is no longer allowed to swim in their waters – an enchantment nothing will ever replace.

In winter we lived cosily gathered round the big table in the hall. My mother busy with her pillow-lace, deftly moving the bobbins (little carved sticks holding the linen thread, with a hollow wooden sheath to protect it), pinning down the criss-cross weave with long steel pins anchored in the cardboard design strip wound round the sausage-like cushion. She was teaching the *pensionnaires*: 'Croisez, épingle, passez fuseaux de gauche. . .' the litany went on and the stupid girls got into stupid muddles. Just hearing the ritual I picked up the craft and soon qualified for a lace-pillow of my own. It was a soothing occupation and I enjoyed endowing my bobbins with obedience to the power inherent in the pattern of the lace. My mind wandered into patterns of life itself, incongruously linking them with the dumb tools in my hands. Through this work my starved fantasy seemed to find an outlet.

Winter also brought its special joys with snow and ice. Rushing home from school, we seized our sledges and slid down steep streets generally free of traffic, as few horses could be trusted over frozen surfaces. There was a dangerous slide which led straight to the railway lines on the brink of the lake. Having savoured the brush of fear, one dug one's heels in to brake at the very last moment.

One very severe winter the lake froze right over its eastern end. I was given my first pair of skates, then clumsy blades of steel attached to criss-cross moveable metal strips which were fastened to the boots with clips and leather thongs. These had a tiresome habit of coming undone, just in the middle of long sweeps. In those days few attempted ambitious figure-skating; we just covered the ground like birds in flight, with the keen joy of speed and conquest over this new mode of transport. We had a good friend, son of M. Suchard, the chocolate king.

He stretched out a long rope which we gripped with eager hands, then led his serpentine band of youngsters far out over the grey-blue crackling ice.

The site at nearby La Tène had been discovered in 1856 and identified as a fifth-century BC cradle of Celtic culture. How I wish we had known this; it would have lent wings to our imagination. (It is now a popular beach in summer, with coca-cola booths and brown bodies stretched out worshipping the sun.)

Chaumont, rising just behind Neuchâtel, provided a wonderful playground for practising skiing. Climbing the 1300 metres or so by *funiculaire* we hired skis from the Grand Hotel, built up a ramp and threw ourselves into the air – to land sometimes upright, on a gentle slope of snow.

My brother had contrived to build a bobsleigh; the winding road was noisy with the clamour of fast descending bobs. As a great concession, he allowed me to sit at the rear and to work the hooter which I pumped assiduously, greatly fearing disaster. All this had to happen without my father knowing of it, specially as I was forbidden to wear my brother's trousers. As if one could go skiing or tobogganing in a skirt! He never found out, so, luckily, we avoided his wrath. In those days, he seemed bent on exercising a strange tyranny of restrictions, to us incomprehensible, and therefore resented.

My mother was petite, neat, pretty and gay; too practical to be very feminine (like Tante Juliette who was alluringly so), never idle and never ill. She used her hands in a great variety of handicrafts such as surface-sculpting and also, much in vogue at the time, what was called pyrogravure, done with a small platinum heated point at the end of a pencil-like handle, decorating flat surfaces of wood (Victorian arts long since discarded). She also later learnt the art-work known as metalloplastie – and taught it to us and to her pupils: the metal was a thin sheet of malleable tin spread in reverse on a soft surface, and with a small curved tool modelled to almost any design, mostly leaves and flowers, adding little beads of coloured glass for fruit; it was then filled in with plasticine, to preserve the moulding, and fitted over frames and caskets, serviette rings and useless paraphernalia cluttering the rooms. This was delicate work, absorbing the long winter evenings as we gathered under the lamp. I became skilful at it and remember enjoying the work, more than the eternal cross-stitch I was set to do before I could indulge my own ploys. I felt mentally corseted as physically I was, having to wear a stiff back-piece hitched to my shoulders by loops round the arm-pits: to keep my back straight.

As the *chanson* has it, '*Les enfants s'ennuient le dimanche*', and in fact so do grown-ups. Boredom is a universal malady, and Isaac Watts rightly wrote:

> In work of labour or of skill
> I should be busy too
> For Satan finds some mischief still
> For idle hands to do.

Maybe my mother was right to impose handwork as the universal remedy. Ethnologists now call it 'displacement activity' as it exists in the animal world – a bit of grooming, of feeding, of preening, to lessen emotional tensions. And so she filled the idle hours by exploiting the skill of hands, by teaching them useful tricks and giving them important functions. Gratefully, now, I salute my nimble hands, which have given me so much reward and many creative joys.

My mother was a born teacher, her pupils adored her, confiding their troubles to her for her wise advice. Somehow she did not seem deeply interested in *my* troubles, though she loved me and I loved and feared her as the centre of my universe. With the constant and heavy demands made upon her which she considered it her duty to fulfil, perhaps she just could not include me among her charges. In fact, as soon as I became a teenager, she relied on me to write her business letters, according to my lights.

She read few books, as she lacked time for such distraction

and did not encourage us in what she considered a waste of time as well as a dangerous occupation for the young. And, among books, the one she most objected to our reading was the Old Testament. She kept it out of reach, and when we had to look up a text for school work, watched like an eagle that we did not stray. She just did not think it '*convenable*'; she thought it improper. For my mother was prudish to the last degree, never mentioned sex in any form, nor any of the facts of life.

Yet, although to be *convenable* was her guiding principle, she had very curious opinions as to what a child could put up with by defying convention. Somewhere in the family we had a relation who became a *diaconesse* (hospital nurse) in Turkey. I wish I knew more about her, but she was never mentioned after marrying a Turk. She once came to visit us, and presented us children with a Turkish fez. We had to wear this unusual headgear to go to school, and pretended not to be aware of the amused stares of the good Neuchâtelois. We also at one time had to wear the Scottish glengarries sent by Tante Juliette. My brother conveniently lost his unconventional headgear, but I was more docile, and went through with the ordeal.

On Sunday afternoons, if Alex and I had not been punished by being kept in copying hundreds of lines, we were taken, together with the *pensionnaires*, for long walks in the Jura mountains, to Chaumont, to the Gorges de l'Areuse, to the Château de Valangin. This last one was a great favourite: a medieval castle perched on the Gorge du Seyon. There was a torture chamber on the top where prisoners spent their last night. They then had to stand against a post to have their skulls smashed by a beam. There were also what they called '*oubliettes*', just a well opening on the Seyon far below into which miscreants were thrown, hacked to pieces by projecting knives before reaching the bottom. These places had a horribly frightening fascination for us, and usually gave me nightmares for weeks after. But the afternoon was crowned by a splendid *goûter* at the patisserie, where we devoured *cornets à la crème* of remembered deliciousness. On the way back we generally took the high road above the gorge, a steep climb concealing its descent. Not knowing that the Earth was round, I was certain that this was the point from which we dropped into nothingness – and clung to my mother's hand for reassurance.

Jean-Jacques Rousseau once stayed at the Champ du Moulin, a lonely farm at the head of the river Areuse. We knew practically nothing about him, but he had become a tribal hero and we visited his shrine. Trout play in the shallows before the river grinds its rocky bed through a narrow gorge, between high cliffs. At that point we walked on a path cut out of sheer rock, above the coil of the dark, massively urgent element. Incidentally, it was this same Areuse, tamed at Boudry, which turned my grandfather's engines to shape the *couleuses* he had invented.

Another of Jean-Jacques' refuges was the Ile de St Pierre on the lake of Bienne. A leisurely voyage in the steamer took us there, through the reed-fringed link between the lakes. It was a charming pilgrimage to the only farm in the place, boasting the desk where possibly he wrote *La Nouvelle Héloïse*. He also loved botanising and delighted in the rich flora of the Jura, visiting his friend Du Peyrou above Cressier, in what Rousseau called 'un salon sur la montagne'. The house, Bellevue, became the home of my school-friend Baucis de Coulon, the painter; Julian and I spent many happy days there, wandering in the woods scented with wild cyclamen and finding rare orchids.

In autumn we became involved in the harvesting in the vineyards; we had a friend at Boudry who needed all the extra hands he could get, and we flocked to his aid as a special treat; starting early in the morning, stooping to the bunches of grapes hiding in their leaves and deftly plucking them off. A strong man followed with a hamper into which he tossed our full tubs, and woe to anyone who had left a bunch unpicked.

By old custom, the punishment was a scratchy kiss applied by the *vigneron* who had allowed his beard to grow to make it more memorable.

Then came the three nights of the Fête des Vendanges: all that remains in the reformed cantons after Calvin's disastrous suppression of all expressions of joy. Still in full swing in the Catholic cantons the old-fashioned Carnival lasts for three glorious weeks of therapeutic exuberance. But here, in Neuchâtel, it was considered to be *convenable*. My mother, therefore, allowed herself to take us all to town; under her watchful eye we could observe the antics of students and young citizens, unrecognisable in masks and fancy dress, out for mischief and stealing of kisses, cavorting to the noisy tunes of trumpets and drums, throwing fireworks and confetti. The dimly lit streets of the town became alive with surging masses, the scent of roasting chestnuts filled the air – guiding us to glowing barrows where we warmed our hands. There was beer and wine, the restaurants were full of revellers and bursts of student-songs, and things going on unseen in the dark. How much better it would have been had we been allowed to join in the revels, in fancy dress too, like the bouncing clowns and dancing Columbines, to prance ourselves out of our stuffy selves . . . Soon we were rounded up and marched home again, to our safe and proper little bourgeois nest.

My father suffered more strokes of ill-luck. He was a defeated man, more and more withdrawn into his private world, detached from his invaded home which my mother ran, most efficiently on her own.

Alex and I were sent away, separately, for the long summer holidays, to stay with convenient *pensionnaires* or their relations. No books or pastimes were provided and we were just left to our own devices. These, of course, ended in trouble for me. I remember my furious indignation when spanked by a red-headed *jeune fille* whom I had plagued beyond endurance. But there was also Zäziwil, a thriving village in the Canton de Berne where I spent a long summer holiday at the Gasthof zum Baer. It was a large wayside inn, old-fashioned and opulently hospitable where I could persuade my 'guardian' to let me serve beer to the country folk gathering there after work. I loved turning the tap till the foamy white froth ran over from the tankard. Sometimes there would be singers who set the whole gathering off into song, with a harmonica spilling its joyful notes. I sat enthralled, my heart beating with patriotic fervour or with the unknown fever of love, sad and pining for the unattainable. German songs are profoundly sentimental and I revelled in them. To my sorrow I could not join in the singing, my unmusical ear cowed into silence. Of course I soon picked up the *langage de la tribu, switzerdeutsch,* to my mother's deep disgust. She spoke *hochdeutsch.*

One of the sons of the landlord ran a busy butcher's shop behind the *gasthof* and, having nothing else to do, I would sneak out there to watch him – with curious fascination – killing an ox or a cow. It was swiftly and neatly done with a heavy blow of the mallet on the forehead of the passive animal. It was like felling a tree.

I wonder how I could actually watch the death of a large animal with such utter detachment. Though prone to dark terrors of the night, I was never haunted by this simple function of a working butcher.

When I was about six, I was haunted for a long time by the death of my loving godfather. I was told he had 'gone to heaven'; this implied that he was up there, all-seeing, like God, and in a way more than God as he knew me personally, which I never felt God really did. Parrain, therefore, knew all my wrong-doings: my pinching of sugar, not brushing my teeth, hiding when I was called for some detested chore, losing that button, and so on. Small crimes, but all punishable. I developed a deep sense of sin, of Big Brother watching me, making me feel a prisoner to my own conscience – until it became like a sponge – soaking up other people's misdeeds and for ever accusing. A sense of guilt is a mysterious plant, growing out of capillary roots which spread far and wide. It has followed me throughout my life, and became even more active later on.

My mother, and also my dear grandmother used a form of blackmail to bring us to heel: 'You'll be sorry when I am dead.' The fear of their death, especially of my mother's, weighed heavily on these childish feelings of guilt. So it did to Huckleberry Finn: 'It don't make no difference whether you do right or wrong, a person's conscience ain't got no sense and just goes for him anyway. If I had a yaller dog that didn't know more than a person's conscience does, I'd pizon him. It takes more room than all the rest in a person's insides, and yet ain't no good nohow. Tom Sawyer says the same.' I have found the presence of my sense of guilt a tiresome, burdensome, weakening shadow. It may be the basis of the all-important sense of right and wrong, which my mother's puritanical make-up cultivated to a high degree, conditioned by worn-out standards; but I often wish it was a 'yaller dog' and I could 'pizon him'.

*   *   *

Returning home and back to school, we discovered a new hero: Buffalo Bill. The magazines in which the serial appeared were loaned around, and my brother and I read them avidly, hiding in the wood-shed. Our games became full of scalping Indians, unerring arrows, sticks one rode across chasms, better than any living horses, and of course at the crucial instant of mortal danger, the miraculous arrival of Buffalo Bill. We became adept at scouring the vast prairies of the *Farouest* – shooting from the hip and living in danger. The merest idea of human justice never crossed our minds. The Red Indians were villains, Buffalo Bill was Right – just as any folk-hero always must be.

Our magazines were of course discovered, we were spanked. My mother had a strong arm with a carpet-beater made of wickerwork: she dealt on bare bottoms many a painful blow. 'Couche-toi là-dessus,' she commanded, and we bent over a stool reserved for the purpose. I have it here now, innocently used to stretch tired legs on. It is a pretty old Louis XV stool which I would not part with for worlds.

She had read somewhere that children should not be beaten in anger. I had been guilty of some misdeed, and she announced that my beating would take place at six o'clock that evening. The hours spent in waiting are burnt in my memory: the hope that if I anticipated her every wish she might relent; the watching of that clock with no sign of her appeasement or forgiveness; and finally the inexorable 'Couche-toi là-dessus'. I made a point of never crying when she beat me. My brother on the contrary howled lustily. I suspect it earned him some alleviation. My mother had pale blue eyes which, when she was displeased, seemed to turn into hard round pebbles. On that unforgettable day, they stared right through me, as if watching my humiliation; more likely, though, regretting the postponement of my beating but unwilling to weaken. We never talked of many hurtings – in all our life. She never repeated that lesson.

I remember but one occasion when my father beat us, and that was for a serious crime. My brother, tired of having absolutely no pocket money, helped himself to a secret little hoard my mother contrived to save, for extra needs. This was of course soon discovered. I became somehow implicated though completely innocent. We were marshalled before him, in awe and fear. I remember that he hardly touched our bare bottoms with a small stick, to our immense relief. I also remember howling as never before. But I never forgot the prestige chastisement for the black crime of stealing.

After that, a very small number of centimes were allotted to us each week as pocket money. I spent my first on a lovely red apple at the market, on my way to school.

And so we grew up. By other standards ours was perhaps a deprived childhood. Yet, knowing no other parents and their ways, we were not unhappy. We were fed, and clothed and housed, intermittently loved by our mother whose first response, however, was *always* to the *pensionnaires*; mostly ignored by our father. Our minds were left unguided except for what we learnt at school and at play with our age-group.

We vaguely knew, from childish gossip, that children were made when parents lay together in bed. My little friend Dédée and I often gave birth to our dolls after lying stiff as pokers (oh Freud!) on a divan in the verandah. It was just a ritual, inaccurate but unperplexing – sufficient unto the day. It satisfied our sense of putting facts into place: not a morbid or excessive curiosity, but the need to ritualise. The dolls were left to sleep as any well-behaved baby should, and we went on with our geography game; this consisted in calling out a name from a world-map hanging on the wall, and challenging each other to find it. Madagascar, Vladivostock, Timbouctou, Nijini-Novgorod, etc. evoked obscure, remote and savage places; names which have stayed magical even until now.

Alex was a poor scholar, always in trouble, but utterly without stimulation or assistance from either parent, though both could easily have given help. He was an unhappy waif among too many girls, and bullied me in defiant retaliation. I was nearly three years younger, and there was no love between us. It was decided to send him, at seventeen, to be apprenticed under Oncle Ferdinand, who was then foreman in a large tin factory. (He had escaped from the Boudry workshop now run by two other sons of Anton Ortlieb.) Alex had no choice but to obey, but his heart never was in the profession he was thrown into. When Oncle Ferdinand uprooted himself to found a new factory in Buenos-Aires, Alex followed him out, and we never met again. But that was a long time later, after the First World War.

My father, dispirited by his own cruel experiences in early years and suspicious of a higher education, wanted me to follow Tante Juliette's footsteps and leave school early. But my mother, bless her, would not agree, and sent me to the École Supérieure des Jeunes Filles where I was to finish my *bachot*.

Herself always absorbed by some practical labour, going from one to the other with no respite, their urgency an escape from her own thoughts, my mother kept me busy too. After school and piano practice (which I never was much good at), she sent me on errands, set me to do boring handwork, to help with housework – anything she could think of; and only after all the chores were done to her satisfaction did she reluctantly allow a book. Yet she never spoke of matters of outside interest, never asked after school friends who anyway were never invited to the house. And if a short moment of intimacy was sought by me it was invariably interrupted by one of the *pensionnaires* calling 'MADAME' which had her instant attention.

Looking back on our childhood, I see a house with no cohesion, nothing to feed the veins of imagination or the hunger for understanding; nor was there any religious grounding. My mother's beliefs were incidental, she turned to Le Bon Dieu when she felt in trouble, and warned us He would punish us for our misdeeds. My father was an agnostic – and neither of them ever went to church. However, we children were sent to Sunday School, and learnt the New Testament parables though with little understanding. At fifteen we duly took our first Communion, prepared for the ritual by our pastor who instructed us mostly in our duty as Christians. I do not remember being moved by a sense of spiritual power or mystery or even praying with any conviction. Nevertheless I must have expected to discover some light, some guidance to heavenly ways, for I remember my feeling of deep disillusion when I was given Communion. The place was a public hall, there was no altar and we mumbled the responses kneeling backwards against our seats. The spark of faith was not lit by the very casualness of the occasion, neither were the words I heard inspired by the joyful gift of divine love.

I wonder how much Calvin's fierce puritanism, from his stronghold in Geneva, succeeded in destroying the inspiration of a sacred living Power throughout so many generations. (It is more than probable that my personal experience has coloured these reactions and I stand here in ignorance of the meaning of religion in French Switzerland.)

Much later, at the age of nineteen, I was writing a letter to a boy-friend with whom I discussed religion. I was just coming to the words: 'I am not sure that I truly believe in what the church tells us of G. . .' when a very strange thing occurred. The room shook, the pictures on the wall swung from their nails and the lamp swayed drunkenly. It was one of the very few recorded earthquakes in Switzerland. I never finished that letter – nor, strange to say, did that curiously timed quake change my heretical attitude. I have never believed in the God of the Church, the God of the Old Testament full of revenge for men's misdeeds; the God of Genesis, creator of our world. I believe in Jesus, son of Man, one of the greatest lights in our darkness. But I turn daily to what, for want of a better word, I call the Power of Life – indescribable, but to me absolutely real, urgent, universal. It is a cognition of an immensely great, impersonal and inescapable power. Man's knowledge can never reach or explain it: to me the supreme mystery unapproached by anything in this world. We live, we love, we suffer and survive – and finally we die, because IT is there. It leads us, each naked ragged individual, into our understanding.

*   *   *

When I was about sixteen Rosy came from Bâle. A year older than me, she had lost her mother, her father had re-married, leaving her without a loving home. In this, we had much in common and became deep friends. Her friendship, in fact, was my salvation, for being more mature, she helped me to become independent of my mother's strangling discipline, of her obsession with her *pension*. Rosy came just in time, yet the destructive marks on my brother and me during our vulnerable years never healed.

Fortunately, Rosy stayed with us for two whole years. She

was gifted and adventurous in discovering creative joys such as drawing and painting, designing and making amusing clothes, sharing my love of the lake and exploring both the lovely country around us and what, in our narrow experience, we called life. My mother was relieved for I was growing up and becoming a problem; she trusted us.

We went together to the École and loved it. I think the curriculum was superior to and wider than English education. We were taught biology by a scruffy Professor Jacquet-Droz who had an infectious enthusiasm for his subject; we learnt physics and chemistry, but I am afraid mathematics, with algebra and trigonometry were a dead loss. The best of our teachers was the Director of the school, Dr Paris, who taught history as well as art-history; he was an inspired teacher, loved Italy and re-created for us its alchemy of genius and beauty. A determined Miss Prissnal blew us fiercely through English, making us speak as well as translate, and read poetry with imagination. All we learnt in those early years made me want to know more and laid essential stepping stones, stimulating me to further discoveries – and that, after all, is what education is for.

Our school stood half-way up the rue des Terreaux, and twelve o'clock was the general signal for all students to emerge on their way home with a satchel of books under their arms. The boy-students from the Collège Latin assembled at the bottom of the hill, scrutinising the girls with good-humoured cheek and showing off the emblems of their Order: green velvet bérets for Belles-lettres and red casquettes for Zofingue, worn at a rakish angle. Many of us girls wore our hair in coils over the ears, a few harboured large knots of ribbon at the nape of the neck and we all wore competitive hats. We had just two hours before returning to class; there was no lingering between the camps and never a word exchanged, but we didn't miss a trick.

My mother was strict about bedtime lights out by ten. But it was then that Rosy and I set up our theatrical performances, behind the safely locked door of the dormitory wing. With the most rudimentary props and knowledge, we re-created plays we had read or heard of, inventing passionate dialogues or heart-breaking soliloquies, to the assembled *pensionnaires* piled on the beds. We must have been convincing enough for we reduced them to tears, and they constantly asked for more. I cannot imagine now how we ad-libbed our way through *Madame Butterfly* or even *Athalie*, and magically found the response in each other. My mother, of course, never knew.

*   *   *

The garden flat had long been too small for the growing number of *pensionnaires*, and we lived in the whole house. In her gallant way she had created a good *pension*; assembling a group of intelligent girls, keen to learn all they could. She took us all to the theatre (my first play was *Cyrano de Bergerac*; the acting seemed for me alone, sitting in the front of our little theatre, sobbing my heart out); to lectures, but never to concerts; to dancing classes where we inevitably met young men of our age and kind. Occasionally we set off for joint picnics with a famous young men's *pensionnat* run by a most formidable *directrice*.

I was just sixteen when I fell in love with a young Englishman learning French for the diplomatic service. He probably just wanted to practise his French, and we discussed the universe between meaningful silences.

The day was perfect. The party walked to a charming château perched between vineyards and then we all dined on fresh fish at Auvernier, my birthplace; he and I arrived first at the head of the pier where the paddle steamer was to pick us up: a still soft night with the immense moon of mid-summer, trailing its golden path over the dark satin of the lake. That first kiss was *fulgurant*, ineffable and unforgettable. Ecstasy pervaded my very soul with its piercing radiance.

My mother quickly saw the stars in my eyes; it was not difficult to guess the cause: she questioned and I answered. She said not a word, she did not warn or deplore, forbid or encourage. But it was suddenly decided that I must accompany my grandmother on her yearly visit to Tante Juliette in London. Grandmamma had done the trip many a time before – and always happily alone – but it was claimed that she had had a recent illness which made a companion necessary. I cannot imagine how, at sixteen, I could have been any use if anything went wrong, but anyway, go I did – never guessing why.

All went well. The twenty-four-hour journey took us safely to Victoria, where Uncle Dick picked us up in a hansom cab and brought us to St James's Palace where he lived with his wife, Tante Juliette and their daughter Elaine, always called Baby. Tante Juliette by then had lost some of the glamour my brother and I invested her with in our childhood, but she remained a dominant personality – even until the last years of her long life, dying at ninety-four. She was the youngest of that large family of Anton Ortlieb, my mother being the eldest. Not by choice, but by fate, she became a sort of lynch-pin on which we all depended. One after the other, my cousins from Boudry – all four of them – were found jobs in England. And all of them, in their diverse ways, flourished, thanks to that concern of Tante Juliette. I too joined the band of grateful nephews and nieces when my time came to sally forth.

This holiday in England was my first experience of the land which became my adoptive home. My cousin Baby was about seven years old, and I invented for her a Monsieur Jules who lived in her dolls' house. We walked together in Green Park, when my aunt was not taking us further afield. Baby was very pretty, with Titian-coloured hair kept in curls. She spoke French to her mother and grandmamma, and English to her father, was much loved in her home, but not spoilt: my aunt was strict, but expansively affectionate, very unlike her sister, my mother; she was gay, loved the theatre and dressed exquisitely.

The house where they lived was a small part of the complex of the old Palace, its bricks blackened by time, its windows fighting the pervading soot. Two sentinels were always on guard in Ambassador's Court, changing watch every three hours, with loud commands and presenting arms. Access to that court is now closed, but in 1912 there was no forbidding gate; it was secluded from St James's Street, evoked ancient privilege and, to me, romantic fantasy. The house, filled with objects picked up by Uncle Dick on his many voyages with the King, was very pleasant, but bore no trace of its great age.

Uncle Dick was tall and handsome. He was superintendent of King George V's wardrobe. He had three valets under him to prepare the suits and polish the decorations chosen for the various royal occasions – and had to know the ritual and its apparel. A midshipman when the then Duke of York chose him to be his batman, he remained faithfully devoted and dedicated to his King, to whom he gave absolute loyalty. His life at Buckingham Palace was a confidential world from which never a word escaped. This was very tantalising but his manner defeated the most persistent curiosity.

Years later, he allowed himself to take Julian, Aldous and myself to the private rooms at Buckingham Palace. He held the only keys of the drawers where the jewels, Orders and medals were kept. There was among them a slender beaker, once the Grand Mogul's, given to Queen Victoria: an exquisite object of vertical thin gold ribs filled with emeralds. And there were many Indian treasures lavishly studded with precious stones; swords and daggers dripping with diamonds. I also remember a superb pendant in enamel of St George and the Dragon which, it was said, had belonged to Queen Elizabeth I.

The King's bedroom was austere as one might expect of a former sailor, which of course he had been when Duke of York. The small bed was plain; over it hung a reproduction of Holman Hunt's *Light of the World*; between two tall windows, an old master which Aldous recognised as a fine Titian. It was

1. Myself aged about 34

3. Julian with Anthony and Francis, Oxford 1923

2. T. H. Huxley, his son Leonard and grandson Julian

4. Lady Ottoline Morrell at Bedford Square about 1912

5. Mme Baillot, Frieda, D. H. Lawrence and Anthony at
Diablerets, 1928–9

6. H. G. Wells, his son Gip and Julian, working on *The Science of Life* at
Wells's home, 1927

7. Anthony and Francis on London Zoo postcard

8. Julian and Myself circa 1940

9. Julian and pelicans at the London Zoo

10. The Brains Trust (circa 1942): Julian, Sir Gilbert Murray and
Sir William Beveridge

11. Looking for gorilla in Uganda, 1960

12. Julian's first party as Director-General of Unesco, in Paris, 1946: with Walter Laves, Assistant Director-General, and his wife from USA

14. Myself (Photo: W. Suschitzky)

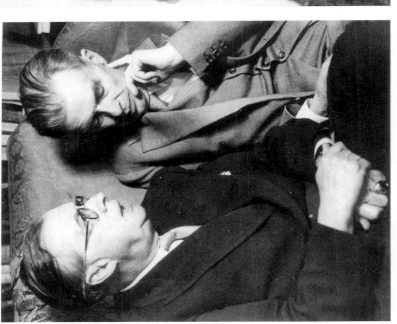

13. Julian and Aldous, circa 1950 (Photo: W. Suschitzky)

hardly visible against the light which Aldous deplored. By the door stood an illuminated glass-top case holding a quantity of walking-sticks; the variety was infinite and unselective, as a favourite collection should be. Uncle Dick's room was large and full of wardrobes and cases, all locked of course. The round table in the middle was covered with newspapers, uppermost of which was *The Times*, heavily marked with blue pencil for HM's attention.

My first visit to England was a great event. I remember Hampton Court, the Maze, the splendid Mantegna Orangery, the pompous State rooms, the crowds milling about on the wide paths. And indelible on my memory, the curious hat which Tante Juliette forced me to wear. It had frilled white lace stuck on the underside of the crown, a wide brim and blue velvet ribbons joined under the chin. It was much stared at and I swore never to wear it again.

Then we went to Madame Tussaud's. All was well until the question of visiting the Chamber of Horrors arose. Tante Juliette warned me strongly against it but I meant to show a superior state of mind and disregarded her caution. She gave me the sixpence needed for admission and I went jauntily down those stairs. I lasted less than ten minutes. Charlotte Corday knifed Marat in his bath. The fully documented criminals stood like inhuman beasts. Crippen and Jack-the-Ripper forever re-enacted their foul murders. My exit was a good deal quicker than my entrance. And for the rest of my stay at St James's, every step of the sentries doing their guard duties in Ambassador's Court marked time with my sleepless hours, my haunted torment. For death by murder terrified me beyond bearing, my fermenting imagination living through the utmost suffering of the victims.

We went to Bembridge on the Isle of Wight; swimming in that wonderful sea was pure joy; not so, however, was the book I had brought with me, Victor Hugo's *La Légende des Siècles*. Lost in the avalanche of resounding words, I soon abandoned the attempt: baffled, as was André Gide, when asked who was the greatest poet in France, and forced to reply, 'Victor Hugo, hélas!' Then came the time for me to return to Neuchâtel, back to school to finish my *bachot*. My mother again said not a word about my budding love affair. Silent resistance was ever her way. But I had turned a corner, and though cherishing the small silver-framed photograph of my enchanter, I knew it could not be. I wrote him a pompous little note asking him 'not to write and to forget me'. So he disappeared from my life: I grieved, but knew it wise.

*   *   *

Two years passed; my mother's *pensionnat* was now well established and flourishing. In the early summer of 1914, several Russian women graduates arrived at the newly elevated University (it had been an Academy until then) to polish their French. They stayed with us, and a tingling freshness swept through the home, with their adult minds, keenly interested and alert. They started to teach me Russian, insisting I should one day go to Russia and marry a Prince. Then came rumours of impending war – and suddenly they were gone, their audacious Swiss venture ending in anguish. One of them, Miss Garbatov, had no money for her journey and my mother lent her the gold coins then in favour against which she left a box of oddments. None of the Russians ever came back, and after the war we opened the box: I remember a thick felted blanket which later my babies crawled over, a very small diamond in a ring, and a jacket made entirely of pillow-lace in complicated patterns. I wore this a lot as it became an amusing relic in the 1970s. Poor Miss Garbatov – her father was a General in the Tsar's army, and God knows what happened to them all.

My father became ill and mostly remained at home, sitting in the garden when the sun was warm enough, his little dog Zephyr at his feet; his very soul darkened by approaching war; talking, with friends who visited him, of '*les sales Prussiens*', '*les canailles*'. The doctor spoke to my mother, but I was never told about his illness, nor how grave it was. I often sat with him, in the silence of strangers, unable to penetrate his reserve, his detachment. The day war was declared (August 4) he quietly slipped away. He was forty-seven, I was eighteen and a half; shocked, haunted and frightened. A good friend of his took his ashes and dispersed them over the lake he had loved. The little dog Zephyr was destroyed by my mother's orders. The collection of books, many early Voltaires, was packed off to the Penitentiary. It was not her way to explain.

I have often bitterly regretted not having tried harder to get through to my father, to help gentle away his last lonely months, ashamed of my pusillanimity. My mother remained silent, unresponsive, apparently unaffected.

We wore deep mourning for a ghost I had never known. The thought of his loneliness, his being made to feel an intruder in his own home, feared by his children and seemingly not wanting their love, tore at my heart. Years later I had a dream, not once but several times; he had become what I wanted – a real father, joking and laughing with his children, loving and loved, sharing happy experiences. The father I never knew returned to me in that dream so vividly that I woke to a new reality; it was a profound comfort, a blessed fulfilment. And who is to say that it was not a response, a true gift of love, annihilating the perplexing years?

$$*\qquad*\qquad*$$

During 1913, my mother had acquired a mortgaged villa at Bel-Air, a rocky hill dominating the town, from Uncle Ferdinand who had built it, then only the second house in a charming oak forest. He was going to Argentina to take up a new job. This house had a superb uninterrupted view of the moody lake and the imperious background of the Alps. My father loved the shore and refused to move there. When he died, however, my mother temporarily disposed of the *pensionnat*, and we went to perch at Bel-Air.

The villa never became a place of the imagination as the

house at L'Evole had been, with its wild garden, its *souterrain* and mysterious legends, its solid character and thick walls of dressed stone making a sheltering ambience for us children. Brand new and convenient, it had three good apartments and verandahs opening to the southern landscape. The stretching of the horizon high above the lake gave a new dimension to our lives.

A garden was planted round the cluster of native wild oaks, as well as several fruit trees, apricots, succulent pears, and a sturdy vine whose roots throve in the rocky soil. A high wall supported it above the new road climbing steeply from the town. My mother had always loved the high place: the move was for her a much-needed respite. For me, too, it marked an important change.

The war had begun in terrible earnest, still glamorised and heroic. Belgium had been invaded, refugees were pouring out and the Swiss frontiers were fully armed. My brother was called up and spent the whole of the war in the army, and for a time in hospital where many soldiers died of a virulent flu. But until I finished my studies in 1915, it was only through news-papers that we heard of its horrors. Swiss neutrality was a shield behind which we went on living our lives of stolid worth, hard work and limited ambitions. I remember much poverty and slums, with only private charities to help the dis-abled and sick – things are very different now.

2

Life at Garsington

I had done just well enough with my exams. My highest mark was for composition for which the Director commended me; but, somehow, I never thought that I might pursue this line and make writing my profession; besides, in those days, a girl had little choice – or advice. Although, in a way, I longed to go on to the university with my friends I was in a sort of no-man's land, undecided what to do with my life, except wanting to learn English well. Moreover my mother was not prepared to meet any extra cost and I was now to go and earn my living and help to pay The Debt. A modest trousseau was prepared for me, with a modest amount of broderie anglaise but no threaded ribbon, then much in fashion. I was nineteen and a half.

My train went through Paris and on to Dieppe, where I saw the helpless casualties of war, pale young men on stretchers carried across the gangway and out again at Dover where fleets of ambulances took them away. It was a grim sight under the spring sky.

Tante Juliette took me in hand. She still lived at St James's Palace, with the sentries marching to and fro, night and day. My dear grandmother was there again, and I slept in her room, she smelling of milk and honey, kind, plump and gentle, doing much sewing and reading herself to sleep. She had a passion for books of discovery like Sven Hedin and Aurel Stein but she read in German so that I could never share her enthusiasm. My cousin Elaine (Baby) was under ten and her mother was determined she should be a ballet dancer. Every morning, before school, she had to practise for an hour at pirouettes and standing *en pointes, entrechats* and attitudes Queen Mary, whose goddaughter she was, disapproved of this, and therefore Uncle Dick barely condoned it. My aunt, however, always managed to win any decision on that score. Elaine became a graceful accomplished dancer, later joining the Shubert Ballet in New York. She was forced to abandon her career when she grew to be over six foot tall.

I was taken to an agency to find a job as a governess. My curriculum vitae was noted, my cerebral luggage listed, for better or worse, and addresses were given me for interviews. I remember being interviewed by three possible employers. The last was Lady Ottoline Morrell and she asked me to meet her in the first class waiting-room at Oxford station.

I duly arrived and waited some time in a musty solitude. It then struck me that there was another waiting-room on the down-side of the station. I made my way to it, and there found two imposing and distinguished persons, obviously expecting someone. Lady Ottoline and Mr Morrell (for indeed it was them) greeted me graciously and the interview began.

Thinking back now, I wonder that I was not more intimidated, more surprised, for indeed they were, to my Swiss eyes, extremely unusual, statuesque and beautiful in a most singular manner. But I was a foreigner in a new country and I accepted the strange impression as part of a new experience. The fashion then was for long dresses and Lady Ottoline wore a pale flowing dress and a wide hat over her Titian hair. There were several strands of baroque pearls on her bare neck and she wore long cream suede gloves. Mr Morrell, with his clean-cut face and slightly hooked nose, was definitely what my mother would call '*un bel homme*'.

Lady Ottoline spoke French in a deep, modulated, vibrant voice, a voice which seemed effortlessly to tune in with one's inner listening. It was as unforgettable as it is impossible to describe.

I was told my prospective pupil was a girl named Julian aged nine. She was still a little delicate and had spent a summer at

Leysin: she would therefore not be expected to do strenuous lessons but needed a companion-governess who would share her life and teach her more French (she had learnt some at Leysin with a Swiss girl) as well as general subjects. The salary was £60 a year.

A few questions were asked about my curriculum vitae but oddly nothing about my experience of teaching. Instead, Lady Ottoline asked me about my journey over and I told her of the ambulance-trains and the haunting faces of the wounded on their stretchers. To quote Ottoline's words in the second volume of her memoirs:

Mademoiselle Juliette Baillot came to us to be a companion and *soi-disant* governess to Julian. The first time I saw her was at Oxford Station where we sat together on a bench – a tall, slim, very pretty, shy, severe and composed Swiss girl, with plaits of fair hair done in two buns on her ears, she seemed almost absurdly young, but she herself seemed quite confident and I wanted someone young and cheerful and active for Julian. She came and was perfect . . . she took part in all our life and with her lovely simplicity and intelligence wound her way in and out of the various visitors, much liked by everybody . . . I can never forget her lovely slim figure as she dived into the pond, her long yellow hair making her look like a water nymph or a picture of a silvery saint by Crivelli . . .
Juliette and I have always remained great friends and I know her to be one of the most loyal and faithful women that I know.*

It was late May 1915. Soon after that interview I was invited to go to Garsington and take up the position. I had a large wooden box full of my precious books, little thinking how incompatible my small hoard of knowledge would be with the requirements of my job. I had of course never learnt to teach, let alone in a different culture. I arrived at Wheatley Station to be met by a groom and dog-cart; my luggage and I trundled on and we reached the top of the hill and the gate of the Manor, opening on to a court bordered on both sides by a tall hedge of

* *Ottoline at Garsington*, Faber & Faber, 1974.

yews and, facing the gate, the Tudor grey stone manor with lemon-coloured curtains at the windows; through the hall and into a room filled with the glow of Tudor-panelled walls painted Venetian red; sunshine filtering through yellow curtains, the pale Samarkand rug throwing up a softness of tone – and there was Lady Ottoline in a painter's overall.

I was struck again by the strangeness of her beauty: the long face, dark blue eyes, reddened lips, the lower one slightly more definite than the upper. Her copper-red hair was curled in a low coil on the base of a small neck. She moved with dignity and grace, tall and queenly. In all the years I knew her, I never once saw her hurry, fidget or fuss.

On top of a ladder, looking down at me, a young girl of about eighteen was painting the grooves of the panelling with a thin gold line. She was, I wrote later, 'small, rather plump, lovely beyond words, with large blue-green eyes matching an Egyptian scarab on her long finger; delicate slightly aquiline profile and a small pointed chin under a full mouth. Her hair, cut short by Philip Morrell (the fashion was just beginning with the Slade students) hung like a dark fringed helmet. She had the vulnerable and defenceless face of a beautiful child with a mature body.'

She climbed down the ladder and was introduced as Maria Nys. She was the eldest of four girls whose mother had sought refuge in England just before their country, Belgium, was invaded by the Germans. Her father had stayed to watch over his textile factory at Bellem. The painter Balthus helped to find homes for the family and asked Ottoline to receive Maria.

Lady Ottoline then took me to my rooms. These consisted of a large bedroom in one of the gables facing the court, the schoolroom, which was another large room opposite, facing the lawn and the distant horizon, and Julian's small bedroom next door. Julian was in the schoolroom: a slight child with golden hair cut short, like Maria's, by her father. She had delicate classical features with a mouth which smiled an uneven and most attractive smile. Julian was called after

Mother Julian, the Abbess of a Cornish nunnery, a saintly person whom Lady Ottoline had known and much revered. It was explained that Julian and I would be downstairs for meals, except supper, to be served early for Julian, who would be put to bed by her maid, while I had mine in the schoolroom on a tray. 'However,' Lady Ottoline added, 'you will come down tonight and share our dinner at eight.' This invitation was renewed the next evening and I never had my supper on a tray. In fact the evenings became a wonderful part of my life at Garsington. I was then left to my own devices, to learn my job and to fit into this new life. I do not think I was frightened but I was certainly awed.

After lunch in the front hall, which was also Tudor panelled, painted a soft grey with a faint pink undertone and hung with cerise curtains, Julian and I went for a walk round the grounds. The house stood free on a wide rectangular lawn, descending under a vast ilex to a rectangular pond reflecting the sky. It was immediately enchanting, with a brooding austerity I came to love more and more. Mark Gertler caught this mood in a beautiful painting. Trimmed yew hedges had just been planted round the pond. (When I saw them last in 1974, they had grown like walls shutting out the horizon.) We wandered round the great square kitchen garden, a little shy of each other, exploring both the garden and our way of communicating. Julian knew a good deal of French; there would be no difficulty in teaching her. She was quick, intelligent, interested, not yet selective. We did the usual lessons, both of us learning yards and ounces, and I mugged up English History out of J. R. Green to spare her from William Tell and Winkelried, Charles the Bold and the French Revolution. But I must confess that as a 'governess' I was not really up to the mark: inexperienced, young and too freshly out of college to have learnt how to dispense what I knew except in the broadest terms. And when, during the next year, a little cousin of Julian's, Lalage Lysaght, was added to the schoolroom, I found it even more difficult as she knew no French at all and lessons had to be constructed to fit two very different pupils. Curiously, neither Mr Morrell nor Lady Ottoline ever investigated our work closely.

Being, as I had been warned, 'delicate', Julian was prepared for bed at six, after which her mother came up and read some poetry. Blake was a favourite: I can still hear the deep modulations of 'When the children are heard on the green' and 'Tyger, Tyger, burning bright'.

Lady Ottoline was a very different mother from my Tante Juliette, who was possessive of her child and ruled her very closely. Elaine was ordered about, kissed and hugged and scolded all day long by her mother. Not so with Lady Ottoline. There was a restraint in her bearing, a formality in approach, which instinctively discouraged possible childish tantrums. Julian was not spoilt in any way; she was undemonstrative, attentive, thoughtful and private; very much an only child. I do not remember her having any dolls, but she had an adored little pug dog called Socrates (Soey for short), who was hugged and kissed on the nose, appearing indifferent to the affection lavished on him. He neither courted nor resented it, just submitted and snored away most of the day. There was also a charming little Pekinese called Nutty, who slept on my bed at night.

Julian loved reading, and had many books. Soon after my arrival, Lady Ottoline asked me to choose a new selection of books suitable for Julian. I had never read any English children's books and looked with perplexity at the library list from which I had to make a choice, finally listing all the books which had had several reprints and were obviously popular.

Though Julian rarely played with toys such as Elaine's (dolls' house, tricycle, dwarf cooking stove, etc.) we enjoyed terrific games of double demon, rummy, halma, snakes and ladders. Later a bicycle was given her, and I steadied her while she learnt to ride it. I then had to learn to ride as well, and Lady O. lent her very tall bicycle for the purpose. After falling into many a bush before I had acquired sufficient balance to launch out, Julian and I went for lovely rides through the country; sometimes with Ottoline and others, including Dorothy Brett, called Brett, of whom more later.

After Julian had been tucked up in bed, we dressed for dinner. Copper cans with hot water, covered with cosies decorated with vivid crocheted flowers, were brought to all the bedrooms by Milly, the head parlourmaid (there was then only one bathroom in the Manor, and the gardener had to come in specially to pump up the water for the weekly baths).

I was still wearing mourning for my father, and had one very simple black dress with swansdown round the neck. Later Lady O. gave me a discarded dress of hers, a Venetian gown by Fortuny, stencilled all over, with hundreds of small bead buttons, worn under a grey voile sleeveless long tunic. *Couleur du temps*. I loved that dress.

Lady Ottoline often designed evening dresses for herself: draping a brightly embroidered Chinese shawl on one shoulder to fall straight down her tall slim figure; a sheath gown of brocade, in which she looked like a medieval princess. High-heeled brocade shoes added to her caryatid image. She always wore her many-stranded pearls and drop ear-rings. She also loved exotic tunics and wide trousers gathered at the ankles, collected on her travels. Her maid, Eva, made most of her clothes, never fully following the fashion of the day, but giving all she wore a particular style which suited her personality. Her taste has been much discussed and criticised. She would have looked arresting in almost anything, and was sufficiently interested in her 'image' to create an original, a striking appearance. Some of the published photographs bring out a false note, though there is no doubt that she sometimes was careless – but how lovely she looked in a cream crêpe-de-Chine Grecian dress, very simple with gold braid at neck and wrists, a wide belt on narrow waist and long flowing skirt; or in a Russian peasant full-skirted embroidered linen dress – or a gauzy white muslin floating precisely with her unhurried movements.

The summer that year was warm and pleasant. We swam in the pond, Julian often naked, a lovely little Donatello. The water was never warm, and I remember Lady O. descending the steps with quiet determination, accepting the gradual shock of the water. She wore a pink *maillot* covered with a peplum-style tunic in soft rainbow colours.

Weekend visitors invaded the house: many Slade students, Dorothy Brett, Carrington, Barbara Hiles (later Bagenal), Mark Gertler and others. Though the men often swam with us, they were never allowed to sun-bathe on the roof with the girls. Lady O. was not seen without clothes, but drifted among us. By then, statues – 'rude figures' the village called them – had been set round the pond and one day Carrington posed naked on a pedestal for a photograph. She was solidly sculptural, a little short for perfect beauty. Little did we know that the villagers were watching behind the hedges with shocked delight! . . .

*   *   *

Julian had a music teacher in Oxford, about six miles away, where we were driven in the phaeton either by the groom or by Lady O. herself. This was a great experience. She drove with superb panache, often within inches of other vehicles. In those days, there were but few cars; the High Street in Oxford was a superb almost theatrical vista, and many eyes turned in surprise at the sight of her, sitting high, in her wide hat, holding the horse at a proud pace. I loved watching her, skilfully controlling its impulses with the same calm self-discipline that she controlled her own with.

Driving with the groom was very different and, later, Mr Morrell decided that these excursions for Julian's lessons took too much of the coachman's time. I was briefly taught how to drive, and was sent off in the phaeton with my pupil. We put up at Blackhall, where old Mrs Morrell, Julian's grandmother, lived, handed the carriage to the man in the stables, went to the lesson, possibly to the Ashmolean, did some shopping and returned in the evening.

One rainy day, as I was driving out of Blackhall with Julian and Gerald Shove (a Cambridge don who was a conscientious objector and working on the land at Garsington), the horse slipped on the wet road. The phaeton lurched to a sickening stop. No harm was done to the horse, who picked himself up, but the shaft of the carriage was broken. I shall never forget the shame of having dropped the horse, but Mr Morrell took it very calmly. Nor did it discourage him from perching me in the dog-cart to take visitors to Wheatley Station and I incurred another small disaster when I once drove Brett along at a gallop to catch her train.

Later Julian was able to cycle the six miles to Oxford and back and we became more independent. I also cycled once or twice a week to Magdalen College to hear Sir Walter Raleigh discourse on Swift. This was a cherished experience, but sad to say, I have forgotten every word I heard.

So much has been written about Garsington, true, false, good and bad. I wish I could capture in words the enchantment of that extraordinary place. I lived there for two years during the First World War which drew its shadow over everything, yet this time was for me a truly germinal experience, rising in memory with renewed beauty and flooding me with nostalgia.

In all its seasons and moods, Garsington Manor was alive with inner beauty: its colours, its glow, the pools of light under the wide lampshades, its faint scent of incense enhancing one's sense of privilege, of living in a 'habitable work of art'. And reigning over all this loveliness was Lady Ottoline, whom I adored entirely. I was of course much too naïve to understand her full character, her self-discipline, or defeats. She was, and remains in my eyes, the most wonderful person I have ever known.

Her strong religious feeling, though not dogmatic or formalised, lasted all her life, and was deeply influenced by

Mother Julian, the Abbess of the Little Sisters of the Poor in Cornwall. She also searched for mystical truth outside the Church. We often went to the village church where, as squire, Mr Morrell admirably read the lessons. The parson thundered loud and clear of a vengeful God who punished all sorts of iniquities. There was no sympathy between the vicarage and the manor; in fact the parson seemed to address his most virulent sermons directly at what he believed the manor represented. As his notions were mostly based on rumours not much notice was taken of them.

When the family moved to Gower Street, Lady Ottoline often went to All Saints, Margaret Street, to pray alone. Yet she was deeply influenced by Platonic ideals – perhaps their victim. She told Rosamund Lehmann that she and Philip 'lived for beauty'. That was, of course, an impossible quest, but she pursued it in poetry, in all forms of literature, in the Classics, in art and, often with punishing results, in people. She wanted to be at the source, to be near the fountain of creative art, of that world of beauty proclaimed by Socrates in Plato's *Symposium* – the Banquet scene which I so well remember her reading aloud to us.

Ottoline gathered her circle of friends from among writers and artists, whose genius she often recognised long before their actual achievement; this distinguished her from other hostesses who collected people already famous, for reasons of prestige. In these creative people Ottoline found some reflection of her own ideals and endeavours. She was not blind to the difference between the world as it was and what she felt was the world intended by Plato's demi-urge. This conflict could have contributed to the dreadful neuralgia she suffered so often.

She was laughed at by Katherine Mansfield, by Lytton Strachey and Clive Bell, by Carrington (though at first defended by her), and, later, by Stephen Spender and many others: this wounded her deeply, yet she bore it all with tolerance and dignity. Why did these writers, one wonders, use her in this inhuman manner? They absorbed her generous hospitality, and caricatured her without mercy. Some of them, probably Aldous Huxley in particular, may have been unaware as they wrote that, in the process of creating their characters, they used some of Ottoline's features and mannerisms.

She stood apart, in her singularity. Of course, she was envied. She was the daughter of a ducal house, brought up in a rarefied aristocratic atmosphere to behave in a tolerant but superior way towards the less fortunate. But she had reacted against this to become approachable: that made her vulnerable, 'fair game'. She was betrayed again and again, and curious myths grew around her, nurtured by malice. She herself longed to be creative, to be able to express her deep feelings in some art form, some tangible creation. But where I think she succeeded beyond anything else was in her contact with people, with any class of people, be it her aristocratic political circle, the so-called bohemian circle, or many shop girls, to whom she spoke on equal terms; with her gift for drawing out the best in her companions.

Take, for instance, this letter of Virginia Woolf:

Asheham, Rodwell, Lewes,
Sunday 18 August, 1918

My dear Ottoline,
I think you must be the only hostess who actually thanks her guests for having enjoyed themselves! As I always believe you have a conception of life which is far more magnificent than any that can be realised with the sort of material available. But it is superb that you should go on trying to make us out more beautiful and brilliant and humane than we can ever possibly be.*

This was not done obtrusively – it was her personal magic, whatever this much-abused word implies. She created a sense

* The Letters of Virginia Woolf, 1912–1922, *The Question of Things Happening*, The Hogarth Press, 1976.

of uniqueness, of quality in living, aided I suppose by her appearance and her environment, but mostly radiating from herself. And this is where one comes upon the inexplicable in human beings, in works of art, in religion, in love, in scenery. She dispensed a sense of grace which it was a blessing to receive.

Ottoline in her journal describes herself 'creating' this 'small and perfect dwelling'. She rightly calls it a 'lovely romantic place'. Both Garsington and, later, Gower Street were works of art in themselves, creating their own special climate. For where Philip mostly chose the furniture, it was Ottoline who assembled the lovely colours, the harmony, the pictures, the shades which threw their light of intimate appeal. She gave the breath of life to her decor and within these walls which reflected her personality she moved with her own particular dignity.

Truly I feel that I owe her everything; that in a deep sense she gave me the awareness which forms my being. She was endlessly kind to me – but these words cannot convey the radiant essence of her influence. She lent me books to read, specially her own precious green vellum copy of Plato's *Republic*. Often, in the evenings, she read aloud to the two or three people assembled by the peacefully crackling log fire. I remember her reading *Deirdre of the Sorrows*, and never think of Deirdre but as Ottoline herself, enchanted in an Irish mist. Poetry was always kept alive, be it Keats, Herrick, Dryden, Donne, Dante, as well as French poets. She shared their potency. How else can we explain the magnetism that seized us in such moments of awareness, of awe, of illumination of things outside ourselves?

I was, of course, not the only one under her spell; Maria 'gazing at me with great adoring eyes', as Ottoline writes in her journal; Brett, who lived at Garsington for so many months; Lytton Strachey; Bertie Russell for all his life; and, of course, Aldous Huxley who wrote in 1917 when he left after several months of so-called work on the farm:

Dearest Ottoline,

I did so genuinely mean it when I told you that my stay in Garsington had been the happiest time in my life. And I think it has also been the period when I have been conscious of the best and most fruitful development of myself. I won't try to thank you and Philip, because I can't do it adequately, can't even begin to do it. When I look back on these last six months I see it as a crowded hour of glorious life and all the rest relegated to comparative namelessness. I have learnt so much from you – so much from your inspiration that I feel I shall never be able to compute the full amount of your giving. From Maria I had a great and violent emotional self-discovery; from you something slower, more diffused, yet very great. You have given so much and I have been able to return you nothing, I fear, unless a very deep devotion counts at all in the balance against all your gifts of inspiration, almost of creation.*

Katherine Mansfield in another evocative key:

Your glimpse of the garden – all flying green and gold made me wonder again *who* is going to write about that flower garden. It might be so wonderful – do you see *how* I mean – there would be people walking in the garden – several *pairs* of people – their conversation, their slow pacing, their glances as they pass one another – the pauses as the flowers 'come in', as it were – as a bright dazzle, an exquisite haunting scent, a shape so formal and fine, so much a 'flower of the mind' that he who looks at it really is tempted for one bewildering moment to stoop and touch and make *sure*. The pairs of people must be very different and there must be a slight touch of enchantment – some of them seeming so extraordinarily 'odd' and separate from the flowers, but others quite related and at ease. A kind of, musically speaking, conversation *set* to flowers? Do you like the idea?. . .*

I expect many of Ottoline's 'thank you' letters showed this consciousness of something indefinable, enchanting and yet disturbing. Did Ottoline possibly suffer from what was said of Cardinal Retz: the terrible gift of intimacy? Discretion may

---

* Both letters from *Ottoline at Garsington*, Faber & Faber, 1974.

have failed, on both sides, and the unforgivable betrayal
followed.

★   ★   ★

What do I remember of those two years? I kept a journal which
later, in a suicidal mood, I burnt. I wrote extensive letters to
my mother; in one of the early ones I remember telling her that
I was happy to be at Garsington, in a very interesting but, I
thought, 'more or less ordinary British household. . .'! She,
likewise, for reasons unknown burnt these letters years afterwards. So, faced with all these ashes, I can only rely on what
surges in memory, only vaguely dated and with many gaps.

I was green as an unripe apple and utterly naïve. Foreigner
that I was, there must have been, of course, much to surprise
and bewilder me, shaped by a narrow Calvinistic ambience,
not allowed to read the Old Testament but having 'done' my
French classics; having never been actually told 'the facts of
life' but by a sort of osmosis among my age-group, having
grasped the essentials. Added to which, the image projected
by creative geniuses seemed to me sublime – they could not
but be as perfect as their creations. The thought of a *living*
author or artist pertained to the man-in-the-moon, and that of
actually meeting one an utterly improbable and petrifying
experience. And yet, by the sheerest accident, here was I,
within that unimaginable circle.

Weekend parties invaded the house, and sometimes every
corner, including the Bailiff's Cottage, was inhabited by some
fascinating personality.

One such very early party is clearly etched in my memory.
It was a very large party, including Clive Bell and Mary
Hutchinson, Duncan Grant and Vanessa Bell, Lytton
Strachey, Carrington, Bertie Russell, Brett and Mark Gertler.
Dinner on the long dark oak polished table, with candles
shaded with little red paper hoods; brilliant conversation,
punctuated with Clive Bell's shrill gusts of laughter. Bertie
Russell's high cackle, the chorus of all the other guests. I do

not remember what they talked about; absent friends were named and absurd stories told, Gertler specially good at mimicry. Maria and I never said a word (Ottoline used to reprove us about this). After dinner coffee was served in the Red Room (it was one of my jobs) and then Philip sat at the pianola and with his usual panache began to play Tchaikovsky and the Hungarian Dances. Soon the party drifted out to the lawn: there was a full moon, stars in a great still sky and the dark ilex tree brooding like an ancient god. The music floated, powerful and alluring, through the open windows, its rhythm pulsating; one after the other, the guests obeyed the compulsion, threw themselves into Russian ballet stances, while P.M. went on pounding out the flamboyant music. One by one outer clothes were stripped off for action, shawls became wings, smoking jackets and ties abandoned to a strange frenzy of leaps and dances by the light of the moon.

I was transfixed with shock. Returning to the Red Room I found Ottoline helping Philip to change the rolls; I primly announced that 'Ils se déshabillent et je monte me coucher'. 'Well, bonsoir, Mademoiselle' was kindly said, and I climbed up to my room.

Later, of course, I got to love these impromptu dances with P.M. at the pianola, and a wonderful dressing-up chest of exotic garments opened for us to choose from. There was never, even on that first occasion, any indecency; it was simply the confrontation of my narrow Calvinistic background with 'Bloomsbury' which shook me. The scene remains imprinted on my mind like a slightly faded photograph – a vision of *Le Grand Meaulnes* – a flash lingering from some dream. And I can hardly believe that I was that solemn girl in her little black dress and hair coiled over ears, suddenly transplanted from my Swiss bourgeois confines, still so much my mother's daughter hearing her say, 'Mais ce n'est pas convenable!'

Indeed, what was *convenable* began to undergo a profound evolution in my absurdly narrow little self. Whereas until then, I had been pretty well ruled by its laws, whether consciously or not, the very word ceased to have any meaning at all. And when Tante Juliette, alarmed by my letters, wrote warningly and advising me on my behaviour, I promptly and humourlessly retorted that she could have no authority over me, and we could either be 'friends' or behave to each other as '*hommes d'affaires*'. It is a measure of her understanding that she became a friend.

What mattered, and of this I became intensely aware, was to be alive, to absorb the essence of vitality, an awareness of life flowing not only through one's veins, but in all tangible things, in the soil one walked on and the air one breathed, in the flight of birds and the frailty of petals. Above all in the books one read, the words one heard. For there were stored all the treasures one could hope to approach, the discoveries and the search, the eternal seeking for meaning and understanding.

Conscientiously and punctually, I did my job as best I could, preparing the lessons and thinking out ways to teach what I could teach. I had absolutely no guidance, and often floundered. Looking back now on those two years at Garsington, I do not feel that I really taught Julian, and later Lalage, very much of any value, except perhaps French. And it seems ironical to realise that it was I who learnt so much, drank so deep from the spring, instead of my pupils.

*   *   *

Maria and I did not form any basis of friendship. She was a silent, undemonstrative and rather vague inhabitant of the house. I think it was in 1916 that she was sent to Newnham in Cambridge, to try for entry. She failed, having had no regular coaching, being perhaps unwilling to try. In her memoirs, Ottoline is not always understanding of the lost child that Maria was, uprooted early by the war from her home, parted from her mother and sisters and a beloved grandmother. Somehow, Maria did not fit into the pattern, and it was only when Aldous declared his love for her that she confided in me.

She was baffled and frightened, and I believe lost in her 'otherness'.

Years later, when she and Aldous, Julian and I motored to the Dolomites, we all talked of Garsington. Maria confessed that she had often been deeply unhappy there, being teased by Ottoline for being plump, whilst also suffering from a complete lack of money. No one thought that she might need a pound here and there for her own needs – her mother least of all. All her clothes were made at Garsington by Eva, and practical expenses met by the Morrells. I at least had my job and monthly salary – but in a sense, we were both anchorless, living on a sort of spiritual charity, not in our own right as in our own family; we were suspended on the fringes of another world, to which we were artificially attached. We both loved Ottoline, no doubt, for our own very different reasons, for she was the focus of our vision of life. Maybe it was harder for Maria, from whose loving family she had been taken at the beginning of the war, becoming a 'refugee' through the good offices of Balthus, the painter (no relation to Maria's father Baltus). It was all well meant but, looking back on it now, must have been a testing time for one so vulnerable and young. Yet even though Maria was about a year younger than I, she had, already at Garsington, a clear perception of what was going on. Or perhaps she came later to realise what Sybille Bedford described as 'what we now call permissive'; and the thought that 'sexual freedom of action was a prerequisite of being civilised' . . . Wrapped-up as I was in my adoration of Ottoline, I never suspected any of this, let alone encountering any of its manifestations. There is such a thing as being *too* naïve, unlike Maria who wrote to Matthew in 1952:

And why did I who was so horrified by those Garsington men (and women), I who was so squashed by the English and terrified of them, why did I let Aldous approach me, then wait for me though I never thought he would come back to me considering the theories of the world of Ottoline's: just flit around for fun; why tie each other down? Why did I not get for a single moment entranced by the

Italian men and women and easy life and certainly less terrifying
intellectual strain of it?*

★   ★   ★

Bertie Russell spent the months of the winter of 1915 at the
Bailiff's Cottage and much time at the Manor. In the evenings
after dinner during the week, when the flurry of weekend
visitors was over, our lives took a different rhythm. Ottoline
sat in the armchair under the wide-shaded lamp, smoking
cigarettes and sucking peppermints at the same time, with
some handwork she was engaged on. It could have been
crocheting one of the many-coloured counterpanes, or
embroidering the coverlet she describes in her book; Bertie in
the corner, reading aloud from *Causeries du Lundi* by Sainte-
Beuve, in his faultless accent, vividly, absorbingly; Maria and
I also doing some handwork, contributing to that coverlet of
exploding flowers, for which Ottoline had an array of exquisite silks to choose from, all designed from an Italian fragment: we were allowed to select the colours. I quote from
Ottoline:

> I sat in my special chair under the lamp with a piece of embroidery,
> and all my coloured silks spread out around me. Maria, when at
> home, sitting at my feet and perhaps she would be allowed to
> embroider a flower in one corner of the vast bedspread on which I
> was at work, Juliette at another corner. How much is woven in that
> coverlet! How intense the feelings as we worked at it. What interest-
> ing and vital ideas were blended with the silks and woven into the
> pattern of gay flowers. Some flowers must still be bright with
> poetry, some dark and smudged with war; others vivid and bizarre
> with thoughts of life; and a lovely rose will always speak of the
> fragile beauty of love and friendship . . . with thoughts of Blake's
> 'weary of time'. Maria's flowers are red and sensual. Juliette's gay
> and multi-coloured, but perhaps rather *too* pretty.†

The golden hours spun by, till it was time for Maria and me

* *Letters of Aldous Huxley*, edited by Grover Smith, Chatto & Windus, 1969.
† *Ottoline at Garsington*, Faber & Faber, 1974.

to go up to our rooms. Maria drifted away like a little shadow, there was sadness in her silences. Ottoline and Bertie remained, bound still in the meshes of their great love affair. I never suspected any of this. I only knew that his talk was a perpetual feast, a fascinating exploration of ideas, sometimes outrageous and iconoclastic (to me, at the time); he was the epitome of intellectual power, of knowledge for its own sake, of the widest freedom of ideas. His sense of humour was immediate, explosive and, alas, elusive – and his laugh was like crackling fire, contagious and unaffected. I was deeply influenced and impressed by a mind that flowed so sumptuously often above my comprehension, embodied in a puckish figure with a face curved into a sharp nose, a skin tight over bones, a wide mouth and a slant in his eyes; quick, responsive, with a shock of springy hair.

The 'friendship' between him and Ottoline appeared to be the ideal bond of minds, quickened by a sympathy of ideas. As I sat there I was aware, in my own green way, of an ideal empire of mind, based on much thought and learning: a triumphant and wonderful world, for which my admiration knew no bounds. That this was not entirely so appeared in Ottoline's memoirs.

I was fortunate in knowing Bertie Russell throughout my life. His shock of hair grew white but the vigour of it remained, as did, until my last visit to him at Penrhyndeudraeth in 1970, his extraordinary vitality. During the war, he often came to stay with us at Pond Street, and meals were a rich communication of ideas. 'Isn't it nice to *know* things,' he would say, when some esoteric point was made, and one could feel and share his relish. He communicated this fiery radiance in his unmelodious but compulsive voice, with a dry cackle of laughter, as naturally as he breathed, with every word he spoke. I never met anyone like him. He has been compared to Voltaire – what we know of him in print and in his bust by Houdon – same glinting eyes and long thin lips *philosophe riant*. Maybe there was some likeness in both their minds. Bertie was unique, immensely and absolutely alive.

I am not unaware of the vagaries of his life; he never claimed to be a saint or better human being than the rest of us. I have neither the ability nor the wish to qualify his achievements. He was of our time, he sat at our table, and he was our friend.

Another remembered occasion was a great Christmas party (was it in 1916?) with D. H. Lawrence and Frieda, Middleton Murry and Katherine Mansfield, Mark Gertler and Philip Heseltine, Gilbert Cannan and his wife Mary. After dinner, Katherine Mansfield organised some tableaux vivants including Cophetua and the Beggar Maid. I was the Beggar Maid with a dark frayed tunic lent by Ottoline. Who was Cophetua? I think it was Philip Heseltine, and he was also the Beast, wearing on his head a wickerwork waste-paper basket and glittering clothes, to my 'Beauty'. I remember bending over his reclining 'dying' form and releasing my impromptu 'love-chant' and the waste-paper basket flying off to reveal his red sweating face.

This began a strange correspondence between us, in his small neat handwriting, which at first flattered and bewildered me. 'Tread softly, for you tread on my dreams' – but his letters were so divorced from reality that a deep instinct warned me of danger. One of them also mentioned Lady Ottoline under the offensive name of 'the Ott' – and as I saw her only in a perspective of admiration, my loyalty to her was outraged.

He was an unusual young man, unsure of himself and wasting himself in many pursuits, perhaps part angel and part demon. D. H. Lawrence wanted to rescue him and I rather suspect that Katherine Mansfield arranged the scene to throw us together. We met briefly in London and he took me for my first walk on Hampstead Heath; also, at my request, to the famed Café Royal in Regent Street. Tante Juliette lent me her fur coat for the occasion, which was, on reflection, not as extraordinary as Bloomsbury gossip reported. We sat and drank beer among unknown noisy people reflected in mirrors around us.

I became frightened and broke off our relationship, not gently but finally. A little later, Ottoline questioned me about it, and I learnt he had a mistress who was pregnant with his child. We never met again, and I burnt all his letters. He became a most original and exquisite composer of music under the name of Peter Warlock. Years later, I had pangs of sadness when we learned he had died by his own hand.

Lytton Strachey was also a frequent visitor. He suffered from various ailments which demanded a special diet, hard to come by in wartime London or at Cambridge. He invited himself to Garsington where all the needs were met, and was a most entertaining guest. At the same time, he created the myth that Ottoline had lured him to Garsington, implying her need to be consoled from various disasters which he confided to his Bloomsbury friends.

Elongated and fragile, myopic, long-haired and long-bearded, long-fingered, voluptuously buttering his home-made Melba toast with a gourmet expectancy and popping it delicately through the bushy aperture of his lips, his curiously soft, high-pitched voice commented on writers, books and friends with a slight, affected aspiration between phrases. He was deeply and lovingly learned in literature, especially French, and like Bertie Russell, spoke it with the slightly unnatural charm of a foreigner. He could be aloof, fastidious and unapproachable, but he could also be very kind, and was to Maria, whom he tried to coach in Latin before she went to Cambridge, and to me, whose eyes he opened to the treasure of English poetry. He advised me to learn poems by heart, special favourites like Keats's 'Nightingale', and we read all of the *Rape of the Lock*. As a teacher he was unequalled, linking the achievements of the epoch, re-creating a long-past society which inspired future generations, and bringing out their genius. He also dealt kindly with my clumsy attempts at writing verse, with corrections and guidance.

Yet, according to Gathorne-Hardy who edited Ottoline's *Memoirs*, Lytton was chiefly responsible, with Virginia Woolf, for much of the malicious gossip created about her, still detectable, like a snail's smear, in many of their comments. They played a game, in their letters to friends, and to each other, of deriding her and scurrilously amusing themselves at her expense; to her face, they were flatteringly appreciative and affectionate.

There are many gentle and lovely letters to Ottoline in these volumes as well as many cruelly destructive and maliciously descriptive ones, as if a sort of conspiracy had been set afoot among those friends who graciously accepted the comforts of her hospitality at Garsington and repaid them by sneers behind her back. How deeply do these lightly flung words affect the essence of a personality – alter its character, leaving their mark, obscuring the real image, so that today few people remember Ottoline's courage and proud tolerance, her generosity towards her friends and the unique quality of her being.

The religion of Bloomsbury was above all anti–bore. To be a bore was The Crime, the horror of horrors which put one beyond the pale; to avoid such a calamity, gossip took wing and malice sharpened every telling. Of course Ottoline was a gift – with her looks, her vibrant voice, her strange clothes; also her passionate involvement in many people and causes added to the deep divergence between her class and upbringing and the bohemian habits of her chosen circle. She was fascinated by their iconoclasm, which excited her longing to know, to understand, to feel and share their emotions. While giving every practical help she could with generosity, did she fully apprehend the obligations thus created?

But how can one disentangle the multiple motives and facets of a personality which set her apart, often at her cost, above and beyond the fair and true judgement of her friends? To Lytton's baroque sense of humour she was the perfect target, yet their deep friendship flowered to their mutual delight until fresh intimacies divided Lytton's attentions. His were not the only stones, cast light-mindedly, to leave their wound – Virginia Woolf's were more obscurely sharpened by a curious rivalry and maliciousness.

Of course, in those days, no one at Garsington suspected that Carrington would become the devoted companion of Lytton, finally choosing to die rather than live without him. With her bell of fair hair and her round blue eyes, her slightly affected way of speaking, aspirating, as it were, the words which came to her mind, her stocky healthy figure and amusing clothes, she was thought of as a young woman buzzing around with Mark Gertler, with Brett, with the pretty Barbara Hiles; not very articulate or unusual. It is when reading her *Letters*, edited by David Garnett, that one realises the piquant sense of humour, the acute perceptions and the deep feelings of a remarkable woman. As David Garnett writes in his book *Old Friends*, her greatest work of art was the life she lived as the closest companion of Lytton, with its dangers and rewards, its duties and constant changes. She could have been a fine painter and was highly gifted, but chose instead a dedicated life to a dedicated homosexual. Her style of writing was inimitable and ingenuous, spontaneously word-alive, profound and moving in her personal revelations. Her best letters are those she ordered their recipient to 'burn at once', and which survived her request. One is grateful for such disobedience.

At that time Ottoline was blameless in my eyes, behind their rosy spectacles. I remember her as self-contained, self-assured, self-disciplined, running her household of about five servants with easy authority and a personal concern for the lives and happiness of each of them. She was often crippled with headaches, and her doctors would send her to Harrogate and other spas, where she dutifully followed the various treatments, generally to no avail.

In the morning, she retired to her boudoir, a small room lined with books in vellum bindings, with a Chesterfield sofa, gay-coloured cushions, armchair and writing-desk. She received and wrote innumerable letters. She also held long private communions with one chosen person in this sanctum which reflected her particular taste as a jewel-box. One had to be invited there, and I remember the sense of gravity I felt when I was summoned: a problem to discuss, comments on a book she had lent me, sometimes advice, or a message sent for me. She once called me down rather late at night to read to her while she was feverishly finishing a *petit-point* embroidery for Siegfried Sassoon (he and Robert Graves turned up in their military kilts one winter's day, their knees red with the cold); this was a charming vision of deer and hounds followed by a young hunter through an open forest, designed by Brett. It had to be done by morning. I read the whole of Molière's *Tartuffe* into the small hours while her fingers stitched the bright scene. It was wonderful.

Dorothy Brett was there almost all the time throughout my stay at Garsington. She had a delicious pointed, witty nose, slightly protruding teeth and a delectable sense of humour. She was also, in her independent casual way, more friendly than the usual *habitués* of Garsington, and I felt at ease with her. For my position in the household, as I said before, was somewhat ambiguous; like Maria, I was a foreigner. In any case, the schoolroom was where I belonged, but Brett often came up for a chat and, sensing my bewilderment or unhappiness, was a wonderful astringent. Her loyalty and affection for me were infinitely precious.

She wore jodhpurs and bright-coloured jumpers and, being rather deaf, listened with a capricious ear-trumpet she called Toby, never minding mis-hearings which made everybody laugh. She painted with sensibility and imagination – I remember a large picture of pregnant women sewing: a lovely group with white and black contrasts unifying muted tones. She also later painted a head of Ottoline, very small, with the hair of a Medusa and pools of burning eyes: a vision of a near-demonic being, disenthralled from human bonds. I often wonder what became of it.

Brett's life was full of curious adventures and events. They are outside 'my' Garsington and do not concern this tale. I met her last in Taos, New Mexico, in 1958, when Julian (H.) and I found her in her cabin just outside the tribal museum town. As the Indians absolutely forbade photographs or sketches of their ceremonies, she was recording what she had seen from memory – bringing out in her paintings an understanding of the mystique of the Navajo.

It was a strange reunion for me, like arriving in a film show for the last reels without having seen the intermediate scenes. They would have been unnecessary, for Brett was the same Brett etched in my memory, Brett sitting by the log-fire in the Red Room, smoking her churchwarden pipe, half-listening half-brooding, watching unobtrusively with humorous wisdom. She was now content in her little untidy house, with a faithful dog, living the life which had chosen her and adapting herself to its moods.

Mark Gertler the painter was another semi-permanent visitor at the Manor. He had quarters in the old monastic buildings, which the Morrells had made habitable. (This has since been replaced by Tudor imitation kitchens.) He was subject to TB and had to rest a good deal, but no one could have called him retiring or exclusive. He bubbled over with histrionic gaiety, re-creating episodes of his fortuitous life, avid to learn almost anything and everything, and turning all into a personal aura, a glittering persona. Cézanne was then his hero – he read voraciously all he could lay hands on about this great genius and, though he never copied him, he was constantly inspired by him. He read the Bible, all of it, from Genesis to the Apocrypha (being a Jew, this was taboo) and was infinitely amazed at the magnificent trickery of the ancient Jews. 'And there was Jehovah,' he would say, 'rubbing his gigantic hands in praise,' adding the gesture to the words and shaking his mane of dark curls. He wanted to learn French and asked me to guide him, choosing Voltaire's *Candide*, and mischievously pressing for direct translations of scabrous words, to my prudish embarrassment, which he relished.

He came back from short visits to London with fabulous tales about D. H. Lawrence, Katherine Mansfield, Murry, the mysterious Kot (whom I got to know and love much later), Montagu Shearman, who was very generous to him, and many others, as well as night scenes at the Café Royal where all these demi-gods assembled. But he was not malicious; his touch brought people to life in a vast comedy of predicaments with, more often than not, himself as the mug. He was the daring clown with a broken heart, for all the time he was desperately and hopelessly in love with Carrington.

I used to visit him at Rudall Crescent, then at Willoughby Road, where he had a studio and where he showed me his work, which intrigued me for its curious patina of colours. He explained that all his subjects were painted with a mixture of similar basic colours – shades reflecting a brilliant tone while the high lights borrowed reflections from the darker. It was never Seurat's pointillism, but a much subtler interpretation of tones which gave his painting the quality of a new visual language, an essence mellowed and intermingled like under-water vision.

When he killed himself partly because of unbearable neuralgias, it was a deep sorrow to all our little world.

*   *   *

It was in 1915 that Aldous first came to Garsington. He was then a last-year student at Balliol and bicycled over for lunch on a Sunday. His six-foot-two seemed even taller because of the slenderness of his body and his slight stoop. Under the thick brown hair his wide face was pale, with full lips and blue eyes which had an inwards look until one realised that he was totally blind in one eye and not seeing fully with the other. I remember Ottoline announcing the visit and telling us he was the grandson of Professor Thomas Huxley. I also remember asking who Professor Huxley was, having never heard of him, and Ottoline explaining Darwin and evolution. This was all Greek to me, and to Maria.

On this first occasion, he was mostly silent but when he spoke, the mellow quality of his voice and the quality of what he said was surprising. The unusual beauty of his face, unself-conscious, with its elusive gaze (best said in French *un regard intérieur*), a slightly detached serenity – not shy, but self-contained, and added to this his strange name, Aldous, made a memorable impression.

The next thing I remember was taking Julian Morrell to tea with him at Balliol – in his narrow long room lit by a neo-Gothic window. He entertained us with delicious lemon tea and crumpets, speaking impeccable French, as well as reciting Lewis Carroll, *Struwelpeter, Max und Moritz*, all the cherished bits and pieces which had nourished his childhood. Half-teasing, half-serious, he treated us with a special courtesy.

He soon became a favourite and frequent visitor to Garsington. And after he took his brilliant First at Oxford, he joined the group of conscientious objectors to whom Philip gave work on the farm, though he was not yet one himself. He had been rejected for active service, and was marking time until something turned up or he made up his mind about his future. It was the winter of 1916–17.

Wearing straw-coloured jodhpurs and pale stockings with a dark brown corduroy jacket, he looked absent-mindedly but absurdly romantic and beautiful. Even in those early days, he often seemed to be living in a remote and secret world, yet a word could spark off a brilliant discussion, revealing his astonishing erudition and memory. He also enjoyed the occasional malicious gossip of Bloomsbury visitors. He was, even among his own particular friends, the onlooker, the Jesting Pilate, relishing human foibles and suspecting the heroic.

*   *   *

Looking back at those early years at Garsington I see that it was for all of us a time of growing and expectancy, of disquieting and inspiring awareness. D. H. Lawrence's early novels *Sons and Lovers* and *The White Peacock* were full of this

urgent complicity with the impulsive dreams of youth. Ottoline and her vivid spirit, the visitors, the brilliant talk, the
reading and the music, everything seemed to conspire with the
house and its décor, even the peacocks screaming like possessed spirits. It was as if the world were offering a festival of
dangerous but rewarding experiences to our hungry youth.
As Aldous wrote in 1918, in the 'Defeat of Youth':

> Scarce knowing what they wait for, half in fear;
> Expectance draws the curtain of their fate.

For me, especially – obviously I cannot assess the feelings of
others – it was an unforgettable experience, an ebullition of
ideas, a discovery of poetry and new learning. Under the
influence mostly of D. H. Lawrence, with his sensual description of nature, his heady world of freedom from conventional
principles, my Calvinistic background exploded into fragments. I read insatiably.

After a long eventful life, I can see now that what one calls
education is a multiple, unending process, experienced by
most people in their own personal way and appetite; and I am
certain that my own experience is common to many. The
plough opens the soil for seed and germination, and the
eternally renewed miracle of growth, of life itself revealing
unimaginable new complexities, bursts upon one, like a fiery
awakening.

So it happened to me unexpectedly one summer day, as I
was walking in the silent garden: the awareness of participating in the boundless pulse of life, conscious of a fusion of my
spiritual roots with the very soil I walked upon, its daedal
vegetation and imprisoned minerals, while at the same time
perceiving the infinite treasures of the mind of man, in another
dimension and reality. The illumination flooded me with
intense gratitude, with grave eager joy and anticipation. As
Traherne wrote:

> I within did flow
> With seas of Life, like wine.

3

Enter the Huxleys

Late in 1916 Aldous announced the return from Texas of his elder brother Julian (another Julian, curiously); he had been compelled by an inner urge to take up some war work, though Aldous wrote to him he had much better stay where he was. Julian Huxley came to Garsington to visit Aldous. On first encounter, he was very unlike Aldous: but then, on this first visit, he was determined to make his mark, laughed and told funny stories, ebullient and full of spirit, a little insensitive and Americanised. In fact he still spoke with a slight American accent, which he finally rubbed off by imitating Aldous's enunciation. He lacked the pensive beauty of Aldous, his face immature, his head definitely dolichocephalic.

He seemed to climb up to the schoolroom quite often, and I was surprised that he should, wondering what he found in little Julian to merit his attention. I never guessed that it was me he came to see, as anyway his approach was diagonal. He drew pictures of baroque animals for Julian, recited limericks, Edward Lear and *Alice in Wonderland*, teased pug dog Soey to rouse Julian's protective instincts, while all the time he was observing me surreptitiously. He confessed much later that he had written in his diary that he found me unusual and charming, and that I had 'no back to my head'. This offended me deeply. I do have a back to my head, in fact I have a perfectly regular brachycephalic round head, but the middle parting of my hair into ear-flaps could only show a bare outline.

After that visit, he wrote to me from his various posts. He took me to lunch when we both happened to be in London, all dressed up in a smart uniform (he was by then a lieutenant):

tight jodhpurs and slim-fitting jacket. He later said I fell in love with the uniform. Most of the time, he covered up the serious side of his personality with superficial banter and made me laugh at his anecdotes. His letters were somewhat impersonal, perhaps a little disappointingly so, but they were frequent and attentive. He seemed to enjoy mine which must have been quaintly romantic.

*   *   *

In those days of mixed emotions, sweet and sour, grim with war news, I saw a good deal of Fredegond Shove, Gerald's wife, who lived like a Spartan at the Bailiff's Cottage while he worked as a CO on the farm. The work was mostly cutting logs with Aldous, and the two of them did not form a happy team. Gerald was sacrificing his intellectual prospects to his pacifist principles with a grim taciturnity – hardly lightened by visits to the Manor. Fredegond was a delicate creature, a delicate poet, a delicate friend. She did not discourage my ambition to do something with my life, and suggested my trying to enter Newnham College, Cambridge, even writing to the Principal for guidance. But of course I had no money, and felt I could not ask my mother to support me: she had curious feelings about money; I was to earn my living and save up to repay the old debt to Tante Juliette, incurred when my father's partner defaulted. By dint of strict economy, I just managed it on the eve of my wedding, but it was a handicap, an unfair ransom on my youth.

The dream of university was abandoned. I talked of it long afterwards with Mrs Amber Blanco-White, who herself was at Newnham earlier in the century. 'Oh,' she said, 'you would have been so bored at Newnham after Garsington . . .'

But the time had come for little Julian, now aged over eleven, to go to school; she was sent to St Felix, Southwold. Maybe she too found it boring after Garsington – anyway she only stayed there a year or so.

The Ranee of Sarawak, Brett's younger sister, then asked

me to look after her family of three daughters while she hoped to rejoin her husband, the Rajah, at Sarawak. Leonora was seven, Elizabeth five and little Valerie (Vava) three. My job was to teach them French and be a sort of surrogate mother in her absence. This would allow me much free time, as there was a nurse and nursemaid, with cook and housemaid as well. I welcomed the idea. Soon after that, the Ranee left Wimbledon and set off for Cape Town where she was to embark for Sarawak.

I was instructed to find a house for the family at Callander in Perthshire to be near the grandparents, Lord (Reginald) and Lady Esher, retired in a lovely old manor house with French-pointed turrets, called the Roman Camp. (It is now an hotel.) This was duly done and we all moved up to 'Glengarry' in the winter of 1917.

I taught the two elder girls for about two hours in the morning, then took them to the Roman Camp for a daily visit to the grandparents, who acted as guardians. They were kind and hospitable, loved the children and followed their progress. Lord Esher offered me the free run of his splendid library, which was an unexpected and magnificent boon. In the afternoon, Nanny took over till tea-time. I got a bicycle and roamed the hills, going as far as I could, to the lake beyond Callander and up into the larch-covered valleys. Sometimes, when the weather was fine, I took Leonora on the bike and we went exploring. This was later stopped as the Eshers thought it dangerous.

Leonora was a lovely child with flaxen hair and an inquiring young mind: it was a joy to teach her. Elizabeth, two years younger, was like her mother, with dark hair and magnolia complexion, a curiously Eastern little face. Vava was very babyish and jealously guarded by her nurse.

Maurice Brett, Lord Esher's second son, had married Zena Dare, the beautiful actress with a mellow voice; their family was also at Callander, and we often joined forces. Brett came up from the South; we enjoyed each other's company: all the same I was much alone, but not lonely. Reading, writing letters, learning English by trying to translate, absorbing the wonderful country with fresh understanding.

In the summer of 1918 I was told to rent a holiday house in Argyllshire, and Aldous suggested my writing to Mrs Bruce, his stepmother's mother, who had a house, Mactalla, on the shores of Lake Etive at Connel Ferry. We took the house for about four weeks and Zena Brett and family joined us, also bringing the lovely Phyllis Dare for a holiday.

The place was fabulous and enchanting. Loch Etive flowed beneath the windows and under the new bridge a tidal bore heaved its regular battle against the dominant cascade. Unearthly northern lights played ever-varying luminescence on hills and water, and I often went rowing into the haunting, lingering light which never seemed to darken, the dome of the skies becoming green glass, spangled with stars. There was magic in that Celtic land, obsessively bewitching.

Across the water, over the long narrow bridge which one had to pay a toll to cross, and some miles beyond stood the ruins of Ballahulish, the old vitrified castle where Deirdre of the Sorrows was said to have lived with her lover Naoise and his brothers. There was not much left of this savage stronghold, a few stone walls moulded together by a process now forgotten. It stood on the edge of the water like an ancient pleiosaurus, grimly guarding its secrets in the dark ruins. I remembered Ottoline's haunting voice reading Synge's play aloud to us, and felt her presence, her searching spirit, among these ruins.

The Trossachs were not far away, and Burn's poems still sang their soft craggy beauty. I wrote of my enchantment to Julian in Italy, in answer to his letter about the disasters of Caporetto and his surprising walk within yards of the Austrian trenches of Monte Grappa. The war was still in its full horror, but I must confess that up there, in Scotland, among the ancient cults rooted in the ancient landscape, much of it passed us by. A few newspapers came our way, but of course there was no radio, and the Eshers talked little of it.

During long solitary evenings, I made the most of my explorations and wrote impulsively and romantically to Julian who had known the same haunted world when staying with his father and stepmother at Mactalla.

And he, in the middle of a somewhat alien camp, on the edge of battlefields and under constant threat, found some release from the boredom and discomfort of his days in my letters. He wrote:

> *GHQ Italian EF*
> *4 September 1918*

My dear Mademoiselle Baillot,

It is because I am tired and heartily incapable of work tonight, and because when I got your last letter I experienced a curious sensation of renewing my youth and poetic feeling through touching yours, which you described so well there, that I write this letter, feeling the need of the same medicine again.

This is a strange life I lead out here; if only I were really fit I would enjoy it pretty well – but I oscillate between days when I realize the value of all things easily and vividly, and feel myself as a current of thought and being that is worth while, that will grow, that will now and then overflow the present – actual with the illimitable and untimed fields of art – and other days when I am just something without true individuality groping in the dark, not feeling any feeling but one of physical tiredness and spiritual incompleteness and discouragement. You see, for years and years I have been hypnotized by the disbelief in my own powers that came from complete breakdown, and then last year I have been doing my work and learning much – not to mention being much exercised over the world and the war (I wish I could take things easily! – but knock-out politicians, and stupidity like that in the Irish question, and the hate and folly that this war let loose both in England and America, get on my nerves) – not only that, but I have been becoming a self again, if you understand me: and the double effort is sometimes too much. Sometimes I walk on the pinnacles of mental being – only to fall into a nothingness that would be animal if it were not for the knowing that height and light exist – on other days.

I used to be haunted years ago by the verse of Lucans 'Virtutem
videant, interbeseantique relicta' and I am still, only it is not *virtus* but
vita that cludes now.

Poetry will not fill the void – and besides so often after work I have
no energy to read another man's thoughts.

But enough of preface. If I have said that I was feeling gloomy and
tired and that in such circumstances it always cheered one up to write
to young ladies with pretty faces, feeling minds and cultivated
intellect – then perhaps that would have sufficed! only I so dislike
empty compliments that I end by disliking them all and find it hard
to utter them.

However, if you will write and cheer me up, and in fact be *une
petite marraine* ocassionally to *un bête intellectuel* suffering from the
cafard, you will help tide him over the war – which can be very trying
even in such a safe and emboscaded place as G.H.Q.

I am starting to read some Molière on my lighter days – he is great
in a way I never appreciated when I tried to read him before. I hear
Squire's Poems are some of them very good but for poetry I am
confining myself to Shakespeare and Petrarch for the present.

No more – I must to bed. Do write.

> Yours v. sincerely
> Julian Huxley

Among the many letters we both kept during those curious
months of exploration of each other, and our own identity, the
next one from Julian, of September 13, was a further revelation. I quote the relevant part:

. . . Your advice about not grumbling etc., is, I am sure, well
merited: but sometimes difficult to carry out. Shall I give you in
words why? then perhaps you will understand me a little better.

I had this very bad nervous illness in 1913 which had been coming
on since 1910 and was partly caused by, and partly the cause of, a
terrible lack of self-confidence. Since then – all the time I was in
Texas, till 1917 – I was never well – in mind. It is only since the
spring of last year that I began to get confidence, first in my physical
strength, then in my mental; that latter has been coming back very
much since I came out to Italy; but one must have been frightened of
the world in general or been *outside life* (if you understand me) for so

long to know what it means to discover suddenly that there is no cause for it at all. It is like a starving man suddenly discovering a mass of food: and the same temptation to over-eat, and consequent ill-effect, follow.

I was often realizing in a burst that I had a great deal of talent (I state a fact, and don't intend vanity!) and then finding that I hadn't the energy or perhaps the mental training, or even perhaps the mere endurance, to employ that talent, that led me so often to get depressed and stupid: and being out among strangers doesn't help it.

There! I have done: but I wished just to make my explanations and apologies.

When I was on Garda, I made schemes for two novels – and then the one I had time and energy to do in U.S.A., besides my work on birds, was to work out a fairly complete philosophy of religion in biological terms – e.g. what idea and what value can be attached to the idea of God, etc. But it all remains in my head!

I must bring some of my other poems to show you if I come up to Scotland. Send me a card to say if you will be and would welcome me . . .

> Yours v. sincerely, and in haste
> Julian Huxley

Other letters followed, on much the same theme, and the last of October 3 crossed mine, proving once again that there is no greater fallacy than believing one human being can fundamentally change another, and also that to be invited to do so is one of the most subtle forms of flattery.

In September Julian suddenly arrived on a short visit, and I found him lodgings in Callander. We went for a wonderful exhilarating day-long walk above the valley, by the joyous waterfall I visited constantly, through the mellowing larch-woods and up into the heather, now richly purple – a day stolen out of time. I still remember my delight in discovering through his eyes treasures I had missed. Later, he wrote:

Your letter of Oct 3rd, forwarded from Bracknell Gardens: Thank you, my dear for it and for your confidence and your friendship and your desire to give – I think I am perhaps greedy of affection – I have had so little of it for so long – and probably selfish too . . . It is your freshness and poised, dewy youth of feeling that means so much to me – I must give up mine, apply its energies perhaps, to grinding at facts and the skeletons and machineries of Truth. Meanwhile, if I am to keep young and balanced I must now and then touch it, have it for mine for an instant. I did that evening when I touched your lips – or shall I say your spirit? So is man renewed. You say you seek to give me what you can. Give me one of those touches each day. They will be my communion with the Peace and Life and Virginity, ever fresh-renewed of the world.

Yours Julian

And so, on this quasi-medical basis, we created a regular correspondence, exchanging impressions of our so different lives, with enough affectionate concern for each other to create a bridge of solidity and response.

My dear [he writes in October] How I have to thank you for just being there for me to write to – It is by writing that I clear my mind, help it to see, purge it of obstructions, help it to operate. I never really understood till I was writing this the full extent of the analogy between the minds' microcosm and the universe's macrocosm – nor the beauty and the necessity of order and harmony. They were half-words, half unreal to me – now I see them in a picture, a vision, with colours and forms and active reality, operating and existing. . .

Soon after, he sent me his first book, written in 1912, *The Individual in the Animal Kingdom*, inscribed to J.B., 'to improve her mind. October 1918'. I read it without stopping, spellbound. It certainly did improve my mind with the elation of understanding. It lit up a convincing order of organic life which richly added to my scant basic knowledge, absorbed in the far off days of the Ecole Supérieure.

His letters became more personal; we exchanged spontaneous confidences, rather like two exiles sharing a hungry loneliness. We knew very little of each other, but a definite attraction bound us together. Julian, repressed romantic, was clearly refreshed by my romantic excursions and explosions; I discovered his intellectual character and the acuity of curiosity which filled his mind. We exchanged photographs, and I remember choosing one of my plainer self (shades of Calvinism?).

These letters filled my life, and clearly meant a lot to him; we relied on them more and more, heightening our impressions, setting them apart to share in quiet moments, responded to and understood. The end of the war was in sight – everyone was excited, vibrating with expectations of one knew not what, except that Peace was near, about to burst upon the world like a promise of unbelievable joy.

Armistice day saw us rejoicing with little flags at Callander, on a grey November day. Julian wrote that he would be at St Mark's in Venice, and would think of me. I felt flattered and equally deflated when he confessed later that he had been too absorbed by the service. But on the day after, the 12th, he sent what he called a Futuristo-Cubistical Ode – an explosion of words written in different colours, absurd, tantalising, nonsensical:

Peace! . . . Peace. Scabby brown scales fall off the mind. The real mind emerges. It blinks its eyes: it has not seen the light of God's day for so long. Buds, buds little buds sprout . . . out – all along it . . .
Freedom comes on swallow's wings, with the sound of
    all singing birds
up from the unknown abode of its winter exile,
To nest once more in the green freshness of its own
        true home.

            What is life now?
            It is a tasting of scarce remembered
                Freedom.

– Speeding through the mountain gorges, where poplars raise their yellow selves like flames on the green grass-slopes. There the corpses have been gathered in, the more enduring corpses of iron, – the guns, ugly, terrible, are taken away to rust as shows for peace, or to melt and be reborn for her service; and the people return, scarcely believing the truth, on their high-piled waggons, and the desecrated homes take the first consecration of old simple life renewed.

Speeding through towns where flags are a glory by day and by night, light wakes again to call the dreams out of old palaces, to unveil the mystery and the promise of spires and towers, in the markets and the halls of learning.

. . . and so I might go on forever and ever – Amen. But I won't. So you see others can be as mad as well as Miss J.B. and the Honble Brettkin.

– Life is flowing back into the desolated world. Let us go on the flow of things, I know it is often hard to perceive it, often hard to keep in it even when perceived – but there it is for us.

At any rate, trusting it with you has done much for me – Whatever the future brings, you have done good to one human being, and given water to one thirsty soul. I even started this evening to write a sonnet. I think Poetry is coming back to me too, and this time fledged, soon to fly effortless in the air around her nest in me. Good night, dear child. I shall be vulgar enough to express sentiments in the conventional manner, viz xxx

He rushed up to Callander as soon as he was released; he seemed drugged by the very air he breathed; and suddenly, after a few days, he proposed to me.

This was a very long time ago. I felt dizzy, as if carried off my feet – an image which became visible to Julian that evening. For having blindly accepted his proposal, I felt the need to rush out for a walk alone and get myself back into myself. I had been swept by a major force into what I felt was a dangerous acquiescence. Snow covered the ground, and I then always wore white stockings. Julian, also walking off the turmoil of the hour, saw me as if floating over the snow, insubstantial as a dream.

We came together and were soon in each other's arms. But this feeling of being swept along without my volition persisted, balanced by Julian's assiduous ebullience filled with plans. No sooner had he left me to go to his lodgings than he began writing little love notes, to be delivered the next morning, full of future plans. We were to be married in three months, and he had already decided where to spend our honeymoon. He wrote letters to all his friends and family, and letters came back; his father was bewildered and unhappy at the total secrecy of Julian's intention, and an old friend of the Huxleys', Mrs Haldane, deplored his choice of a foreigner, when there were so many lovely English girls to choose from. (She later became a most generous friend to me.)

Aldous wrote a curiously impersonal note, which added to my sensation of living in a dream. He sent us his new poem, *Leda*, which Julian read to me sitting by the warm fire, and to which I replied with flowing feeling. I got the following snub:

1 *January* 1919

. . . I am glad you like Leda – though I fear your critical faculty may have been a little warped by your personal feelings! For you seem hardly conscious of the profound and painful irony which is the thread on which all its beauty is strung. You must read it again later. It is certainly very good! – but perhaps not as good as your feelings.

Yours, Aldous

We went for wonderful walks in the snow, even climbing Ben Nevis, wreathed in fog, and suddenly I felt we were lost up there forever. But Julian safely guided me back to our own footsteps, and a profound reassurance.

The Ranee returned, having failed to get to Sarawak because of the naval dangers to shipping, and having been stuck for several months at Cape Town. We then all returned to London, Julian to his father's house at Hampstead, I to Tilney House in Wimbledon.

He came there often, and the Ranee deplored my engagement. She lost no opportunity of pointing out Julian's unsuitability in almost every aspect of marriage, his unparalleled self-will which she prophesied I would never be able to cope with. I would, she said, simply be eaten alive. She also painted in glowing terms the chances of greater happiness out of his orbit, tempting me with Sarawak and its half-tame headhunters, its deep jungle mysteries. Small and neat as an exotic princess (though she was of course the younger daughter of

the Eshers), she sat by the fire at Tilney House and warned me
by the hour. Her affectionate concern troubled me, but not
sufficiently to turn me aside.

I was taken to stay at Hampstead, where Julian's father
Leonard was most endearing and welcoming and Rosalind,
Julian's stepmother, deeply kind, understanding and helpful.
Aldous was curiously silent.

The days passed. Our wedding date, March 29, approached. I left Wimbledon and lived at Tante Juliette's, Julian
at Hampstead, whirling me every day to relations and friends:
to Mrs Humphry Ward who paralysed me with her grand
style; to Uncle Harry (Leonard's brother), whose large family
just swallowed me up; to Aunt Ethel Collier (the Dragon),
eldest daughter of T.H.H., at St John's Wood, where I
shocked her husband, the painter John Collier, with my taste
in modern art; to Aunt Nettie, the very venturous Huxley
who was said to have become a Muslim in order to divorce her
husband quickly; to Aunt Rachel Eckersley, another Huxley
daughter; to Ted and Ria Haynes, Ria being granddaughter to
T.H. and Ted a florid solicitor of great erudition in
eighteenth-century oddities. Friends of all sorts: a large party
at Balliol College Oxford; Mrs Haldane, mother of Jack and
Naomi, a small but very decided lady whose opinion ruled the
roost; the Gilbert Murrays on Boars' Hill; and many others.
Sir William Osler, the famous surgeon, took me aside: 'Feed
the brute,' he advised. After my long solitary months in
Scotland, it was a grand ordeal. There were also museums,
exhibitions of all sorts, a constant injection of Julian's
favourites, of visits to the altar of his gods, a deployment of
The Family, both Huxleys and Arnolds, which I became so
confused about that I mistakenly adopted Wordsworth as an
ancestor and felt ungrateful not to like all his poetry. Books on
birds, on T.H.H., on Matthew Arnold were pressed on me,
and plans of every sort tightened round my bewildered small
self. I looked and felt much younger than twenty-three years –
Julian was thirty-one. It was a whirlwind courtship which

Rosalind tried in vain to moderate: Julian was irrepressible. With hindsight and the experience of further crises, I know now that he was going through a period of acute euphoria. At the time even the word was unknown to me, let alone its meaning and consequences.

It was impossible to stand still. I felt unqualified, out of my depth among these famous people, I who had no flag to wave and no ancestor to worship. I was also aware that Julian's lovable but complex character did not include a high degree of understanding of others, did not allow for the margin of human errors, and demanded implicit acquiescence. He was, of course, as merciless to himself as he was to me, driving all before him, arranging voyages and meetings, writing innumerable letters. Hoping for some miracle of leisure, I even bought him a bottle of Sanatogen, but it did not work. 'The lady who rides the tiger cannot dismount.'

He rushed to Oxford and found us handsome lodgings in The High; fixed his job, which was to be Fellow of New College and Tutor at the Museum under Professor Goodrich, all to begin in the Spring Term, early May. Our honeymoon was to start in the Lake District where Dorothy Ward, Aunt Mary's eldest daughter, lent us her cottage, Robin Ghyll, at Langdale. After a week or so there, we were going to Frensham, and he was planning some Great Crested Grebe watching on Frensham Pond to round off his studies of that fascinating bird.

He was then an obscure young man, untouched by fame, except by a remembered reflection of his grandfather T. H. Huxley. After three years as first professor of biology at Rice Institute, Texas (1913–16) he had spent the last two years of the war as Lieutenant in the Intelligence Corps at GHQ in Italy; as some friends reminded him, Intelligence in that Corps merely meant Information.

Yet, under the modest, unassumed, charming, endearing Julian, with his explosive laughter and amusing anecdotes, was the resolutely ambitious man whose career was to be, as his parents had ordained since his infancy, worthy of Grand-pater. The three boys, Julian, Trev and Aldous, and their little sister Margaret, all carried the mixed genes of Huxleys and Arnolds, a privileged but heavy inheritance, exacting its crusading trophies, achievements, and punishments.

Unaware of so much, immature and very naïve, nearly ten years younger than this tall man I barely knew, and who barely knew himself, I felt deeply confused yet also deeply attracted. Nothing was simple any more. I was fascinated by his urgent mind, his passionate curiosity, his contagious vital-ity. But I feared obscurely that I had not the mettle to cope with this whirlwind, that I was chastising myself into wish-fulfilment, into 'happy ever after' illusions. Full-to-the-brim days flashed by, unripened by communion with the inner being, burning up energy and leaving me spent and breathless; Julian, blindly supercharged, galloping at full career.

Nothing, in fact, could ever be simple any more and his daily letters poured out more confusion, problems, a sense of imbalance, the turmoil of his emotions and his distress at being over-tired. Advice was proffered to me by his relations: 'Don't let him have his own way', 'be very firm', 'stick up for yourself', and so on – by all. As a child he had enjoyed the reputation of being, in Mrs Humphry Ward's words, 'a child of legendary naughtiness, but combining the inheritance of Arnolds and Huxleys'.

Finally I offered my doubts to this temperamental possessor of my being: my fears of so complicated a future, my need to wait, even perhaps to turn back. He wanted none of this, but to get on, to have faith in him and his need of me, to get married – when all would be well.

I cannot think why I did not run away, run for miles, but remained spellbound under the flood of his words, like a rabbit bewitched by a stoat.

*　　　*　　　*

Aldous was staying at Bracknell Gardens, desperately looking for some suitable job to enable him to marry Maria. He hardly spoke – deep in one of his curious abstractions, seemingly unapproachable. Julian was possessive, both of his brother and of me. It was indeed a strange time, as if a spell had been laid on us, dampening our sparks of communication, numbing our emotions. On top of which the house was almost unbearably cold, the early March winds whistling through every crack.

My mother meanwhile arrived from Neuchâtel for the wedding. She met Julian for the first time: 'Il n'est pas beau, il n'a pas de beaux yeux,' said she oracularly. 'Mais il a un beau regard.'

At St James's there was a curious silence about my marriage. No word was ever said. Clothes were tried on, invitations discussed and sent out, wedding presents arranged in a special room. Only Uncle Dick watched me with sympathetic concern, as if he guessed my quandary.

The day came, 29 March 1919, the point of no return. I remember waiting, trembling, in a corner of the room, for Uncle Dick to take me to St Martin-in-the-Fields – all dressed up in white satin with sleeves and a basque à la Charles I. A grand party followed at St James's.

Aldous was our Best Man and faithfully accomplished all that is generally expected of a Best Man, finally bringing our luggage to Paddington where we joined him. I remember him standing in his best suit by the carriage door, and Julian announcing that I was now the sole legatee of his modest savings – no longer, as previously arranged, Aldous. It was a curious time to speak of it, embarrassing for both Aldous and me. Aldous smiled, rather ruefully; I felt that we were all acting a play whose script had not been written, while the curtain fell on an empty stage with Aldous terribly alone, desperate, numb and lost.

He did go to Belgium in the summer of that year, and there was a grand old-fashioned wedding with all Maria's kith and kin, but none of Aldous's. Sybille Bedford wrote a moving account of the event, and of Maria's feelings of apprehension about her husband's world:

How very unenglish Maria must have appeared to the world! and how well she knew that this precisely was the original sin.

The family was very much aware that both the Huxley brothers – Leonard's boys – had married foreigners, and it took the best part of half a century to live it down. It is now conceded that they made excellent wives.*

Yes, both Maria and I appeared, and were, 'very unenglish', and the English have never approved of foreigners: London especially was divided into cliques which were choosy and exclusive. Maria was not happy among them. I was luckier in Oxford, but felt an odd disfranchise when we came to live in London. Curiously she and I never compared notes – possibly both feeling a loyalty which might impair the implicit destiny of our lives.

Though under the same roof at Garsington, we were not very close; for one thing, we were profoundly different in character; a difference accentuated by our different experiences. After Garsington, Maria's life in Italy had made her worldly, socially sensitive and responsive, while my solitude in the wilds of Scotland had given me a limited outlook and reaction. I was unsure of myself, and not socially at ease.

Very soon after their marriage Maria became pregnant, and had to rest a good deal: Aldous often came to visit Oxford and stayed with us, but the warmth of our friendship changed. Unconsciously but very positively, Julian took possession of his brother, leaving me out of their orbit, their tribal quirks and links. No word was said, no door was positively closed, but a light went out between Aldous and me and remained so for many years. It is too late now to seek answers to elucidate the mystery, to consider my sense of loss, of treasure wasted.

When Aldous died in 1963, Julian edited a small memorial

* *Aldous Huxley: A Biography* by Sybille Bedford, Chatto/Collins, 1973–4.

volume. Amongst its pages, I find mine, 'Aldous at Garsington'. What had become a cloudy memory of time long past shines now with a new vividness, almost a new meaning. His affectionate letters were a constant joy to me while in Scotland. A simple comradeship inspired in them a gentle concern free from flirtation. Re-reading them now, I find an Aldous who disappeared from me for many years, as if, by becoming in-laws, we had destroyed a spontaneous friendship and trust in each other.

Garsington became an enduring memory; for Aldous, a source of inspiration, for many of his early novels derive from the experience of those months. It is clear that his inward-looking eye missed nothing of the curious evolutions and complexities of so unusual a group of people. His receptive genius was absorbing and digesting, not so much living in a remote world of his own (as we thought) as in the incandescent flame of re-creation.

No one's life, in this world, is an open document – neither to others, nor to ourselves. Our private memories black out essential links, which we seek for in vain, in a kind of despair.

> We shall not cease from exploration
> And the end of all our exploring
> Will be to arrive where we started
> And know the place for the first time.
>
> 'Little Gidding', T.S. ELIOT.

4

Honeymoon,
Grebes and Oxford

You see, a dream is dreaming us*

Immediately after our wedding, we shot up to Langdale for
our honeymoon, both very incompetent apprentices in the art
of being married. I was still afraid and insecure, hiding behind
rocks to cry. But then Julian, who had not apparently noticed
my absences, devised a walking tour of three days,

over Styhead Pass, struggling through snow up to our middles, with
Angle Tarn beside us, covered with great sheets of pack ice, and
Bow Fell's cliff above merging with the clouds. It was a frozen and
awesome world, apart and utterly lonely: we two, who had been
somewhat diffident of each other in this adventure of marriage,
shared the joy of being together in overcoming the external difficulties. It remains one of the most wonderful memories of our joint
life.†

Reading these words again and reliving these distant times I
am moved as I was then, when I so needed the comfort which,
to my joy, he gave in rich measure. There, by the brink of that
bleak cup of the black frozen tarn, we found in each other the
response and the warmth of our love. It was a moment of pure
communion with each other, deeper than words and so
memorable that neither he nor I ever forgot its radiance.

The long walk afterwards was pure delight, for Julian had
the gift of seeing with the inner eye, of discovering hidden

---

* A Bushman proverb from Laurens van der Post's *The Mantis Carol*.
† Julian's *Memories*, Allen & Unwin, 1970.

treasures in grass and tree, of knowing the name of everything. Plants and birds, rivulets and villages, they became
one's own because he knew them. The scenery was full of
surprises, endlessly variable with deepening shades, endlessly
beckoning to further horizons. Julian never stuck to the
planned miles and stops, but wheedled just a little further, to
that small valley or the top of that hill, where another view
unfolded its new temptation. It was no use protesting that one
had walked already much further than one meant, until he
himself gave up from sheer exhaustion. We returned to Robin
Ghyll tired out but blissful.

This was the first of many wonderful tours, walking,
cycling, riding, exploring, which Julian planned for us:
the first tour and the most exhilarating, the most inspiring,
opening a whole new world of indescribable richness and
joy.

Surrey and the Frensham Pond was our next step. There
Julian erected a very small bird-watcher's canvas hide, just big
enough for one. He settled in every morning, equipped with
telescope and notebook, to watch the Great Crested Grebes at
their ritual courtship and display. I joined him later, marking
time in the bitter April wind. The birds did not display,
defeated by the cold wind, and I was bored and frozen. The
grebe, of course, as I only discovered later, was Julian's
seraphic symbol: the bird whose secret he unravelled, writing
his first paper in 1914 (reprinted in 1964), a paper which was an
historic milestone in the study of animal behaviour and which
later led Konrad Lorenz to refer to Huxley as one of the
Founding Fathers of ethology. As Julian wrote in the original
paper:

A good glass, a notebook, some patience, and a spare fortnight in the
spring; with these I not only managed to discover many unknown
facts about the Crested Grebe, but also had one of the pleasantest
holidays. 'Go thou and do likewise'.

I dare say many enterprising youths set off on such

adventures, but it was Julian who touched the wand and to whom was given the understanding. It was Julian who had the quality which germinates what I suppose one might call vision, indefinable as that power may be. Whatever it is called, it was certainly not apparent to me in those early days of our marriage nor could I have any understanding that he should want an absorbing interest outside ourselves: as I waited for him by the small hide, I felt hurt at his total disregard for my feelings. And yet, what could have been more natural?

Later, this became a recurring pattern. He could be loving, enchanting, amusing, full of superb vitality and gaiety, generous, adventurous, keen to open doors for one's imagination, concerned and gentle. But he could also shut one right out, impatient of intrusion or contradiction and of the very existence of others. Neither of us understood that a word could make a bridge of acceptance, and teach us both to live within our own freedom and co-operation.

*   *   *

We stayed at the Cherry Tree Cottage, in Frensham. In the afternoon the grebes were abandoned and we bicycled all over Surrey. We saw a snipe and heard it drumming over the lovely river Wey. Surrey had been Julian's stamping ground, and he and Trev had known every corner of it. This was as much his own re-discovery as a displaying of it to me: the Punch Bowl with its crust of heather, the little dancing hills, the sprawling commons with their old trees and marshy lakes, the dark pools and ancient Hammer ponds, used for smelting, the Dye House at the corner of the road, the Tilford Oak as old as The Domesday Book. By many paths we threaded the treasures of what was still an unspoilt and semi-wild country, its sandy ground holding back the surging urban crowds.

*   *   *

All too soon, the Oxford Term began. We got into our lodgings in the High, Julian took up his tutorship and demonstrated zoology at the old laboratory in the Museum built by Ruskin; I enrolled as a home student in Professor Goodrich's first-year class for zoology.

There I found a good deal of the ground already familiar from my days at l'École Supérieure, when dear Professor Jacquet-Droz expounded the fascinating world of biology to our class – but I had never done any dissection before. A dissected frog became a work of art, an intricately packed mosaic of organs, each fulfilling its different function in perfect balance and meticulous order within the limitations of its body-space. I enjoyed these hours of laboratory immensely, and regretted not completing the course. But events fell otherwise.

The afternoon was mostly spent on social duties. As a bride, I was called upon by resident wives, headed by the Junoesque wife of Warden Spooner; wives of Fellows, old friends of the Arnolds and the Huxleys, young friends of Julian; the calls had to be returned within three weeks, after which one might be asked to lunch or dinner. In a way it was an excellent ritual to introduce one to Oxford society, but I must admit I was always delighted when the calls were negative and the parlourmaid in starched cap and apron regretted that her mistress was not 'at home'. When she was, I left my bike at the door and hastily pulling on white gloves, was taken to the drawing-room where we sat for twenty minutes, getting acquainted. I was very shy and it was a bit of an ordeal.

Julian gave his tutorials at home and the students just walked in: our door was never locked. He had a most interesting and intelligent group of keen young men, some of whom had just returned from the war. They almost all became distinguished in their careers and later often told me how much Julian had contributed to their success.*

* When Julian died in February 1975, Alister Hardy wrote in *The Times*: 'There must be many, some of them leaders in diverse fields of science, who owe much of their success to that balance of reasoned judgment and enthusiasm which he to an outstanding degree has been able to impart. As

* * *

But the end of that first term was not easy. One day one of Julian's brilliant students, Pip (C.P.) Blacker, rang me from the lab to say he was bringing Julian home as he had fainted during the class. Pip also suggested (I expect to get me out of the way) that I go and get some ice. When I rushed back, there was Julian in bed looking very ill, with the doctor and Pip at his side. Nothing to worry about, the doctor said, it would soon be over, but he had been under stress.

Actually the trouble was serious. Julian was beginning a nervous breakdown. He was deeply depressed, could not sleep or make any decision; when the doctor and Pip had gone he looked at me with a sort of detachment. 'And you so young', he said, as if to himself. Not only was I absurdly young, but I was also desperately inexperienced and frightened, not knowing what to do for help, help at all costs. Ottoline, with whom we had kept in close relationship, came to the rescue. She suggested my taking Julian to Dr Vittoz in Lausanne; he had a reputation she herself had tested and found reliable. He could advise and cure Julian.

And so, three months after our marriage, our first journey was to see a doctor in Switzerland. We landed first at Neuchâtel, where my mother was as much in the dark and distressed as I was. Julian was not a physical but a moral invalid, absent from himself, indifferent to everything, exhausted and drowning as if in his own inertia. Why did I not remember his letters of 1918 when he so clearly defined his divided self? He tried to describe his condition in his book *Religion without Revelation*:

one of his first pupils on his return to Oxford after the First World War, I would like to record, since his period in academic life was comparatively short, what an effective and exciting tutor he was; he bubbled over with infectious enthusiasm for this or that new advance in research.

'I remember too the wonderful charade parties Julian and Juliette held – together they remained lifelong personal friends of those early pupils.'

Whatever the precise cause may have been, the phase of conflict ended with that crash known generally as 'a nervous breakdown'. From the standpoint of the psychologist who observes them, most disorders of this type are apparently paralysis of action caused by the mental house being divided against itself, and squandering all its energy in civil war; this is combined, for most of the time at least, with extreme depression, worry and self-reproach. To the sufferer they are the extremest blackness of the soul's night, a practical demonstration that not only heaven but hell is within us, and that neither the one nor the other need seem deserved. Job, in extremity of physical suffering, would have cursed God and died. The break-down patient has not even the energy to curse; but he knows, or thinks he knows, himself accursed, and finds his thoughts set upon self-destruction, as the only way of removing the cause for himself and the accursed life from being a burden to others.

Meanwhile, I was going through a state of deep anguish in which, possessed by my faithful sense of guilt, I was persuading myself that Julian was in this state because he had married me. He never gave me the slightest reason to think that this was so. It was only later that he confessed discovering that his basic knowledge of biology had suffered from three years' absence from any scientific connection, as became apparent when giving his lectures to his zoology class. He could not always give valid answers to questions asked, and did not feel equal to his task. It worried him intensely, kept him awake with a feeling of inferiority which, at the time, he did not wish to confide in anyone, least of all in me. His vulnerable *amour propre* was involved and wounded, and precipitated the crisis.

This was the time when he needed, desperately, not a pretty girl-wife, but a strong, undefeatable mother-figure. Was this to be my destiny?

Neither of us – least of all Julian – recognised this important fact during our short and hectic engagement. It took me years to find it out for myself, years and years of bewilderment and hurt.

Why did he, knowing so many of those lovely English girls Mrs Haldane had hoped he would marry, choose me? (Maria asked herself the same question about Aldous.) I believe it was partly the solitary romantic girl, living almost entirely on her own inner resources, reading, walking and absorbing the wild beauty of Scotland, who attracted him:

Vision in Absence★

I see you floating on a sunset sea
Among the Western Isles. The flaming clouds
Curtain the bedtime sun, whose mellow glory
Hangs where the insubstantial mountains melt
Into the purple radiance of a dream.
And his diurnal path of gold he sends
Across the smooth Atlantic, where it sleeps,
The roof of fishes and the ground of ships,
The sea-gulls' mirror and the only home
Of all the great and salty waves that be.

He built his own romantic dreams around this insubstantial figure, endowing it with a maturity beyond its experience and age. And I, at the receiving end of his lively Italian experiences, was dazzled by his quick mind, his dwelling among so many circles of knowledge, his voracity for learning, just as I had been dazzled by Bertrand Russell at Garsington. We had curiously fused our needs on a common ground of a romantic love of nature – each profoundly unheedful of the true character of our intimate urges. Did we not perhaps need to find, I, the father I really never knew, dead at forty-seven, and he, the mother who also died at forty-seven? A fragment of Julian's journal recalls her dying, he seeing the light from her window, overcome by compassion, yet incapable of walking the few yards to her room and putting his arms round her. An unforgettable reticence of love.

During our short engagement, Julian had leapt into his euphoric paradise, without the ballast of foresight, im-

★ *The Captive Shrew*, Julian Huxley, Blackwell, 1932.

petuously expecting his needs to be fulfilled without even clearly perceiving either them or me. I had been swept along despite my doubts, under his powerful attraction.

*   *   *

While the treatment was taking place in Lausanne, Julian wrote me a letter every day. Re-reading them now, nearly sixty years after they were written – he in his lost-soul state, and I receiving them in my bewilderment – brings back the feeling of helpless anguish. This was his first letter:

> *Pension Charliez, Avenue Agassiz, Lausanne.*
> 1 *August* 1919

Darling girl:

One day gone. It is going to be hard to stand 13 more without you. Pray God I may be fit and strong in mind when it's over! . . . I got to see Jeanneret at 4 this afternoon. It is little exercises I have to do every hour – I am afraid I don't get the trick yet, but that will come. It is all a deuced funny business . . . I slept quite well last night, thank you, for me – but still have a bad 'barre'. . . . No letter from you yet. I didn't know how lonely I would be! But it is all for the best. As long as I am irritable with myself and with you it is better I should be away. I thought of you last night when I woke up early – and that sent me fairly off at last instead of feeling depressed.

Enough of my feeling! 'Coelum, non animum mutant qui trans mare currunt' said Horace – 'They change the sky above them, not their soul, they who go across the seas'. But here I am changing my mind, at least I hope so.

I see you working at your lace-cushion, rather sad, but full of patience. I want you never to forget one thing – and that is that it would have been difficult for anyone to be more brave or more patient that you have been – it has been the kind of trouble which is infinitely wearing, I know too well – but you have never grumbled once. Take that to yourself and keep hold of it. Mrs Haldane said to me 'She is a rare plucky one' and said that I had done her a service, and that was introducing you to her – so there you see! That is quite an honour, isn't it.

Now I am going to tell you another thing. I like you to be stern with me sometimes and I still more often need it. It is bracing, better than a tonic. I am glad you told me not to swear the morning I went away – Let there also be rebukes for me when my love is not full and fine and when I am rude. The more you stand up the more I shall have to stand up against you – by this I don't want you to become one of those hen-pecking women – far from it. But somehow it is possible to raise the self-respect and pride not of either of us, but of us *both together*. Tu comprends? . . .

your loving husband Julian.

Then 9 August 1919:

My dearest Juliette,

I have just got your second letter. Thank you. You must forget my miserable state and my wild thoughts. I had no will, no control, no anything. Yesterday was, I hope, the end of the crisis. Dr. Jeanneret [he took the place of Dr Vittoz who had to leave Lausanne] came today to see me in bed and we had a long discussion. It finally comes to this that he could help me and I couldn't help myself. This morning he forced me up and out and I did my very best to follow his instructions – with the result that I did really forget myself for a bit. He has made it quite clear what it cost me that bad week to perceive, that I mustn't dream of real work at present, or of any *true* life. I must fix myself on to the little silly things of the outer world quite stupidly etc etc. It is the chance to take and I must take it. He is most emphatic that the one thing that matters is not to rest, not to enjoy oneself, but discipline – and this morning for the first time I *feel* he is right – just a little bit of feel, but not rebelling as before. So I shall not come back on Monday. I am going to stick to this as hard as I can, as stupidly as I can, and not put obstacles in the way if I can help it.

One morning, the daily letter failed to arrive. I knew something was wrong and, full of anxiety, leapt onto the next train for Lausanne. There I found Julian in deeper trouble, on the point of giving up. I decided to stay with him and to share, as much as I could, the slow ritual of the treatment. I sold a little diamond I had in a bracelet given me by Uncle Dick, and we managed somehow.

Julian obeyed the exercises dictated by the treatment invented by Dr Vittoz. These were many and varied, being physical movements like bending the arm with a voluntary consciousness, or taking a few steps with the definite sensation, in his brain, of putting his right and left foot forward alternately, realising the movements of leg and body, teaching him to know whether that movement was sufficiently supple and easy, making the senses conscious. (Vittoz was, in fact, projecting the treatment made famous in the 1930s by the Australian, Dr Alexander.) Then came concentration of the mind on simple figures like circles, triangles or squares, followed by the elimination, one by one, of a number of visualised objects. These were to be practised all through the day, as often as could be managed. During the sessions with the doctor, each exercise was checked on the forehead of the patient, where the doctor claimed he could feel, by the palm or the vertical side of the hand, the blood pulsing into the brain. When the exercise was successful, the pulse was firm and steady. When not, it became irregular and jumpy.*

Exercise for sight, the brain being taught to register what quickly passed before the eyes, and to describe it correctly, and likewise for hearing, by concentrating attention on some particular sound like the ticking of a watch or the hooting of a car, were also to be practised, only for short seconds at a time, but always consciously, *with intent*. As Dr Vittoz wrote:

Let us now consider what effect the control of his actions has on a neurasthenic person. At first sight it would appear that this continual attention to all daily acts is something quite abnormal, which could only produce some new unhealthy symptom; but this is not so in the case of a person whose brain is not under control . . . When his brain is always concentrated on something definite, it will become less and less troubled. He will regain confidence in himself and his mind will always be under control.†

* This can now be precisely tested by a small instrument placed on the forehead.
† *Treatment of Neurasthenia by Means of Brain Control* by Dr R. Vittoz, Longman Green & Co. Ltd., 1927.

At the end of the month in Lausanne Julian had mastered a great deal of the treatment, and certainly did his best to co-operate with the doctor; it was hard work, needing both discipline and faith, and constant watchfulness.

Luckily the summer was fine, the lake satin-smooth and blue, and the excursions all round the canton pleasantly refreshing – in fact it would have been difficult not to fall under the spell of its unspoilt charm. Ouchy was a little harbour where one could hire rowing boats, and we often followed the coast of Lac Leman, with its sandy beaches and poplar-shaded nooks. We lived in a small pension with a garden where one could be private and I brought my pillow-lace to ease the idle hours.

Julian was slowly getting better, yet still unsettled by doubts and fears. The time was coming when we had to return to Oxford and he to his teaching. I remember my anxieties as we travelled back to London, then a journey of twenty-four hours, with a tedious night on the train. To get back and face his responsibilities when not yet entirely recovered could have been a disaster, but proved successful.

These long past and forgotten principles which Dr Vittoz was one of the first to practise, avoiding all use of pills but appealing to the will-power of the patient, are now once again in favour, together with many ancillary disciplines, such as Yoga, meditation, the Alexander treatment, and others. Looking back on it, and re-reading the simple manual, translated into English in 1927, I am sure that Vittoz had tested a valuable treatment for nervous imbalance and depression.

*   *   *

So we returned to Oxford. It was probably the best cure: to have to face the music, and trust providence to see us through.

Julian reacted with great courage. The cloud lifted. He managed to borrow the notes of a colleague for the zoology courses he was giving, and even set up an experiment in the Lab. We moved to Beaumont Street lodgings, as the High was too expensive after the costs in Switzerland. Soon after, we heard that Merton College was letting a delightful house called Postmaster's Hall in Merton Street and we were lucky enough to get a short lease of it. This was a happy nest-building time collecting furniture and making curtains, while Julian developed a routine which kept him afloat. We moved in the spring of 1920.

The house was a rare treasure fulfilling my biggest hopes. It had been lived in by the famous antiquarian Anthony Wood in the seventeenth century. There were two lovely Tudor panelled rooms and mullioned windows. Horses were still kept in the stables next door; their homely smell was sometimes a little overpowering. It will always remain in my mind as a house of hope and joy. We unpacked our wedding presents, and found a wonderful store of furniture kept through the war by an imaginative dealer, from whom we got attractive and useful things. Julian gave me a free hand with curtains and covers and, inevitably influenced by Garsington, I chose them bright and gay. The Morrells were just selling their unwanted furniture from Bedford Square, and bought in for us four Louis XVI armchairs and a stool which had not met their reserve price. They are still with me, after many new covers.

By that time, the solemn calls with visiting cards had abated and we had discovered a happy centre of warm friendship and hospitality. We gave a house-warming party, which was taken over by the irrepressible Neville Talbot (Dean of Balliol), insisting on masses of hot water and teapots. The guests brought all the cakes and we just about managed for cups. I remember Jimmy Clark (later Sir George Clark, Emeritus Professor of History who had once coached Aldous during his blindness) and his lovely wife Barbara; dear Mrs Haldane, with her closely cropped hair, bringing her daughter Naomi, married very young to Dick Mitchison, and soon famous for her books on Greek youth (*Where the Bough Breaks*, *Cloud Cuckoo Land*, etc.); Jack Haldane, booming among Fellows of New College; Vera and Austin Poole from St John's; Robert

Graves and his first wife Nancy Nicolson, down from their greengrocery shop at Islip; the Cyril Baileys of Balliol; J. A. Smith the charming unconvinced Professor of Philosophy, confessing to Julian that he wasn't quite sure that there *was* such a thing as 'metapheesics'; the mysterious Urquhart whom, his name escaping me, I introduced as 'Mr Sligger', much to Julian's amusement. So many warm and genial friends, pre-war friends, minor titular deities of Julian's undergraduate days and guardians of the spirit of Oxford.

> O born in days when wits were fresh and clear,
> And life ran gaily as the sparkling Thames;

yet also so much more, indescribable, fragile yet eternal:

> And that sweet City with her dreaming spires,
> She needs not June for beauty's heightening.
>
> Lovely all times she lies, lovely to-night!
> Only, methinks, some loss of habit's power
> Befalls me wandering through this upland dim;
> Once pass'd I blindfold here, at any hour,
> Now seldom come I, since I came with him.
>   That single elm-tree bright
> Against the west – I miss it! is it gone?

Yes, Matthew Arnold, it is gone. It is within ourselves we seek the dream; we find visions and nostalgic echoes of a golden age, heightened by happiness, by the reverence given to a great treasure.

*   *   *

The house-warming party put its seal on our being part of Oxford, and Postmaster's Hall, our first home, took on the enchantment of the place. It was a happy part of our life: released from anxiety about Julian's health I felt able to think of the making of our future with unquestioning love and faith in each other.

Oxford was coming back to life after the profound disruption of the war. Veterans returned from the trenches, fresh-men came up from their schools, dons exchanged guns for books and uniforms for black scholastic gowns; shops flaunted luxurious temptations after the austere essentials of wartime. Eager ventures into new ideas, new problems and new personalities added their audacities and genius to the complex rebirth of a vital centre.

New College was to me the most beautiful of all Oxford colleges: the vast front Quad with its perfect chapel on the left, the next Quad opening on the ancient garden encircled by the old city walls, covered with shrubs and flowering things, the trees standing sentinels round the mysteries of the central Mound. The Warden and Mrs Spooner gave a dinner party for us, and gathered all the Fellows and their wives in the impos-ing chambers of the Warden's Lodgings. I wore my wedding gown with its wide Maltese lace bertha, and Professor Bourne paid me a handsome compliment.

Every Sunday, as a Fellow, Julian dined in Hall, dressed up and in convivial mood. Meanwhile, three or four of the Fellows' wives, Barbara Clark, Vera Poole, Marie Wood-ward, myself, and an occasional visitor, took turns in each other's houses to enjoy a frugal meal together. In Colleges, the port circulated in Senior Common Rooms while Fellows comfortably digested their luscious meal and exchanged loads of gossip. Each College formed its special coterie with its own particular character. New College was distinguished by its Head, Warden Spooner. Entering as a student in 1862, he remained as a Fellow until made Warden in 1903, to retire in 1924. We were lucky to arrive a few years before he went. 'All his life', writes Sir William Hayter in *Spooner, a Biography*, 'Spooner looked like a white-haired baby. His appearance hardly changed. He was small, pink-faced and an albino, with a disproportionate large head and very short-sighted pale blue eyes.'*

* Sir William Hayter's biography is an excellent portrait of this lovable and gentle personality.

A brilliant classical scholar and a remarkable Warden during a time of great changes and improvements in the character of the college, his fame mainly rests on a curious word-dislodgment sometimes called 'dysgraphia' or 'metaphasis', but which one can describe simply as a slip of the tongue. But somehow, these slips of Warden Spooner's tongue had a special twist, a surprising opportunism and oddity which earned them a classified description in the OED. A Spoonerism is now recognised as an adventure in language, and the dons and undergraduates animated the cult by inventing delicious absurdities, such as 'erotic blacks' for 'erratic blocks', 'the minx by spoonlight', 'you have tasted a whole worm and you will leave by the next town drain', and so on.

The OUDS (Oxford Union Dramatic Society) flourished with youthful talent, performing ambitious dramas like Hardy's *The Dynasts* to full houses. Other theatrical groups revived, and I was roped in for various roles, playing Iras in a golden wig and dying noisily in Dryden's *All for Love*. John Masefield on Boar's Hill had turned his barn into a small theatre and was busy producing material and recruiting actors in Oxford. Julian and I acted various characters, under his guidance. I remember *Jesus the King*, where I was pushed into the part of Mary because Lillah MacCarthy (Lady Keeble) was unwell, and nearly muffed my four lines because of stage-fright. Sir Arthur Evans also lived in a great house on Boar's Hill, in the midst of his fabulous Cretan collection. He had some of the attributes of a god himself, and gave wonderful parties, introducing the world to exciting discoveries about the Aegean civilisation.

Lady Mary and Professor Gilbert Murray knew Julian from early days: she was a daughter of Castle Howard where her mother was reputed to have made a holocaust of every drop of alcohol from the great cellars, pouring into the lake the casks of choice port and sherry and every rare vintage lovingly housed within the cool vaults.* For me, coming as I did from a

---

* Emphatically denied by Rosalind Henly in the book about her parents.

vineyard land, this was a small crime. But temperance was their ruling principle and example, imperative however unheeded. I was awed by Lady Mary, a tall ascetic figure in black descending from puritanical heights to dispense love and understanding which I, in my own puritanical limitations, was too inexperienced to receive. I read Gilbert Murray's translations from the Greek with admiration and envy of his closeness to the fount, yet when we went up there to tea I was too shy to ask him to talk on his subject.

Then there was the Bach Choir, run with inspired ferocity by Sir Hugh Allen, who tore the last shreds of vocal effort from his adoring singers: Julian singing *The Sea Symphony* of Vaughan Williams, 'o vast Rondure, swimming in space', which transported one into infinity, a sky of lights and the beating of great wings. There was another sort of delight too at Whitham Abbey, where a mysterious millionaire called Major ffenel contrived a group of delectable tents in the woods, complete with heating and electricity, deep chesterfields and bathrooms, while waiting for the lease of the Abbey to run out and enable him to take full charge of the property he had bought. His parties, luxury camping among the tall trees and the complicity of the natural world around us, were enchanting like a fairy-tale. He must have loved that wild island of peace, for he left it to the Ornithological Club as a sanctuary.

Jack Haldane, just out of his belligerent army kilt, gave the first lectures on the new field of genetics, still rather obscure and suspected by the older scientists. He often dropped in on us, reciting reams of poetry (such as Shelley's *Prometheus*) like a train puffing steam, and finally departing, cursing his 'poor' memory. He took an active part in the political quarrels between town and gown, and actually stopped the trams running for hours, marching in the tram-lines reciting the Athanasian Creed in Greek. Harold Acton walked down the High bearing his lily, while the reckless Marchesa Casati shook her red-headed beauty at a shocked and adoring following, leading a pair of cheetahs.

These were also the days of the birth of the crossword puzzle at which dons in New College worked till the small hours, solving tangled problems of words and anagrams. Professor Hardy, the mathematician who later deserted to Cambridge, was a great dab at it and organised a brilliant team which just failed to win the jackpot. Julian's mind, like the others, was baffled by the clue: 'What gives knights nightmares?' The answer was produced by an obscure chap from the Midlands: 'The blot on the escutcheon'.

And, of course, there were picnics on the Cherwell, generally organised by the ever hospitable Mrs Haldane. Undergraduates of all sorts were invited. The long trail of punts wound its way up to the green meadows full of buttercups and marguerites; scones and cakes were devoured and, singing all sorts of songs, we returned in the gloaming. One young man in my punt asked me, 'Have you ever heard of a poet called Mr Keats?' It was Stephen Potter, who blushed when I burst out laughing.

Neville Talbot, then Chaplain of Balliol, sent the following invitation:

A-ONCE-FOR-ALL-IN-MAY
CHERWELL RIVER-STUNT

May 29th 1920

1   The Party will assemble at Tim's Boat House at the end of Bardwell Road in time to start at 2.30 p.m. Be Punctual.

2   Canoes and rowing boats have been chartered.

3   It is hoped to get about Water Easton for tea and return to Tim's by 6.30.

4   Crockery will be provided. Don't bring food unless asked to do so.

5   The party will consist of

   a   The Doctor of Divinity (Neville) and the Queen of the May (Cecil-Mary his wife) who will be accompanied by her mother, Mrs. Eastwood and her brother Charles, the Capitalist.

b Julian and Juliette Huxley – New College, are not his doings chronicled in the Daily Mail? She is very 'chic' and 'Méchante'.

c Freddie Bairnes – full of Balliol theology. Eddie Baines, unfortunately of St John's.

d F.A. Barr, Balliol and U.S.A. see Outline of History part I (frontispiece). [His thick crew-cut induced me to ask him to stand on his hair.]

e A.E.F. Dickinson, musical and therefore charming.

f Katherine Ponsonby, from Lady Margaret Hall. One of the too few spinsters.

g The notorious Jack Haldane, New College. Scientific chucker-out.

h Humphrey Raikes. Exeter. Stinks don – otherwise delightful.

i Humphrey Gilkes Christchurch, awarded grid in France (M.C. with 3 bars).

j Mr and Mrs Russell, New College. For particulars apply to the steward Oxford Union Society, and to Mr Asquith.

k Alan Young, Christ Church, a peach.

l Mr and Mrs McGreggor; Balliol. verra scotch.

m Hugh Robertson, Balliol, Doctor (unqualified) to the party.

n Mr and Mrs W. MacCarthy. Keeble. Sometimes of China; the salt of the earth.

o Geoffrey Bell, Balliol, our one Blue. He likes Yorkers.

p Clive Burt. University. An Etonian and therefore like 'the little girl'.

r Mr and Mrs Harold Woolley. Queens. He a V.C. and still a Christian.

s Mr and Mrs Maurice Jacks; Wadham. He the editor and bad joker of the Oxford Mag.

t Freddie Ogilvie, Trinity. One of the few coming men among dons.

u   Mrs Acton – her husband Balliol, a victim to Schools.
v   Mr and Mrs A.H. McGreer. Queens. A Canuk and
    Army padre, but married in the old country.
6   Come unless it rains.

P.S. It is hoped that Juliette will bring a bevy of gals even
more wicked than herself viz Miss Petersen, Miss Grierson,
Miss Napier of Somerville and Miss Morrell.

Perhaps Julian's father will be there to match Cecil-
Mary's mother.   N.S.T.

I found this faded document and enjoyed retasting the
Neville Talbot humour of those days. He was a large man,
dressed unconvincingly in canonicals, *enfant terrible* and unre-
pentant. He deplored the long skirts then in fashion and once
swiftly lifted mine to see what sort of legs I was hiding. Sadly
Cecil-Mary, his beloved wife, died quite young, and so did his
son Gilbert, named after the brother whom Neville took off
the barbed wire in the First World War.

As I was of the 'married' status, I was often asked to
chaperone girls not always younger than myself. In those
days, as in *Charley's Aunt*, the rules insisted on chaperones in
mixed company. I did not take my duties very seriously, but
was rather disturbed when my 'charge' disappeared for half an
hour during a New College Ball, and on returning asked me to
put a safety pin in her dress. She was, however, a good deal
older than me and knew what she was doing. These were, as
Neville Talbot hinted, the days of the *Daily Mail* and the
axolotl. In his autobiography Julian shortly mentions the fact
of his experimenting with thyroid injected into axolotls.*

---

* 'Having read of Gudernacht's experiments with frogs, in which he
induced premature metamorphosis of tadpoles into froglets by feeding them
on thyroid gland, I wondered what would happen if I gave the same diet to
axolotls. These were strange tailed amphibians from Mexico, often kept in
aquaria as they live permanently as tadpoles, or efts, with moist skin,
external gills to breathe with and a broad swimming fin round its long tail'.
Memories 1, Julian Huxley.

Looked at with hindsight, this curious episode in his life almost directly led to what was to follow: he became a public figure overnight and his name blazed across headlines. Not only Jack Haldane, but many of his good friends and, of course, I myself, were deeply disturbed by this curious turn of events. He took it in his stride, a little sheepishly perhaps, but as lightly as water off a duck's back.

There was to be no going back.

5

Babies and Zoology

Then one day Julian suggested that we might embark on a family. This lifted the curtain of anxiety which had been so heavy during the last summer vacation. He really felt that he had achieved what had seemed impossible – to go forward with confidence in himself. The doctor also assured him that he need fear no genetic complication.

I was blissfully happy when, quite soon, I became pregnant. My mother came over for my last month, bringing with her a Swiss maid, Lydia, small and stocky, quick tempered, an excellent cook and general help. She knew no English, and my mother only a little; we managed.

Julian and I were both equally ignorant of the psychological and physical upheavals caused by pregnancy. We cast around for expertise. There was then in Oxford a Dr Good who practised hypnosis of a kind to allay the fears of childbirth. He came to see me and tried in vain to put me to sleep by his simple methods. He then advised me not to be afraid and to face the ordeal naturally: but I was not in the least afraid, in fact I looked forward to this great adventure and was ready to bear whatever pains it might bring.

No one in those days had discovered the deep-breathing method in delivery, and there were no sources of advice available. My mother told me nothing except to cry out with the pain and, though she brought the little box of white powder from my great-aunt in the Oberland, I never felt justified in using it and so it was carefully returned. I shall never know what it really was.

As it happened, Anthony was nearly born without any

assistance (as I was), though my mother was there and the monthly nurse had just arrived. The doctor could not get to me in time, and Julian was dining in Hall at New College. I still remember the curiously excruciating pains, and then the little warm body surging between my thighs. We were both delivered after a long journey and a final travail, the fragile head forcing its way through the narrow pelvic tunnel, subject to a power far greater than ourselves, the naked force of life.

Julian arrived, and in his hand, which trembled a little, I put the delicate minute hand of our son, perfect to the shiny small finger-nails, miraculous as the shells of the sea. The joy, the tremendous adventure of 'giving' life was intense. I pondered deeply over it, seeing the pictures of the Nativity as symbols of that great mystery and identification with maternity.

I had a woman doctor, Dr Carew-Hunt, one of the first batch of brave women who had to go to Ireland to be admitted to their training. I also had a kind monthly nurse who, however, was a disciple of that monster, Dr Truby King. Knowing no better, and naturally terrified of endangering the frail life of my child, I absorbed her teaching. Truby King had decided that babies are hopelessly damaged by their mothers and nurses fussing over them. He had therefore drawn up a list of rules which one disobeyed at the peril of one's child. 'Never feed baby on demand', 'Let it cry until the time marked for its being attended to', 'Don't hold it in your arms more than an hour a day', 'Nurse it yourself, of course, but remember it is a sort of business arrangement, and not an excuse for coddling' or what he called 'spoiling'. And so, every four hours, the baby was allowed out of his cradle and I could cherish him, for the time allowed and no more. Nurse Williams was very firm and absolutely sure, after all the babies she had helped into the world, Truby King was *right*.

My mother, mercifully, did not hold with it. If Anthony gave any sign of prolonged discomfort or anger she was defiant and dauntless. 'Quelle brigande!' she would say of the nurse, and pick up the crying child. She broke all the rules –

except the feeding on demand – and she gave the baby all the cuddling I was restrained from, spoilt him (if it was spoiling) and earned my undying gratitude, even if, at the time, I was not too happy about the outcome, and also a little jealous. My maternal instinct was too unproven to ignore the practical knowledge of a trained nurse, and Truby King ruled the day.

I know now with absolute certainty that babies should have all the love they can get, that Truby King was a cruel, shallow-minded imbecile not to see how immensely important it is, both for the mother and the child, to establish a loving, tactile relationship, a bond of security for the child, of conscious responsibility for the mother; yet I am afraid he had a great deal of influence in his day.

A short time ago, I was privileged to see the film *A Child Is Born* by the French gynaecologist Leboyer. The child is born without anaesthetics, but the mother controls the pains by breathing and an essential knowledge of what is happening. She is taught to share in the delivery, to understand the meaning of the travail of birth. As soon as the baby's perilous journey brings him into the new world, the doctor holds him secure, massages the tiny limbs, the back and chest, assuaging the cries which occasionally break out. The child is stroked with gentle hands, bathed and caressed, tenderly reassured after its ordeal. Let there be no mistake, for the new-born it is an immense effort fraught with fear. The child cries, not only because its lungs must be freed from mucus, but because it is terribly uprooted and frightened. At the end of the film the baby was clothed and the camera turned on the small, pitifully vulnerable face: a smile, a real heart-moving Buddha smile, curled on its lips, transfiguring it with an expression of blessed acceptance.

I was discussing this with our old friend John Bowlby, the famous child psychiatrist. He tells me that, on tracking down the reason for battered babies, it has been found that a good many were separated at birth from their mothers for health or other reasons. The vulnerable chain of maternal response is damaged, the mother cannot sustain the continuous demands made by the infant, and begins to resent it. It is rejected because the link was not forged with the first and continued unforgettable joy of enfolding the child in loving relief. At long last, we are beginning to re-learn the essential lessons of bringing a new life into the world. Fathers and mothers are bound together in the miracle of reproduction, with a new reverence. This is one of the enormous changes which have evolved in our lifetime.

My mother and Lydia between them became absolute slaves to baby Anthony, who was growing his first teeth and being superbly bright and enchanting. He was about six months old when Merton College decided that they needed Postmaster's Hall for one of their own Fellows, and offered us 8 Holywell instead. I was heartbroken; but there was a big garden with the new house, very close to New College.

As soon as we were properly settled Julian, as he writes in his *Memories*, was almost accidentally lured into an expedition to Spitsbergen:

An ornithologically inclined undergraduate called Paget-Wilkes kept pestering me to go with him to study arctic birds, and had set his heart on Greenland. He was so persistent that, in the end, I agreed to see what could be done. I discussed the problem with my zoological colleague Alec Carr-Saunders and the Rev. F.C.R. Jourdain, a local vicar and excellent ornithologist (though also, I regret to say, an avid egg-collector), and decided to organize an all-round scientific expedition to the Arctic, but chose Spitzbergen as an easier target.

When the idea was first bruited, in March 1921, we treated it rather as a joke – a fantastic project bristling with absurdities. But somehow, the idea 'took' and discussions became more and more decisive. Julian asked for my agreement and, although still subject to headaches and fatigue, it seemed possible that such an adventure would give him just that extra lift and strength. It was about two years since his breakdown.

An astonishing number of complications arose, improbable

needs became essential; time was very short and not one person involved had any experience in preparing for this sort of trip. However, at last they got away.

His first letter was very prompt.

> *King's Cross, May 30, 1921*
>
> . . . I look forward to this as giving me final release from all health worries – you can't, even you perhaps, imagine what that means to me. I will write a long letter from the boat tomorrow . . . I think of you erect and brave walking and waving on Oxford platform . . . I do believe, most really, that this trip will enable me to come back a transformed being to you.
>
> Be brave – and be, above all, happy; to help puff each other's sails of soul is our business this next two months.
>
> All my love, Julian

Later, June 10, on board *SS Irma*:

> . . . The ship is very jolly, and old Pocock quite a good cook. I look forward to it more and more. I will tell you more of myself – just now, only by not doing anything but exist for the moment, I am finding what I have been looking for since my last breakdown – no, really since my first – namely a *self* to fall back upon, a continuing self, a something to bring back to join yours, instead of that restless phantasmagoria, that kaleidoscope to which you have been tied. You will understand what I mean . . .

Letters followed each other from ports of call on the way to Spitsbergen, to Prince Charles's Foreland; letters full of arctic space, glaciers floating transparent under pale skies, nearer and nearer to a sun which never set; often ugly weather buffeting the old ship. These pages are now before me, alive with their vivid descriptions, the joy of discovery and unprepared for discomforts. Phalaropes are late in nesting and as yet no male is seen mothering new chicks – though red-throated divers accomplish a new ritual parallel dance, and flowers blossom in protected corners. They are long fascinating letters, fresh, alive, fluently scribbled in his rapid and almost illegible hand, mostly in pencil as biros had not yet been invented.

21 July [1921]

My heart is full of a great peace – I am coming home. Responsibility is nearly at an end for the difficult and harassing task of trying to get so many things done by so many people with so different aims – and more than all I am coming back to my beloved wife and babe. We should be in Tromso on the 26th . . .

Then from the return ship *SS Richard*, 28 July:

Dear Heart – you know when I went off I wrote to you that I should bring back, I hoped, a peaceful soul and a real *me* for you. I think I am. So much restlessness and worry is gone – gone in the spaces of the Arctic, rubbed off by the necessity of doing and finishing things.

I have roots in the great world that go down deeper than before, and can reach higher up towards heaven because I spread more widely upon earth. We will share all the good things together, and make the rest of this vacation a quiet time full of love and happiness.

And soon after, in August, I opened the door at 8 Holywell to a tall fellow with a vigorous red beard, wearing unspeakably dirty and untidy clothes and carrying a kitbag full of smelly rags, without a penny to pay the taxi. We danced with joy while burning the clothes, and rejoiced in the fullness of our hearts.

The magic had worked: no miracle really; the experience had been totally new, calling out totally fresh efforts and adaptations. Julian's nomadic urges had been exorcised, his restlessness redirected; the haunting of his nervous instability had been purged in this surge of enforced physical activities.

For the present, there was indeed a new Julian, gay and peaceful, generous in loving and patiently perceptive of his little family. But it was not the sort of 'continuing self' he spoke of in June from Spitsbergen. As I was to discover in the years to come, there was a protean daimon within – driving him relentlessly and demanding ever new achievements. He set his aims high and had no peace till he reached the target – and always the intellectual power came first, aggressive and voracious, blunting the relaxing joys of simple pleasures, the sensitive needs of the heart.

*   *   *

Before leaving for Spitsbergen, Julian had started an experiment with frogs at the laboratory in the Old Museum. In his absence, it was my job to call in at night and separate the mating frogs so that the eggs laid should be unfertilised for the experiment. It was truly a ghoulish job, the place lit by dim gas-jets, haunted and deserted. The frogs splashed about in their dark tank and one had to catch those who looked busy with their procreative activity and pull them apart; in any case it was a distressing act and I was not happy for the frogs.

Julian had also started an experiment with the little sea-shrimp Gammarus, which entailed noting the colour of the eyes of new-born young under the microscope. I missed my chance of making a discovery, for I never noticed that the colour changed during the first month, and that red-white may turn black-white. All this, however amateurish on my side, made me realise the amount of unrewarded patience, precision, accurate dating and observation which goes into a scientific experiment. I also realised that I was not cut out for that sort of application and very happily relinquished my duties at the Museum when Julian returned.

While he was away, Somerville College, opened in 1879 with the collaboration of Julian's aunt, Mrs Humphry Ward (Mary Arnold), gave a party to celebrate its fiftieth anniversary. The relatives of the founders and of the first students, among whom was Julian's mother Julia (Arnold) were invited to attend, and Queen Mary descended from London to grace the proceedings.

Anthony, grandson of Julia Arnold, was included and I brought him along in his pram. A large gathering awaited the queenly procession, accompanied by Miss Penrose, the imposing Head of the College, with a smile like the Cheshire Cat's.

When the great ladies making their way down the row of guests came to me holding Anthony firmly in my arms, the usual presentation took place, and the Queen solemnly shook hands with seven-months-old baby Anthony, and pronounced: 'If heredity predicts rightly, he will become a great man.' I curtsied my homage and soon after, the guests dismissed, I departed pushing the pram across the quad. Half-way through, I found myself cutting into the prow of the royal convoy. The Queen peered into the pram, recognised mother and child, and announced, 'If heredity predicts rightly, he will become a great man.' She had learnt her part with royal memory.

*   *   *

With Julian's equilibrium so much stabilised, his health and energy improved as well. With the great help given me by my mother and faithful Lydia, I was much freer to fly off with him on our bicycles and even, rather dangerously, on an old motorbike acquired from Carr-Saunders, Julian's scientific colleague. We explored, camped in wild places, visited friends, went to parties, collected things, and altogether led a very full life, while Anthony continued to thrive under what was mostly my mother's care. Julian continued his experiments and his tutorials and finished his book: *Essays of a Biologist*, published in 1923.

We went climbing in the Peak District with a party led by George and Ruth Mallory, George Trevelyan, the historian (married to Julian's cousin, Janet Ward), Walter Elliot and his wife, David Pye, an old friend, godfather of Anthony, and a few other enthusiasts. I had never done any real climbing, but Julian had had some training from his father who took up the sport when over fifty years old. It was grey December weather and we all set off rather grimly to climb a rock-face. George Mallory went first, like a cat clinging to the almost vertical cliff, and I was to follow on the rope: under his confident guidance I found myself so secure and enchanted that in no time at all I was right up alongside, flicking myself up in the appointed hand and foot-holds without effort or the slightest fear. It was like dispensing with the law of gravity.

George Mallory had just decided to rejoin the ill-fated expedition to Everest, from which he never came back. He talked about the oxygen cylinders that, in those days, were being tested, fearing their weight would hamper the climber, while the risk of the machine breaking down meant certain death. Both he and Ruth had a premonition of disaster, but he felt he could not refuse, and she feared that to try to dissuade him would leave him with a deep sense of frustration. They were caught in the dilemma of their too honourable scruples. Watching him swarming up impossible rocks with agility and fluid, beautiful movements was something I cannot forget. He was admired by his Cambridge friends as a perfect athlete and a man with the gift to delight.

The days in rain and fog up at the Peak were a new joy and discovery. There was this sense of miraculous potentialities in conquering what looked like implacable climbs, and fun in the evenings, sitting round the fire and listening to grand tales of mountains. George Trevelyan was superb, sticking it out with fierce determination in a once-white pullover – his laughter a mixture between a bark and a donkey's bray: he was a careful but awkward climber, whose good humour never failed him.

A few years later Julian took me up a high pass between Courmayeur and Aosta, but I never felt the same exhilaration and fearlessness. Another time, as we were crossing a wide glacier near Val d'Isère, two black spots crawling on a deserted snowscape, Julian fell into a crevasse. Suddenly there was nothing at the end of the rope, not even his voice. I gripped that rope as hard as I could and pulled with all my might, with the power of despair. Then his voice blew up from the icy bowels: 'Stop pulling that rope, you are cutting me in half.' Soon after he emerged, adjusted his glasses and calmly went on: it was luckily a crack only twelve feet deep and narrow enough to wriggle out of. We went on more cautiously, but I was thoroughly shaken.

No, I never became a climber, but Julian and I enjoyed many wonderful walking tours, in Scotland, in Wales, in Switzerland, where we happily left the children with my mother. Julian was contagiously venturesome and loved exploring, always binoculated for birds or distant heights, keeping data, missing nothing. He was also an excellent botanist, and his memory was infallible. With rucksacks containing essentials, blissfully free, we walked into a new awareness of nature, and forgot our own selves. Julian had a gift of enhancing the moment, making a memorable event of an ordinary walk. He was intensely aware of the moods and treasures of the natural world, knew mountains and their geological structures, feeling their bones under the skin of earth and trees. I loved his all-embracing recognition – knitting together the earth and the animal world, including human beings, even though he was not really as interested in people as he was in knowledge, in ideas and, passionately, in birds.

I was a good disciple for his learning and, by a natural process of osmosis, absorbed much without effort. I failed in ornithology and now deeply regret my ignorance. There was perhaps one thing in which I was never docile: the broad conclusions of evolution always seemed to me to leave something immensely important out of count. That something still hangs in my mind when I read, for instance, my son Anthony's book *Plant and Planet*: the inventive cunning, the extravagant adornment, the infinite variety and unsurpassable beauty of that world of plants and trees which seem to have no necessary purpose in evolution. Nor can one really find a reason for the iridescent beauty of the feather of a peacock, for the preposterous fantasy of a bird of paradise; or, taken at random, the feather fish, the magic inhabitants of coral reefs, all the unimaginable small creatures one now has the privilege to see through the miracles of photography, more surrealist than inventions of the greatest surrealist artists.

And from another viewpoint, look at the implacable caval-cade of viruses, defying all rules in order to survive. Consider also the processions of prehistoric animals now extinct and their inexplicable gigantism. Above all, think of Man, Man himself, according to Julian the highest achievement of evolu-tion and, according to Konrad Lorenz, the missing link be-tween Neanderthal and Homo Sapiens: man with his world of consciousness as well as subconsciousness, his urge to love and create beauty, his adventure of awareness and understanding; all that and his fearsome capacity for evil – knowing it evil yet doing it. Evolution, based as it is on the continuous physical adjustment of organisms to constantly varying external condi-tions, explains one broad principle in the process of life, but does it at all bear upon the inexplicable, non-physical pilgrim-age? Julian and I never finished this endless discussion.

★   ★   ★

Oxford in termtime had many pleasures. At 8 Holywell the drawing-room was large enough to allow charades, the special charades invented, I believe, by the Haldanes. They were called Nebuchadnezzars, or Nebuchs for short. An act was played on the first letter of someone famous, and the last act was the full name of yet another great personality. Noah was a great favourite, being short and rich in possibilities of per-mutations. The party divided in two teams, out-vying each other in digging up obscure characters, mostly from the Old Testament. The house was ransacked for props, sheets torn off beds, anyone's fur coat going four-legged, domestic imple-ments and baby's bath or pram dragged up for a full-grown student. Needless to say, these objects were never quite the same again, but Julian was a dauntless impresario, reckless and audacious. It would take long to enumerate our triumphs, but I think Landru, the bald ivory-headed murderer 'took the cake'. The final bit was the burning of his victims in his kitchen stove – in our case a small oil-stove crested with sausages and riding boots: a splendid macabre effect.

Then there were glorious long holidays, which Julian planned carefully and endowed with his own particular touch. Of
course, for me, it was a battle of loyalties between my family
and Julian's exacting demands. He was used to winning, and
my mother was a wonderful substitute for me, but I always
rushed back in an agony of impatience. One lovely autumn
during these early days at Oxford, we went off on a walking
tour from Berwick-on-Tweed to Dunbar, following the
coastline, through forests of sea-buckthorn covered with red
berries; we were both full of energy and the joys of exploring.
It must have been near St Abb's Head that we saw the distant
fluttering of white wings on the beach, which Julian then took
to be strange great birds. Mystified and determined, we leapt
on rocks and boulders to find not birds but large books lying
haphazardly, their covers destroyed by water but their dry
pages shuffled incessantly as by unseen hands, offering clear
printed texts. They were the most improbable *objets trouvés* –
shipwrecked pulpit bibles thrown up by some recent storm on
the rocky deserted shore.

'Have you ever read the Song of Solomon?' asked Julian.

'Of course not,' I replied, 'my mother would never have
allowed it.'

So we sat among the bibles whose dancing pages barely
ruffled the silence, and Julian read the unforgettable Song,
sensuous in its passionately human appeal. Among the
bibles were smaller books, instructing would-be missionaries
arriving on alien shores how to make shelters, to plant seeds,
to start their mission. Further along, the coast was black with
spilt bitumen, possibly from the same shipwreck. We never
found the source of our extraordinary discovery.

One winter we went to Naples and stayed with Reinhardt
Dohrn and his lovable Russian wife Tania. The Naples
Aquarium was then a Dohrn concern though, during the First
World War, the Italians had tried very hard to expatriate the
German family. Julian had spent many fertile months at the
Aquarium after getting his First in Oxford, working in the

laboratories created by Anton Dohrn, with the co-operation of T. H. Huxley. Incidentally, Julian learnt not only the Naples dialect, but from his co-students fluent German based on what he had already learned at Heidelberg. Equipped by Tania with oranges and dates, fresh figs and bread, we wandered all round the ancient pagan land with its colourful Christian rituals – the persistent texture of earth-bound superstitions and Virgin-Mother. Christ died for our unworthy souls, but she held forth the helping hand with the sweet promise of intervention.

We climbed Vesuvius, puffing and panting, and leapt down again propelled by persistent guides. I shall never forget mine, a toothless old rascal who seized me by the waist and took off, down the almost vertical slope of pumice. Barely touching the ground before leaping down another five metres, in a few minutes of ecstatic parabolic leaps we had reached the base. For an instant of time, he had been a winged god, radiantly conquering the world of space. Back on the hard soil, he dribbled his thanks for a well-earned tip.

Then there was Pompeii and its street of tombs, with the deeply worn tracks made by carriage wheels on the stone-paved narrow roads and the atrium where a fountain sang its gentle lament for the ancient calamity. There were the majestic temples of Paestum, vivid in memory; and Amalfi and Sorrento and the tenacious villages perched like birds' nests on craggy slopes. We went to Cumae, the early Greek settlement by the deep blue of the sea, and returned tired after a long walk, hitching a lift from an old cart along a very bumpy road. I was just beginning my second pregnancy and did not relish those bumps.

During the next year, while Julian was finishing his *Essays of a Biologist*, Francis was quietly accomplishing his own little miracle of embryonic evolution, and was born in late August 1923, at Holywell, Oxford. He was another marvel of delight, placid, contented, hardly crying at all, with large grey-green eyes, and melting smile.

Babies are commonplace enough; there are probably too many of them anyway; but each is an imponderable mystery, a prodigy of creation. Subjecting the bodies of both mother and child to the most crucial trial of survival, it is perhaps the deepest experience a woman can have.

*   *   *

At Holywell, before Francis was born, we found the house big enough to take a lodger. One of them was Gavin de Beer. He and I did not like each other. He shared our breakfast while we fought for Julian's attention. If he got in first, we had a scientific discussion excluding me by its depth. If I did, we talked of homely matters. Gavin was truly a brilliant student and became Director of the Imperial Museum of Science, but in those early days, he compensated for his short stature by a curious arrogance which many disliked, including Alec Carr-Saunders. As time wore on, however, both Alec and I shared a mellowing tolerance and I grew to like and admire Gavin. Julian was above these reactions and got on very well with him, later collaborating with him on several books.

Our last lodger was Corliss Lamont. His mother, Florence, was a great admirer and friend of Masefield and thus he came to us, before going to Harvard University to read Law. He left Law for Philosophy, resigned his Professorship at Columbia to be one of the first determined fighters against the McCarthy terror, became a great Humanist and in 1975 gave Julian an important Memorial Tribute at the Ethical Union in New York. There are few precious friendships like his.

6

London, H.G. Wells and The Science of Life

We lived in and loved Oxford until 1925, when Professor Dendy died and Julian succeeded him in the Chair of Zoology at King's College, London. It was sad to leave Oxford, where we had so naturally made many friends. It also meant going further from Garsington, always enchanting and stimulating: not quite the same for me as in those days of my green past when everything had been a new experience and the very air was charged with expectation. I was now married, perhaps dangerously, fulfilled by my two young children; my husband blazing his trail in a larger, wider horizon. Lady Ottoline was my fixed star, concerned, kind and generous though herself going through troubled times, the depths of which I could barely fathom.

I had cherished the atmosphere of a university town, still in its time-capsule. Something undefeatable survives in its lovely colleges and gardens, its scholarly endeavours, its libraries and bookshops, but it can never be the same again. Lord Hailsham, in 1979, described Oxford as the 'Quartier Latin of Cowley', the thriving factories of Morris cars.

London. We spent some time home-hunting, and finally bought, on mortgage, a corner house in the new Holly Lodge Estate, a 'Tudoriffic' enclave on the edge of Hampstead Heath, away from general traffic and safe for our two small boys. No. 31 Hillway was our home for seven years. It was a roomy house, devoid of character, but comfortable enough. Anthony went to prep school on top of the hill, at Byron

House, soon followed by Francis. They sailed their fragile boats on the ponds on the Heath and learnt to bicycle along its safe lanes. Julian took the tram down to the Strand, reading and writing all the way, spent the day at King's College and came back tired and frustrated. King's was not Oxford – his students were mostly youths doing a short biology course before embarking on medicine. His own experiments were not exciting, something had gone out of trim. He thrived at high pressure, using the tension to propel himself forward.

His success with the axolotl was followed by another with planarus (the little aquatic worm continuously reborn from pieces of its body, testing to the full its powers of regeneration) which also made headlines. These gave him a hunger for something more significant. He was like a young lion roaring for his prey.

Ernest Barker, Principal of King's College, wrote to him: 'How easily you dash off lectures and books and letters. There is a kind of leaping grace which fascinates me – all the more as I often get so tired when I try to leap. I am not teasing you – I mean what I say.'

He often felt the need to escape into the country, to walk off his frustrations and stretch his mind, away from the cage of his profession. On one of his days away I wrote:

. . . It will be good to have you home again – yet I am not lonely in your absence, as your letters bring me a joy to last the day. I feel sometimes as if we get nearer each other with these daily shreds of ourselves, nearer anyway than we got last term in London. I love your letters, always read them twice at least, every word. And so I piece together a *you* which is not the tired Julian who comes home just in time for supper, his own spirit asleep under his brain – asleep or anyway, turned away from me . . .

Almost every weekend was spent somewhere without the children, left in charge of their nurse; and if by chance we were at home Julian took us on some expedition to the Zoo, to Kew Gardens, to Box Hill. It was only on rare family vacations that we really could be ourselves, get to know each other and taste the small important acts of daily life.

In between bouts of furious activity I was too idle within myself, aimless in that immense city, discouraged also by Julian's curious habit of often contradicting me in company. I became depressed, unwell, and insecure with an inferiority complex; this annoyed Julian, blind to my perplexities and helplessness. The vulnerable flame of joy was dimmed.

Francis's health began also to give serious trouble. He seemed to catch every illness, including Bell's Palsy, which he woke up with one terrible morning; he also had measles, whooping cough and eye trouble. He bore it all with a strange patience and courage. I was torn with anxiety.

Anthony was a highly strung child, and he too suffered from the lack of cohesion in our family. Quick and very intelligent, he would have responded wonderfully to guidance from his father. But Julian never had the time, nor the patience to give more than moments of intensive play to his children, treating them like super-toys for his own play. Anthony became a problem, difficult, bullying his little brother, refusing discipline. Julian laughed at his spurts of naughtiness, delighted to find so much of himself in his child. I found a precious letter from my mother which sums up the situation, written in October 1926, after we had spent several weeks at Bel-Air:

Pourquoi cette tristesse, Juliette? Oui, je comprends . . . C'est à vous deux d'élever ce cher et précieux petit Anthony, au père surtout; qu'il le fasse le jour, pas avant le coucher. Il faut pour Anthony une vie régulière et sans excitements, de la joie, de l'amour; si l'enfant fatigué de sa journée s'excite, crac, Julian se fâche, et pauvre Anthony crie et devient méchant. Il faut respecter chez lui l'enfant . . . l'enfant. Cette superbe petite intelligence doit être dirigée avec beaucoup de patience, sans demander trop à la fois, car l'enfant se fatigue de suivre une même idée . . . Chez lui, la croissance, le développement lui mange les nerfs; il lui faut le calme, l'eau froide, la vie au grand air, et tu auras un petit homme qui portera avec honeur le nom de Huxley.

J'étais sur le point d'écrire à Julian que tu as besoin de repos car vraiment tu n'es pas tout à fait bien, et c'est là surtout qu'il faut agir; pense comme tu es jeune et pourtant toujours si sérieuse. Voyons ma Juliette, sois jeune pour ton mari, pour tes petits . . . jeune et jolie . . .

This perceptive letter showed my mother in a new light: her own children had not been blessed with such concern nor had my father ever been allowed to interfere with her Calvinistic rule of the home. Free from her responsibilities to her *pension-nat* and the financial strain of the days of my childhood, she opened her heart to her little grandsons, and took loving charge of them when Julian and I went voyaging and left them in her care.

I was evidently far from well, grimly and humourlessly shouldering my responsibilities and anxieties, afraid to talk it over with an impatient Julian. I could not blame him for my failure to adapt myself to the new sort of life we both had to learn to live.

Yet we led a busy social life and met many interesting persons, including Arnold Bennett, resplendent in embroidered waistcoats, with his rabbit teeth and stammer felicitously punctuating his speech. Lady Colefax often asked us to her famous parties – so different from Ottoline's in that chief guests were chosen for their fame. One was always sure of meeting some star, and sometimes introduced to the great. Sometimes not. Didn't St John Hutchinson, on one occasion, suggest that Sibyl Colefax should ask Tom Mix and his horse, and anyway introduce him to the horse? Nevertheless, she was a remarkable woman, with an unquenchable passion for celebrities who enjoyed her gatherings. It must have taken an enormous amount of social skill and energy to organise them so successfully. It was at one of these that I saw Raymond Mortimer sitting bewitched at the feet of the striking Nancy Cunard, pale as a scented lily, glittering with gold and fascination.

We also met H. G. Wells, and that was another turning point. He had just finished his *Outline of History*, a triumphant break into a new vertical vision of history. I remember George Trevelyan, the aggressive historian, remarking that the *Outline* was a sort of blasphemy of history as he knew it – but that he wished he could have done it himself.

H. G. Wells was ensconced in a radiant reputation. He had invented a new type of person in his novels, and no one ever surpassed his Mr Kipps or Mr Polly. They were facets of himself, the part of himself he built on as a youth to become The Mr H. G. Wells. They embody his imagination, his agility, his deviousness, his avidity for learning, his quarrelsomeness, his curiously placed vanity and amorousness and his lovable sense of humour. His real ambition was more serious, he saw the whole world as a mis-shapen Brain-Power which only needed a course of trenchant thinking to put it right. He saw himself as such a thinker, capable of mugging up the necessary facts and drawing the essential valid conclusions. He did, passionately, care about the results of political misbehaviour and desperately sought to give all he could drag out of his clear determined intelligence to 'set the world straight'. By the time we knew him he had outlived the scandals of his illicit amours, though the taboos he had so recklessly disregarded still shook the lives of his loves.

In 1929 we often joined him at meetings of *The Realist*, together with Bertie Russell, Major Church, Richard Gregory, Herbert Read, Alec Carr-Saunders, Malinowski, Gerald Heard, Naomi Mitchison, Eileen and Rhoda Power, Hilda Matheson and others.

I was always delighted to see Bertie Russell again, remembering my platonic passion for his electrifying mind. We danced together at The Gargoyle Club. I wrote in my diary: 'not dangerously, but curiously umbilically'. Malinowski did an odd Charleston which Eileen Power called 'the sexual dance of the savages – as strange as if one were dancing with a tassel'. H.G. only danced on compulsion, and sedately promenaded Hilda Matheson round the floor.

But these are crumbs from more important business. H.G. was an ardent ex-student of T.H. Huxley. Julian as his grandson caught some of the glory which shone on T.H.; H.G. considered him as a possible collaborator for his next venture, *The Science of Life*. This was a vast project, but dazzling. After much thought, Julian accepted, and for over two years our lives were dominated by strenuous, purposeful labour. We spent many a weekend at Easton Glebe, H.G.'s lovely house in Kent. The mornings were stormy with dissection of manuscripts, Julian, Gip Wells and H.G. in combat; the rest of the day given over to games, including the famous 'Barn Game'★ which H.G. and his family had invented.

We also went to Grasse, where H.G. and Odette Keun had built an enchanting house, and were 'honeymooning' between the usual effervescent bouts of hard work. I liked Odette. Of course, she often shocked me, but it was all genuinely noninhibiting, neither unhealthy nor malignant. She was highly intelligent, avid for life, not selective but full of vitality. H.G. enjoyed her fireworks for weeks at a time, then claimed he had business in London and, as she was not supposed to enter the UK, he could conveniently leave her behind. They were a most oddly paired couple, sparking each other off to extravagant displays of wit and temper and sexual attraction. To be a witness during meals plus quarrels was a stirring experience: no holds barred. 'Sale petit calicot!' she flung out and he, unabashed, would throw back her mysterious oriental polygonal career.

But H.G. was a kind host and often took us for long drives into that magnificent country of Provence. I specially remember him taking us to Les Baux, the ruined city perched on crags, deserted for fear of the Corsairs from Arabia in search of slaves, the houses hollow shells, ghosts and hungry cats marching the streets.

★ I cannot remember how this was played, except that any number of people could join in, and a ball had to hit a target to score.

Of course, it all had to end; H.G. was a discriminating philanderer, a taster of many dishes, a charmer with few defeats. Baroness Moura Budberg took the place of the indignant Odette, yet refused to marry him. He bitterly lamented this: 'But, H.G., isn't it perhaps poetic justice?'

7

Les Diablerets
and D. H. Lawrence

We rented the Chalet des Arolles at Diablerets, above Aigle for the winter of 1927–28. Aldous and Maria, their boy Matthew aged seven and a half and his governess were to join us. We had our two boys, Anthony barely seven and Francis not yet six; my mother also came for a short time as well as Maria's sister Rose and my cousin Elaine Howlett. The chalet was roomy and comfortable, and we were well looked after by a local woman, with a girl from Neuchâtel for our boys.

Aldous was deep in *Point Counter Point*, urged to work by Maria after our pleasant leisurely breakfast; Julian equally deep in the *Science of Life*; while Maria and I busied ourselves typing pages hot from the pen. Actually Maria was typing D. H. Lawrence's first version of *Lady Chatterley's Lover*, for Lawrence and Frieda arrived a few days after us, and settled in the Chalet Beau-Site, a few steps away. We met every day at Les Arolles, or on a picnic somewhere up the mountain, joining the Lawrences on our skis.

I had seen Lawrence and Frieda before at Garsington in 1915. I remember Lawrence meticulously copying a Persian miniature and saying that only thus could one absorb the perfection of such works. Frieda was then in her prime, defiantly handsome, wearing a bouquet of parma violets pinned on her fur. Aldous had also met Lawrence at Garsington, and later in London. In fact, in December 1915 he had been bowled over by Lawrence's passionate dream of 'Rananim' – the visionary escape from the war, from rebellion against his poverty, the British way of life, his fierce equivocal fights with Frieda, captured but not subjugated, and finally the terrible shadow of tuberculosis, always vehemently denied but all too true. Aldous had become one of his temporary converts and Lawrence wrote to Ottoline in December 1915: 'I like Huxley *very* much. He will come to Florida.' This immediate response was shared by the Middleton Murrys, Heseltine, Brett, Gertler, and others.

Lawrence's obsessive dream took many years of ripening. In a long letter to Ottoline in February 1915 he had written:

I want you to form the nucleus of a new community which shall start a new life amongst us – a life in which the only riches [is] in integrity of character. So that each one may fulfil his own nature and deep desire to the utmost, but wherein tho', the ultimate satisfaction and joy is in the completeness of us all as one . . . And the new community shall be established upon the known, eternal and good part in us.

. . . And a man shall not come to save his own soul. Let his soul go to hell. He shall come because he knows that his own soul is not the be-all and end-all, but that all souls of all things do but compose the body of God, and that God indeed shall BE . . . *

Many things were to happen after those long past grandiloquent plans were made. Lawrence never went to his Florida; his poverty, lungs and restlessness drove him to New York, to Mexico, to Germany and to Italy where, after some years, he met Aldous again, by then married to Maria. A deep friendship was formed amongst the four of them, and the Lawrences were easily persuaded to join us all in Diablerets.

Out of the way of casual visitors, set in its white landscape which sheltered our simple but fertile life, it was a wonderfully neutral ground. As Julian writes in his *Memories*, he and Aldous took it in turn to read to us in the evenings, with a contagious skill, and got through the whole of the *Pickwick Papers*, which they both relished and knew almost by heart.

* *The Letters of D.H. Lawrence*, edited by Aldous Huxley, Heinemann, 1932.

Many a peaceful evening was spent in that warm room, at the end of the day's work.

Our days at Les Arolles were very full. The three small boys filled the chalet with their growing life, all three speaking French, mildly disciplined by Matthew's governess. After lunch we put on skis and went for a run down the nearby slopes, sometimes joining the Lawrences for a picnic in a sheltered corner, the boys on their sledges or playing in the igloo Julian and Aldous had built for them. The sun shone till about four when the shadow of the Diablerets hump fell on the valley and cooled the air. We always resented that early dying of the day, and sometimes climbed to the Col du Pillon to prolong the blessed sunshine. On the whole, the weather was fine with only a few scurries of snow cleaning the surface of our landscape. Then it shone with its new whiteness, spilling pale blue shadows, moulding the gentle slopes with a great peace. Pine trees took their burden in shaggy bundles and the square roofs of chalets added their own symmetry. Soon the tracery of wheels or sledges, skis or footprints etched their pattern.

At teatime, the Lawrences joined us and my mother took up her handwork, involving Lawrence in designing a border for a cardigan, and Frieda in giving advice. These hours were happy, filled with a gentle creativity in embroidery, at which both the Lawrences were adept. The village had no tourist emporium yet, but I managed to buy a sort of dishcloth which served as a canvas and some mending wools of various colours. Touched by the subtle but definite influence of Lawrence, I wanted to embroider Adam and Eve in their paradise; stitch by stitch the Man and the Woman stood by a brook, with enchanted beasties around them and blossoming trees above pierced by God's gigantic eye. Lawrence finished Adam's genital organs which I had fumbled, adding a black virile business to a perfectly sensible phallus. He obviously enjoyed this last touch and the collaboration which crystallised these precious moments.

There were discussions of every kind: but we learnt to avoid scientific ones, as Lawrence had a very definite dislike and block about everything not based on his primary instinct. The theories of evolution enraged him, even when Aldous gently reminded him that they were proven and based on natural processes. 'It's all BUNK, they may be facts but not truths,' Lawrence shouted, getting red in the face. Lawrence had a firmly rooted personal distrust of evolution. He writes in 1917 to Eunice Tiegen: 'There is no evolving, only unfolding. The lily is in the bit of dust which is its beginning, lily and nothing but lily. Man was man in eternity, has been man since the beginning of time, and is man in the resulting eternity; no evolution, only unfolding of what *is* man.'* Julian had given up trying to explain, and mercifully kept quiet, but Lawrence was always suspicious and tense when his 'mores' were threatened – almost as if he feared to be challenged, even convinced. He loved talking about his Mexican experiences, about Mabel Dodge Luhan, the 'tiger woman', about Brett and her quirks, and about Ottoline – towards whom he felt uneasy, perhaps guilty – and promised he would write to her, after their long quarrel. (He did.)

At the Chalet Beau-Site he and Frieda did all their own housework and cooking: Lawrence was an excellent cook and produced delicious lemon-curd on crisp little pasties for tea when we were invited there. He cooked as he did most things, with a radiating creativeness which was contagious. Even washing-up had its own charm, enriched with the satisfaction of putting everything back in its chosen place, glowing with fresh cleanliness. He had trained Frieda to feel this joy, and that was no mean achievement: Frieda, the proud, arrogant Baronin, scrubbed the table or the floor, with might and power, forgetting that in her golden youth she had never even suspected that somebody did these mean jobs. 'I believe the chief tie between me and Lawrence was always the wonder of living

* *The Letters of D.H. Lawrence*, edited by Aldous Huxley.

. . . every little or big thing that happened carried its glamour with it'★ – the wonder of living which is resonant in all his writings. One could say that it would always have been his gift, whatever his destiny; but it often seemed that it was Frieda, elemental, highly sexed, untamed female, who was his catalyst. She could taunt him by her very laziness into violence and creative power. But the fire was always there, the Phoenix which so truly was his emblem.

Above all, he believed in life, rejecting the Christ Crucified. It was the living Christ he knew, deep in the very roots of his being – the joyful, life-loving Christ who walked through the fields and saw the lilies in all their splendour, the angry young man who shook the people and healed the sick souls.

The cruel years of the First World War had left deep poisonous wounds in both the Lawrences, wounds which should never be underestimated. Paul Delany, in his book *D.H. Lawrence's Nightmare*, quotes a letter from Katherine Mansfield to Brett, describing how he had again become the ideal companion of pre-war days:

For me, at least, the dove brooded over him, too. I loved him. He was just his old, merry, rich self, laughing, describing things, giving you pictures, full of enthusiasm and joy in a future where we become all 'vagabonds' – we simply did not talk about people. We kept to things like nuts and cowslips and fires in woods and his black self WAS not. Oh, there is something so lovable about him and his eagerness, his passionate eagerness for life – that is what one loves so.

His passionate eagerness for life – yes, that was the essence of the Lawrence one loved, in his being, in his writing. He knew life with the innate complicity of root and sap, with the unappeasable love of a man doomed to die young. Meanwhile he wandered from land to land, living his spartan life and fighting his mate for dominance. Frieda was his challenge – and being Frieda, she took up the challenge and fought back.

★ *Not I but the Wind* by Frieda Lawrence, Heinemann, 1935.

Lawrence's nomadism disturbed her but he suppressed her yearnings for a solid house and its furnishings with fanatical rebuttals. Her touching efforts to sink roots in the many lodgings of their life could only amount to collecting a few bits of bright china, a lovely piece of furniture, curtains or a bit of carpet; then came the day of moving – the packing up, and the brutal parting with her small treasures. They were given away to friends or neighbours, ruthlessly left behind, and Frieda had to accept the next resting place, anonymous and characterless. For Lawrence had a horror of possessions – of the subtle power of a cosy familiar fireside, a shelf of well-loved books. Restlessly, he travelled all over the world, to Germany, Italy, Switzerland, Australia, Ceylon, America, New Mexico and Mexico. He travelled far, he travelled light. No clutter entangled him with the place he had left behind. Yet, as soon as they had found new lodgings, he would scrub, paint, tidy and rearrange the place to his own particular spartan pattern. As I knew him at Diablerets, he never talked of his journeyings. He lived day by day, creating his present, aware of its hourly claims. At first, Frieda resentfully lay on the bed, smoking, until once again Lawrence had brought his vital partnership to the tools needed for living, creating their new home. Then she could start *her* nest-building, collect some bright wool and stitch a cushion-cover, or plant a gay flower on the window-sill.

*   *   *

As time passed at Diablerets I began to sense in Julian a restless impatience, an impervious need to assert himself. He was under the strain of finishing *The Science of Life*, and anxious about the future. Our quiet days became charged with tension, Julian playing a part towards Aldous and me – a curious sort of 'I'm the king of the castle' role, excluding others in discussions. Aldous was courteous as always but also a little uncomfortable.

It was not long before Lawrence began to resent Julian's

attitude. One afternoon, when my mother and I were having tea at Beau-Site, he began to speak about what I always felt was my secret world. Profoundly embarrassed, I barely listened because my mother was there, and although she did not understand every word in English, I feared she was hearing too much. Lawrence was hard on Julian: he thought him 'an expurgated version of a man; like so many others; much the greatest danger for men'. Frieda made encouraging noises, and I felt trapped, far too repressed to risk a discussion. What a chance I missed, sitting there frozen and numb . . . '*Par delicatesse j'ai perdu ma vie*' as Rimbaud summed it up. Dear Lawrence. He was full of the unpasteurised milk of human kindness, he blundered into vulnerable situations, knowing that *he* was right and that all would be well if only people listened to him. He believed in taking action whatever the moment, or the results, as he always did when Frieda and he exploded with rage, smashing spiritual and material china at each other, exhausting the flow of adrenalin and finishing by making beautiful love . . .

This, alas, was not my way, nor Aldous's. I wish it had been, for it was in fact what Julian wanted and needed: to release the tension he could not cope with by himself. Aldous was perceptive and, in all the years I knew him, never once lost his temper. He preferred to remain the silent watcher, the observer of human quirks. Besides, he had a younger brother's respect for Julian, his senior by seven years – the vulnerable years when Julian brought home the prizes of his intellectual and athletic successes. It must have been impressive to a youngster at prep school to see Julian getting the Brackenbury Scholarship, the Newdigate Prize, the Oxford Blue, the brilliant First in his final exams. Julian, nevertheless, always recognised in Aldous a superior quality, with some greater dimension to his mind.

It became a strange disruptive time – difficult equally for all of us, yet controlled outwardly by the ritual of the days. The mornings were always busy with Julian and Aldous at their

writing, while Maria and I attended to the housekeeping and
the typing, the three boys at their lessons and, now the sun was
getting warmer, lying naked on the balcony enjoying a sun-
bath. Lovely little growing bodies, in health and spirits, each a
different character. They were becoming rather bored, with
their igloo melting, and the sledges getting bogged down in wet
snow. They too needed a change – our time was running out.

When Maria had at last finished typing *Lady Chatterley*,
Lawrence allowed me to read it. My feelings were very mixed;
being prudish and puritanical, specially compared to Maria
who, though younger, was worldly-wise and sophisticated, I
was somewhat shocked by the exclusive importance he gave
to the sexual side. It was disturbing as, of course, he intended it
to be. And in a long talk we had about it, I said I did not think it
a good novel, being unbalanced, with but little depth, and a
very limited message, although I had found some pages very
beautiful. I also told him he should call it John Thomas and
Lady Jane, because that was really all it was about. He exploded with laughter. He had a very special way of laughing,
tilting his head and pointing his small red beard at one, his
bright blue eyes twinkling and merriment melting out of his
every pore. He than announced that many a wise word was
spoken in anger, and that he would give the novel its new
name. Orioli, the printer in Florence, was alerted – but later
Lawrence was rightly persuaded that it would not be to the
advantage of the book to wave so flagrant a flag. So it went
back to Lady C.

He laughed again when, flapping my maternal wings, I
asked what would happen if Anthony found this book at
sixteen and read its risky message? This, remember, was in
1928, before the permissive society had emerged. I lived to see
my granddaughters reading the book at fifteen in the bath.
Actually, Lawrence knew perfectly well that he had forced the
pace: he wrote to Koteliansky* on December 23, 1927, just

* Samuel Koteliansky, born in the Ukraine 1880, died in London. Came to

before he and Frieda joined us in Diablerets:

My dear Kot,

I do not think this is the low-water mark of existence. I never felt so near the brink of the abyss. But in 1928 something is *bound* to begin new: must. We are trampled almost to extinction – we *must* have a new turn soon.

As for my novel, it's half done, but so improper, you wouldn't dare to touch it. It's the most improper novel ever written: and as Jehovah you would probably find it sheer pornography. But it isn't. It's a declaration of the phallic reality. I doubt if it will ever be published. But certainly no English printer would print it. When one is in despair, one can only go one worse. I am driven to *le plus plus pis aller*.

Oh dear, why are you Jehovahish! I could wish you a little Satanic I am certainly going that way. *Satanasso*! It's a nice word. I am weary of Jehovah, he's always so right.†

This letter is explicit and interesting, for Kot was not a man to be fobbed off with phrases. Lawrence meant every word of it – and this 'when one is in despair, one can only go one worse' brings back to mind all the misery and poverty Lawrence had to endure all his life – and the 'satanic' self grafted on to so generous a person. Even so, his bark was ever worse than his bite, and his quarrels soon forgotten.

Later, he wrote me a little poem he called 'Henriette'.

> O Henriette
> I remember yet
> How cross you were
> Over Lady C.
> How you hated her
> And detested me.

London in 1911, never returned to Russia. Loyal friend of D.H. Lawrence, Katherine Mansfield, Mark Gertler, Dorothy Brett, Leonard Woolf, James Stephen, Ralph Hodgson, Dorothy Richardson, J.W.N. Sullivan, Lady Ottoline Morrell, Beatrice Glenavy, Dilys Powell – and many others.
† Letter 295 from the Villa Mirenda, Scandici, Firenze, in *The Quest for Rananim*: Letters to Koteliansky 1914–1930, (George J. Zytaruk).

And now you see,
You don't mind a bit
You've got used to it
And you feel more free.

And now you know
How good we were
Up there in the snow
With Lady C.
Though you hated her
At the first go.

Yet now you see
How she set us free
To laugh and be
More spontaneous, and we
Were happy, weren't we
Up there in the snow
With the world below.*

Of course, Lady C. even in its third rewritten version was
rather a blunt instrument, and suffered all the indignities of
being publicly execrated, anathematised and finally suppressed. It survived underground and by private circulation, until
it attained final reprieve. Lawrence had wanted to shock the
world into admitting the joys of sex. In 1929 it was not a
subject to be discussed. Lawrence launched his lonely crusade
against the ranks of that pliant hypocrisy backed by the
Establishment and hit his Goliath well between the eyes. It
was a grand fight, and he relished it.

He was impetuous and careless, trusting his instinct more
than his manners; another letter to me (28 April) deplores the
fact without admitting it:

I hope Maria doesn't repeat things maliciously. Just had a long
malignant letter from a friend saying all that Maria said I'd said
carried on by Y.F., and home by a sister of the maligned and much
worse than anything I'd really said casually and explosively. It's too

---

* Later published in *Pansies*, Martin Secker, 1929.

bad, of course I say all sorts of things – you yourself know perfectly
well the things I say about people – but they aren't malicious and
méchant things, just momentary. People who *repeat* things are really
wicked – because they always pour vitriol, of their own . . .

But of course, people did repeat things maliciously. And
even if Lawrence thought himself innocent, he was not ex-
empt from furibund outbursts which surprised one by their
violence – sometimes quelled by a burst of laughter. He lived
by thrusting his thoughts into flames; there was something
incandescent about him. Lawrence identified himself with
Frieda, and when she fell off her pedestal he lost his temper as if
he had been betrayed. Even her violent fit of coughing caused
by a crumb in her throat enraged him: 'Stop it, woman,' he
snarled. Tears sprang into her eyes, her large loose body shook
with choking efforts under his white fury. And it was worse
when she said something he thought foolish. But she always
stood up to him and as, elementally, she was the stronger, she
won and had her way. When she vanished on one of her
periodic prowls, he was left vulnerable like an orphan.

★   ★   ★

At Diablerets, the white skin of snow was melting into
prudent green. I even found a gallant gentian blazing its
blueness through a nest of snow. Julian went back to London
and the next chapter of *The Science of Life*; Aldous and Maria
returned to Paris to finish getting into a house in Suresnes
which they did not really like. Frieda disappeared; Lawrence,
the children and I were left to pack up, until he too had to go. I
accompanied him to Aigle as the sudden change of altitude
might have over-tired him. Lawrence had this tiresome cough
which he insisted was purely 'bronchial'. Actually, as we all
knew, it was TB of the lungs, and he needed the pure high
altitude to control it. Nothing would induce him to accept the
fact. If he had stayed so long at Diablerets, it really was because
he was happy. All the same, he longed to get well, and having
heard that coltsfoot tisane was an old-fashioned remedy,

accepted from the boys offerings of the early flowers we picked in rocky crannies.

He got as far as Paris and soon collapsed with a bad bout of pneumonia. Aldous called a doctor who again diagnosed TB, but Lawrence would have none of it. He was indeed very ill, until Frieda reappeared. Aldous described how she blazed in, in the fulness of her elemental vitality and Lawrence leapt out of bed, cured. We wondered at these so often repeated miracles, this spark of Frieda's which kept him alive long after the medical pundits had given him up. Who can tell? Not for nothing did Lawrence choose the Phoenix for his symbol.

8

First Trek in Africa

*We carry with us the wonders we seek without us;
there is all Africa and her prodigies in us.*

SIR THOMAS BROWNE

In London, when I rejoined Julian with the children, *The Science of Life* was progressing, with lively shots from H.G. who wanted, nay insisted on, as near perfection as he could squeeze from his two contributors: it was a valuable experience for Julian, confirming his gift of synthesising material, of organising facts into a language non-scientists could understand. It was a great success, every weekly serial sold out; published as a book it was compressed for a still wider public. The last pages went into print by the end of the summer, and that also meant for Julian the end of a regular earning job. He was now a freelance, though still with a laboratory at King's College, and giving lectures here and there.

Luckily, the Colonial Office offered him a voyage to Africa to report on the possibilities of better education and, at the same time, on what should be done to protect the wild life still abundant, but threatened. Prophetic travellers like Colonel Meinertzhagen, Professor J. W. Gregory, Lord Lugard, Major Church, and many others, described great massacres of elephants for ivory (started long ago by Arabs and continued by Europeans), of rhinos for supposed aphrodisiac properties in their horns, and of antelopes, giraffes, lions and leopards for their depredations to growing villages or farms, or just as targets. The abundant wild animals, which had always been the natural inhabitants of the continent, were being discovered by Europeans – not so much as subjects of immense scientific interest, but as grand game to hunt and destroy. The colonies, started in the 1880s, were taking root, and it was high time that responsibilities were outlined and developed with conscientious appraisal of the needs of the original inhabitants.

Julian was the ideal man for the job. There was always in his make-up, and in Aldous's, a streak of the missionary: not as propagandist of a God-worship, but dedicated to finding the meaning and the way to a better life, and the wider access for all mankind to achieve such a life. *The Science of Life* had been an exploration of the theoretical basis for man's vast possibilities of improvement, a kind of biological blueprint: this was a practical approach *sur le vif*. Julian was full of zeal for this providential mission. I was to join him at Jinja as soon as I had brought the children back to London, with my mother and a nurse, after a holiday at Chaumont, the mountain behind Neuchâtel, where we had taken a chalet for the summer in 1929. Julian went off to East Africa in mid-August.

In his *Memories*, Julian conveniently skipped over what was to be a major crisis in our married life. He wrote:

The boat trip from Southampton to Dar-es-Salaam was unremarkable, except for four facts: the appalling heat of the Red Sea, where the ship had often to turn round to get a breath of northerly air; the presence of a very attractive American girl, with whom I fear I flirted (she took it much more seriously than I did); a set of poems I wrote, in spite of the heat, entitled *A Freudian Faustulus*, in which I tried to set down in verse my own state of mind, and my relations with nature and other people; and the squalor of the French boat, a relic of pre-war days, with such an abundance of rats that they gnawed holes in one of the passengers' trousers . . .

The 'Faustulus', fragments of which were printed in his short book of poems *The Captive Shrew*, I shall refer to later. But that the flirtation he made so light of was a deep explosive experience for him was made evident to me when I reached Port Said a few weeks later, and found two contrasting letters waiting for collection. This is the first:

August 19, 1929.
On the morning of the day we get to Port Said.
S.S. General Duchesne

Dearest –

Here we have crossed all the Mediterranean without the ship having rocked or pitched once. I hope you will have such a smooth crossing . . .

Well, my dear-one, this really looks as if it would be perfectly all right for you to come. I am so happy! You have been so self-sacrificing all these years, while I gadded about; and at last I can make it possible for you to do something really jolly. I think it ought to be the most wonderful trip, and something to look back on all one's life. At last I am beginning to think we shall be there!

Dearest I am afraid I must have been very irritable and nervy these last months; but it has been a real strain, as I have been realizing now these last few days, now that the pressure is off. I am profoundly thankful H.G. did propose the scheme to me – I am proud of the work now it's done, and it has started me off in a wonderful way on this new career of free-lance scientist-writer; but I am also profoundly thankful it's over, and I can be myself again for a little! My temperament is so different from H.G.'s, and Gip's that, while the combination has been doubtless good for the book, the combining process has been rather a trial!

Now, as I say, I can become JSH again, and not only a collaborator in the Trinity. (How annoying and trying Jehovah must have found it when he was suddenly made to cooperate, AD I with Jesus, and the Pigeon . . . !)

Meanwhile, my sweet I have never had anything but love and help and peace from you – bless you! . . .

This is a queer no man's land existence – I have deliberately relaxed, and the result is I feel as in a dream, with Africa in front of us, one reality to make up to, and the home reality out of which I have started the dream! But in the dream you are always there, popping into the background – as I lie awake when it's too hot to go to sleep – suddenly the old reality seems realler than the dream – Juliette my beloved wife – Our marriage has been wonderful in this, that after ten years it is much richer and more beautiful than ever – I want this time to be myself after this long spell of treadmill, and when I come back I shall insist on having some country place where we can get away from London and be our two selves, and not appendages to someone or something else.

Well goodbye and bless you forever.

The second letter (written the day after) which I destroyed went through me like a hurricane. It recapitulated our particular sort of incompleteness: we had discussed it quite a few times before, and agreed that we must both be more open with one another, and more free; now he had found freedom, essential to his personal growth, having met a lovely American girl of about eighteen, passenger on his ship as far as Port Said. The letter stated his wish to pursue this affair, his entire right to do so, while he swore his continued devotion to me, from whom he was taking absolutely nothing, but promised an enhanced relationship for ourselves. It was a sort of Shelley bargain; I was to be reasonable and accept it, as he would accept the same were I to fall in love with someone else. It was, in fact, a rational letter, and my painful reaction to it only showed how little I knew of the man beneath the scientist, the man who was my husband. It also showed how lightly I had taken H. G. Wells's philosophy, and his manner of life, which was to live as fully, as unshackled, as it was in his power to do. Had I not seen H. G.'s home life at Easton Glebe, with his loving and so lovable wife Jane and his two grown sons? And then an entirely different scene in his other home near Grasse where he carried out one of his highly coloured love affairs with Odette Keun, of which he never made a secret?

The recently published *H.G. Wells in Love** takes the reader step by step into the never fulfilled quest for the 'Lover-Shadow'. It never mentions the legal partner in the great adventure. She remains in the background, but on our few weekends at Easton Glebe she was fulfilling herself in devotion to her husband and her two sons, faultlessly and perfectly running the home station. She died of cancer in the last stages of the collaboration between H. G., G. P. Wells and Julian in

* Edited by G.P. Wells, Faber & Faber, 1984.

the writing of *The Science of Life*. I never knew her intimately, but often wondered, now that I was faced with a situation not unlike hers, how she coped, all those years, with her own persona.

Stuck at Port Said half-way from home towards Unknown Africa, I only gradually realised what was happening, as I read and re-read that strange letter from Julian. The ship had docked in port for refuelling, and most of the passengers had gone ashore. I spent the time crying my eyes out. Looking back on it now, I cannot believe I could have been so foolish and so green – nor that Julian could have failed to guess how painfully his letter would hit me. Late one night, at sea, I tore it into shreds and scattered them over the ship's foaming wake.

There are many ways of dealing with a crisis – Julian, voluble on paper, chose to write the unilateral words of that moment of truth. Not prepared for what amounted to a surgical operation, I found myself instantly deprived and lost, an empty shell, aware only of my total deadlock and immense sense of failure. There was no one on board I could turn to for help, and my need was desperate. Yet even if there had been such an understanding friend, I am not sure I would have knocked on the door, and opened my heart. For I was, as many of my generation, afraid of exposing my secret and introverted self. 'Each generation must judge for itself', as T. S. Eliot wrote. Freud probably did us all an immense service when he made verbal communication a normal, accepted outlet, beginning as he did with the couch in his consulting room. At Port Said, however, I was utterly removed from all that.

Julian, in that letter, was breaking the sound barrier; he pulled down the wall we had unconsciously built between us. He was trapped between two loyalties: one to himself and one to me. He took the flying leap, and left me far behind. For I could not, in so short a time, escape from the naïve girl-wife I was into the strong mature personality that he himself needed as his mate. Impatiently, blindly egoistical and rebellious, with a sense of guilt, he too was lost in the storm of emotions. We were both helpless, fatefully divided by our characters.

And so I landed in Africa, not imagining that, for both of us, it was to be the point of departure for wonderful terrestrial explorations, forestalling psychological nightmares.

★   ★   ★

Julian had, most considerately, arranged for people to meet me at Mombasa, sort me out, and put me on the right train to Jinja, in the heart of Africa. At Nairobi I was met by the young Louis Leakey and his wife Mary. They took me to their excavations at Elmenteita, caves full of obsidian knives and scrapers, relics from early dwellers of prehistoric times. They were both convinced that the cradle of mankind lay somewhere in the dark continent, and their enthusiasm was contagious and inspiring.

For me it was also a transcendental experience of exotic landscapes, masses of luminous flamingoes lining the shores of blue lakes, Africans moving with archaic grace in scanty clothing over sculptural bronze bodies. I saw my first streliztia flower, a jewel of surrealist invention; brilliant birds of all kinds, gaudily fluttering before unbelieving eyes. I fell under the spell of Africa, intoxicated by its present realities and yet aware of others uncharted for countless epochs. Treading like yet another pilgrim, step by step over its red soil and time-smoothed rocks, I became a new self – outside myself – in the euphoric delight of an unimaginable paradise.

Julian met my train at Jinja, then the terminus of that famous railway. It was the middle of the night: we motored to Kampala through arched groves of scented trees sheltering villages where the Hindus were celebrating their New Year, carrying flickering lights from hut to hut. The warm night embraced us with its aroma, its conspiring mystery and wonderment. We were transfused by its power – both deeply moved, united in this awareness of the witching moment and its enchantment.

We set off on our safari: John Russell, of the Education Department at Kampala, had been appointed as our organiser; he collected the daily fifty porters to carry our food and gear on their heads, and the long trail of black legs followed us to the Mountains of the Moon, marching our fifteen miles or so from dawn to noon, when we made camp, lunched, rested and explored. The land unfolded itself, an ageless survival from the Pleistocene period. With every sight, sound and smell of that fabulous experience, my heart was filled with elation and delight. Julian was part of the enchantment, he was gentle, loving, infectious in his keenness, interested in all things, from an ant-lion to a giraffe. I have never known anyone to equal his zest for living, his generosity in sharing it, stretching himself to fill the inquiring mind. Threaded as though on a tapestry, the multiple impressions are as vivid now as they were then.

Later I wrote a book called *Wild Lives of Africa*, after yet other journeys in that mesmerising land.

But much more important, and still of enormous topical value, is the book Julian wrote after his three months of that early trip spent, until the last four weeks when I joined him, in visiting schools, laboratories, hospitals, administrative departments of every sort, and taking innumerable notes on whatever subject he was exploring. *Africa View*★ represents an important landmark in the appraisal of problems then dominant, and also in discussions on the outcome of these problems. Direct and Indirect Rule are now a thing of the past, but he brought a prophetic vision to the results of the British administration. I have been re-reading it and find so many of the troubles of today predicted in his pages. It is a balanced judgement of the principles which governed the colonies and mandated territories, of the potential abilities, yet uncalled-on, in the Africans who, he felt, 'should be more comprehensively prepared to take over their share in governing', and of the influence of Smuts in the perilous divisions of apartheid.

★ Chatto, 1931.

His vigorous appeal for the protection of wild animals and their habitat was implemented in the following years by the creation of several new game reserves and national parks. Now, of course, the book is forgotten: a pity, for it contains much valuable material and a wide study of contemporary thought, expressed with the vigour, the omnivorous knowledge and precision of his mind.

Thinking back now on that long safari, I remember the fresh awaking of every day, watching the sun rise in splendour, fully alert to the unexpected, and absorbing each impression with all our perceptions. It was a perpetual feast: striding along with a long stick, every step a communion with the soil of Africa, a personal discovery of its nature, seemingly unchanged since the beginning. Our journey, from Kampala to Ruchuru and the whole of the newly created Parc National Albert in the then Belgian Congo, was through a land but little affected by the white man. Africans were still living their lives in their own way. Sparsely populated, small groups of huts sheltered behind a thorn *boma*, their only visible protection from predators. The lack of so much that we took for granted was extreme: they ate the fruits of their labour, digging the soil with sticks and planting sweet potatoes and millet, drinking the milk of their cattle and goats, occasionally eating some meat, out of wooden bowls they themselves carved. None of us could have survived their complete dependence on nature alone, adapting their needs to the capricious conditions of a wild environment, subject as it was to diseases, droughts or floods, bush fires and tribal wars. They also had to live with insidious fears and taboos, such as the evil power of the witch doctor, offset in part by his knowledge of ancient remedies culled locally, and, until comparatively recently, the threat of slavery. Things are very different now.

The Africans gaily answered our 'Jumbo' and stood and watched us pass, as we marched to our next comfortable camp. This was usually a group of three huts built by the government for the visits of officials to remote districts under their care. An attendant kept the walls whitewashed and the place clean; there was a tap for water and a fireplace where our cook prepared the meal which was carried on the heads of porters, summoned daily by the Askari lent us at Kampala. They were paid sixpence a day, the coins kept in a tin box. Their food was carried in leather bags tied round their necks, and they marched back to their village after dumping down our packs, thirty miles in all for sixpence. We depended absolutely on them and the Askari who ruled them: their loyalty was unimpeachable, and remarkable. Now, of course, roads carry the traveller in Jeeps and lorries across the miles we trudged over.

This walking was the most wonderful experience, revealing an intimate face of the land which has since disappeared for ever: the urgent landscape, vast plains with multiple herds of antelopes, buffalo, giraffes flying away as our scent reached them. We climbed the slopes of Karissimbi, first of a chain of dormant volcanoes; gigantic lobelias, senecio, heather trees and ground orchids gemmed the undergrowth of forests; pigmies showed us the way to make fire by rubbing two sticks together; brilliant-coloured birds and butterflies – everything was memorable and exciting. There was no room here for personal intrusions, for the defeated self which met me at Port Said. The vastness of Africa, its incandescence, filled my heart to overflowing.

But all things come to an end. We travelled back to London, to a joyful reunion with our beloved children, our home life, our various social encounters, and our inescapable personal problems – under the grey skies of January.

9

Home to Troubles

The contrast was stunning and absolute.

What I had found in Africa was a blessed detachment from an uneasy self. Exposed to that epic environment I was absorbed, dissolved in its dominance; it was an integration into the limitless macrocosm of another world, a closely knit world of nature. Africa had become our paradise regained, our escapist's sanctuary – in all its moods, its treasures and delights as well as its threats and pervasive mysteries.

To return to London was to plunge again into a sea of trivialities, man-made rules, futile and meaningless conventions and obligations. Only with our two precious sons, Anthony and Francis, could I find a sense of reality in living my daily life. I had to sort myself out; Julian at once immersed himself in writing his report for the Colonial Office, and then his book *Africa View*. He generously suggested that I take over the writing of the safari and left it for me to fill in. It would have been my salvation – the essential step in breaking out of the chrysalis and forging the self who understood. But I could not do it at the time because I was severely ill with a bug picked up in Africa, and then because of the crisis which exploded between us. At Kampala, when I spoke of my resistance to his intention of having extra-marital relations, he had impatiently brushed it aside, and later accused me of doubting the abiding love which had so blissfully proved itself when we met at Jinja and all through our journey. We were both trapped.

But the words on those bits of paper strewn into the tropic sea were alive, and burning now with renewed intensity. What Julian really wanted was not just a passing affair with a pretty girl, but a definite freedom from the conventional bonds of marriage. This was never explicit in so many words, nor were the implications and consequences of that freedom postulated and challenged. But he regarded my giving him this bond of faith as the highest proof of our love and trust in each other.

Looking back on it now, I see that something explosive was bound to happen. Our truce, so accommodatingly sustained by the African venture, had to break: the crisis was pressing, and I was part of it. Paul Tillich wrote: 'The immemorial experience of mankind, that new knowledge can only be won through breaking a taboo, that all autonomous thinking is accompanied by a consciousness of guilt, has been the fundamental experience of my life.'

Julian, puritan by upbringing, repressed romantic, emotionally adolescent, was breaking a taboo; to do so, he had to disperse the sense of guilt, and to convince me of his absolute right to forge a new pattern. But this was easier said than done: I was far too insecure in myself, naïve and psychologically ignorant within my outworn idealism, to be able to accept the new situation. Instead of calmly facing it, I wore myself out defending dying hopes.

We had been married for more than ten years: the foundation was sound, we had two lively sons, friends and acquaintances, a house and servants. Habit was forming its crust over deficiencies we both knew, differences in our demands on each other, complexes and reticences.

These had not been obliterated by our African journey but had been transfigured by our experiences. Our private jungle now had to be entered and traversed. It was a perilous journey, full of the pitfalls created by our separate characters, upbringing and principles. I can see now, all too late, that Julian, determined to win and with what today would be considered perfectly acceptable reasons for doing so, nevertheless considerately endeavoured to ease my personal travail towards a better understanding and a wider vision of life. At the same time, his missionary zeal was fully marshalled to compel me to accept what I found a profoundly destructive situation. Had I but been wiser, braver, stronger and less vulnerable, what a lot of fuss and palaver we would have saved ourselves, as well as extravagant emotional agony.

*   *   *

The explosion had been triggered off in the five days between Marseilles and Port Said when Julian was sailing to his commission in East Africa. The young American girl, whom I shall call Sandra, as she is still alive, was an attractive girl with short wind-blown dark hair, intriguing exotic features and a sensuous lower lip. She had a glowing vitality, allied to the dare-devil American temperament, was not embarrassed by bourgeois principles, and surrounded by a bevy of devoted admirers.

Julian found her irresistible.

> My crystal limbs and comet hair
> Glowed into birth I know not where.
> Nor care I – enough for me
> My eternal self to be.
>
> This for better or for worse
> I march across the universe.
> Who shall deny that I am I,
> The Self that knows not how to die?*

So defiantly he accepted the challenge, the rejuvenescence brought by new love. She was less than half his age, and when she left at Port Said, surprised and flattered, but rather cool and unaffected, his last words to her had been: 'I shall conquer you with my mind.' And so he had proceeded to do, building up, in a copious correspondence, a magnetic relationship.

Nothing had really happened to the two of us yet except our endless discussions. We bored each other continuously, fierce-

* From 'A Freudian Faustulus', *The Captive Shrew* by Julian Huxley, Blackwell, 1932.

ly enacting every sense of one of the oldest plays in the world.

Having finished his report and *Africa View* during those stormy months, Julian prepared for his lecture tour in America. He left in late October for three months or so. He saw Sandra, successfully wooed her and they embarked on their private Odyssey. Our letters continued the dialogue but did not solve the problem. In fact the problem was never fully discussed, the deep sexual urge was carefully wrapped up and left on the doorstep to be sorted out, when the time came . . .

> *New Haven, Connecticut.*
> 2 *November* 1930

Dearest Juliette,

I am ashamed at not having written since Wed. or Thursday was it? But literally have been hectic. Yesterday, for instance (I am staying with the Harrisons here) I thought having delivered my lecture the day before that I should have some pleasant free time.

Thursday I had to go in again to see Harpers, and then to get some slides I have had to get made, and then I took the Port Said young lady to dinner. You will be relieved to hear that lacking the isolation of shipboard and the glamour of the orient evening, I found the kissable quality had strangely evaporated! On the other hand, I found her as a personality more interesting than I remembered. In the sense that she has astonishing vitality and capability, likes tackling any job that comes along, and apparently succeeds in all of them! . . . I must confess that the combination of adventureness and efficiency with femininity is extremely stimulating to me – and, my dear one, I can't help it and you must make the best of it! Perhaps it is just because it is the obverse of your beloved quietness and insistence on inner quality, and self-sacrificing devotion to others, and your lack of self-pushing – that when I run across it it attracts and stimulates me.

I like and respect this girl – she is a real human being, and I should imagine would do something interesting as she finds her feet. I hope I see something of her here occasionally, and to hear from her occasionally when at home. But I don't think you need worry.

And this thing leads to another thing. I had meant before leaving to get off my chest a talk; but was so rushed, and so mentally tired that I didn't feel up to it. Let's do it now, sweet heart. You remember when you asked me to promise physical faithfulness and I told you I could promise nothing – I think you realized at the time that I wasn't behaving thus out of 'superfluous naughtiness' as the Bible says. Dear love – I want to try to explain. If I'd been dishonest and had wanted to deceive you, I'd just have lied. But I *can't* lie on certain things – not least to the person I love most in the world.

My love – the *one* thing I do not love in you is this belittling of yourself; it isn't modesty. It is a canker and it is, I believe you will see if you think calmly, mostly because you don't trust the spontaneous reactions of our mutual feelings. After years of painful struggle, I have arrived at this knowledge that tolerance and lack of jealousy and all the rest is good, and that the positive good of real feeling is worth everything compared to the negative things like not doing this or that, that it's better to grow at the cost of making mistakes than to shut oneself in with an unattained ideal and not to develop – that in fact though we must have ideals, it's sometimes good to remember that 'Le mieux c'est l'ennemi du bien'. I wasted ten years of my life by being frightened of making mistakes; and now I am learning more each year to go ahead and trust to my subconscious feelings (which won't be true unless a good deal of consciousness and thought has been expended on them first. I admit! but have done that). I am doing that both in my scientific work, in my lecturing, in my personal relations; and I know I am growing instead of fossiliz-ing, as a result, and that being so, a dull sadness and almost anger comes over me when I see you are still unable to avoid the same mistakes I made. Dear love, trust yourself and grow fully into all the richness of which your beautiful spirit is capable.

In one thing I acknowledge my fault. In those two first years or so after our marriage, I hadn't fully found myself, and looking back I feel that I wasn't fair to you, didn't do you justice, was hard to you often, and found myself at your expense; and that this has never cleared from our spirit . . . My God we are such lucky people – think of all the unhappy and dull marriages! Let's for heaven's sake be happy with what we have instead of worrying about what we don't have or what we might lose!

Well that's enough. I wonder if I have put what I mean clearly – which is mainly that life is positive in so far as it's valuable, and that *you must* take the final step over the brink from the natural reserve and negativism of youth to the self-assurance that you deserve and need if you are to realize your life to the full – and *our* life . . .

> Your own husband, Julian.

This was all perfectly true, and hit the nail well on the head. There might have been some other way to guide one to the acceptance of what was so easily commanded – so difficult, at the time, to achieve.

Lovely letter – spilling over with the fire of joy of being loved and loving Sandra, and the whole world, and me – excepting 'this belittling of myself'. Yet how could I, immature and a foreigner, stand up in company to his contradictions to anything I might say? He did it with such authority that one had to believe that he was right – it took me years to discover it might not be so. As his tutor in Zoology at Eton wrote in a report in 1904: 'Huxley, ma, KS. Barring a tendency to think himself infallible . . . '

I suppose, in one form or another we all have a sort of devil which twists our guts and makes us do the curious things we do. In part innate, in part the fruit of old experience, Julian carried a daimon within. Could it perhaps be traced to jealousy of his little brother Trev who, when he was about four years old, began to be a person in his own right, and to absorb more of his mother's attention? Until then Julian had been the sole emperor, spoilt and cherished, especially after a dangerous illness which profoundly frightened his mother. Trev became the rival and, as children do, Julian hated that small demanding life which encroached upon his territory. The guilt of this feeling, which vanished as they grew up and they became the best of friends, may have created the deep-dwelling daimon; reinforced perhaps by the compulsion imposed upon him by his family, to be worthy of both his grandfather T.H.H. and his Arnold parents, so that he was made to feel guilty if and when he failed. It was a terrible burden to put on a child, and marked him throughout his life.

This 'daimon' was a well-rooted secret inhabitant of Julian's mind. A few months before he died, tormented and

tormenting, I said to him: 'Julian, you have a demon within
yourself, and it is destroying you, and me' – to which, quite
casually, he replied: 'Of course I have a demon, had it since I
was four.'

*   *   *

After the letter of November 2, when Julian so clearly con-
firmed his interest in Sandra, no further mention was made of
her. One did not, however, need to be a wizard to be aware
that he was seeing a lot of her – and inevitably in love with her.
I knew it, and could not bear it. I lost my sleep and health, and
felt utterly lost.

Francis, at the same time, became ill with mysterious
infections. The last was a flare-up of surgical TB, for which
the doctors recommended a clinical school in Switzerland. In
deep anxiety, I took him there when Julian returned, spry and
euphoric, from his American tour. He joined me at Villars, in
the blazing snowy landscape. We two went skiing in the
muffled silence of giant mountains. 'Yes,' he said, 'I love her.'
The purity of untouched snow stretched far before me, the
slope took me at a faster and faster pace, towards the unseen,
the unknown, the crazy brink. Perhaps, at the end, the final
leap into nothingness. But one does not, with such bravura,
defy one's fate, nor cure the broken heart.

Although, at the time, the idea of Julian harbouring some
daimon had not crossed my thoughts, yet I obscurely felt that
Sandra had unchained some voracious force in our midst.
Shakespeare's Soothsayer tells Antony (*Antony and Cleo-
patra*):

> Thy demon, that's the spirit that keeps thee, is
> Noble, courageous, high, unmatchable,

and so, in the better sense, was Julian's, who believed his cause
to be noble, bringing him the peace and power with which not
only to 'mellow into fruit', but even, on the buoyant wings of
his euphoria, to carry me too to a new fulfilment.

His libido, released by Sandra, was Jung's 'psychic analogue of physical energy': 'see a man's drives, for example, as various manifestations of energic processes and thus as forces analogous to light, heat . . .'* In almost clinical sense Julian was unconsciously fighting for this 'psychic analogue of physical energy'. Our disaster was that I could not see it that way; and furthermore, that both of us, in different quantities, lacked that precious gift, the imagination of the heart.

I had tried hard to keep my mother from knowing about the rift between us: however the news reached her through Tante Juliette. She was much distressed, but could be of no use whatever in her emotional reactions. Neither did I want to confide in Ottoline who had also heard and wrote me several wise letters, generously concerned and understanding. She discovered I wanted a new dress, and offered to take me to her favourite shop in Knightsbridge. Ottoline was a keen shopper; she loved wandering round to look at fashionable clothes, and to choose materials with which she designed the clothes that her maid made for her. She knew the assistants by name, inquired of their families, encouraged them in their work. Firmly she took me round, and found for me an enchanting red dress with a pleated skirt: it suited me perfectly and we returned carrying the box. Red was the colour I needed, the colour of love and hope, ancient symbol of life, and the dress, in the manner that 'manners maketh man', could have projected me into the new brave self I seeked in vain to be. But I took it back the next day, not even unpacking the tissue papers wrapping it. I often think of that dress, and my obscure rejection, rejecting in so doing also a renewed self. And likewise also rejecting the help Ottoline offered to give, with her precious affection. She was hurt, regretted the red dress but, in her wisdom, understood my need to lick my wounds in the cage I had made for myself.

To distract us from our fruitless discussions, we took a late

* Jung's *Dreams and Reflections*.

spring trip to Russia, on an Intourist Tour. Here again, Julian gives an interesting account in his *Memories*, and also in his book *A Scientist among the Soviets*.* The contrast between the doomed old people, who had known pre-Revolution Russia, and the young, who were bred to the new regime, was striking. One saw it in the Parks of Culture and Rest, in the queues waiting to see Lenin's tomb, in the markets, in the few churches where some worship was allowed. But, in spite of the despair stamped on the faces of the old, one could feel the power of hope among the young, the surge of a new freedom in their dances in the parks, in their laughter and gatherings. The old sat still, dressed in black, tired voyagers at the end of their world. Sometimes one heard singing – old songs heavy with Russian nostalgia, the helpless destiny of the poor. It was even then, fourteen years after the Revolution, a deeply divided country, mostly unfathomable to us visitors, not knowing Russian and always surrounded by interpreters who had to report on our reactions, who were themselves almost too careful not to let out any personal information. One knew they were hungry and deprived – the American-cloth bag ready to pick up any left-overs from the banquets, and their grateful acceptance of oddments like aspirins and soap, made it clear enough. But the real dangers of indiscretion had not yet made their deep imprints and threat.

The sun shone on a luxuriant countryside and we were shown exciting achievements: the Tsarskoe Selo palace, built by Catherine the Great and filled with beauty; we went to Ryazan in a crowded train and stayed with Ivy Litvinov, returning with her on the Moskova River, in a small ship filled with migrant farmers, taking with them kettles and mattresses, precious boxes of old belongings, going to the great city with hope and fear. Later one heard they had died, the Kulaks' slow but sure elimination, in their millions. A woman on the lower deck, among the crowd of wanderers, began to sing that

* Chatto and Windus, 1932.

night, under a quivering light, as we sailed slowly between the dark lips of the river. Her voice rose through the tense silence, a piercing metallic melopoeia; one felt she was singing the dirge of the millions who were to die.

We returned to Switzerland, where we had left the boys, by a very primitive type of aircraft, a veteran of the First World War, bumping and humping its precarious flight via Koenigsberg. We were the only passengers, sitting on folding garden chairs fastened to the floor with thongs, entertained by the loquacious pilot who boasted of being the last of his squadron, and his machine almost a museum piece. I was violently air-sick all the way, watching the birch trees nearly within touch as we flew over the deserted tundra. It was probably a miracle that we got out alive.

*   *   *

If I sometimes felt a measure of cruelty in Julian's insistence on forcing me to accept his right to a Pelagian extension of experience, I also felt, in his concern for me, his sense of fairness and responsibility as well as a kind, one of many kinds, of loving. He had made it quite clear that the freedom he demanded for himself was mine in equal measure, that I could take a lover if I chose, and that he would, implicitly, accept the situation. I was too far gone into an obsessive neurosis to find this funny, or to resist the advice of a woman doctor, Helena Wright, I was taken to see, who told me: 'Take a lover, and I will give you the contraceptive.' 'Take a job' would have been so much more constructive, and I had tried to find one. The difficulties were the boys' holidays and my poor health. Moreover, in those days women's jobs were rare.

So, in a kind of desperation, I broke my taboo and took the lover as a sort of medicine: a kind man, whose grave honesty appealed to me. I was not 'in love' but he held out a branch and I clung to it, thus in a sense restoring a sense of balance and a measure of sanity. It was also my first step into a personal identity, into a situation not overshadowed by

Julian's involuntary but definite autocracy. He was too egocentric to tolerate any dependence on himself, yet he created a sort of centrifugal power which made resistance too crucial an effort for a timid creature like myself.

True to his word, he accepted my use of the freedom he believed in. It was all too soon discovered that two plus two does not add up to four, and that we were still in the jungle. Deeper entangled, in fact, than Julian ever expected to be.

*   *   *

It was about this time that I met the formidable Kotelianski at Mark Gertler's, and finding myself accepted, we became great friends. He was a wonderful tonic, and I often called on him for a cup of tea and an obliging ear. He spoke little, but what he said was wise with an ancient sagacity, an astringent and remarkable brand of integrity. I have never known a person one could trust so implicitly, whose truth was so undivided. I can still see him, sitting before his never dying fire, in his bare spotless kitchen, pouring water from a large kettle into a very small teapot which brewed the best tea: his shock of upstanding hair crowning the great head, his face as hewn out of ancient wood, with piercing eyes which looked straight through one's defences, and forced one to look at one's inner self. He was like a prophet of the Old Testament, a lone fighter for improbable ideals; he never wrote his own books for this reason, but translated several from the Russian. He was implacably faithful to his friends and equally to his enemies, even to people he took violent dislikes to for trivial reasons. His verdict was absolute.

When I began to know him, he was Reader at the Cresset Press, and lived at 5 Acacia Road which at one time he shared with Katherine Mansfield and Middleton Murry. Her faded photograph, the only one visible in the house, serious, distant, stood on the kitchen mantelpiece. He talked but little of her, but one felt the deep protective love he had for her. Her letters to him, now in the British Museum, are perhaps the only sincere unflowery fragments of her personal writing; from his friends, Kot demanded truth – not what he contemptuously called 'literature'.

He always wore a wide-brimmed black hat and carried a cane; in his pocket a tin filled with his own Russian cigarettes, made of expensive tobacco he bought in the city on rare trips, and rolled onto a long cardboard mouthpiece. He lived alone, meticulously clean, washing everything, including his own sheets and even his suits, scrubbing his kitchen, keeping a constant coal fire under the large-bellied kettle and reading voraciously. Marjorie Wells (ex-wife of G. P. Wells, son of H. G.) had so to speak adopted him for many of his later years. She called every day, changed his books at the Times Book Club, ordered his coal and milk, and generally watched over him. Finally it was she who took him to hospital after he tried to cut his throat during a nervous breakdown and rescued him time and again.

Beatrice Glenavy wrote a perfect book about him: *To-day We'll only Gossip*. She lived in Ireland but voyaged to London three or more times a year to visit him. I was told that when he died a packet of letters from her, reportedly unopened, was found in his room – were they really unopened?

James Stephens, the Irish poet, called once a week, driven to the door by his wife, whom Kot refused to see. James was a leprechaun, talked with the mellifluous words of a troubadour; telling stories of his bees, of his flowers, of his learning how to be a tree, a horse in meadows of buttercups, a bird singing in a special language as he himself was talking an enchanted language. Then came the hoot of the wife's car: he leapt out of his chair, his small figure plunging into a very old mackintosh, hardly said goodbye and was gone in a cloud of glory. He was Kot's opposite, yet his twin brother, so tangible was their unspoken solicitous tenderness. James died of a stroke during the war.

Mark Gertler was like a son to Kot – a wayward, difficult but much loved son; but the greatest concern Kot ever felt was for D. H. Lawrence of whom he always spoke with deep understanding and admiration. Lawrence could do no wrong in Kot's eyes – the only thorn was Frieda, who richly returned his dislike. Yet when Lawrence died, Kot did all he could to help Frieda through her complicated legacy, for the sake of Lawrence.

When, in his turn, Kot died of a merciful stroke, attended by ever-faithfully devoted Marjorie Wells, most of the letters he had received were found in neat bundles, some to be left to the British Museum, and others sent back to their writers. Mine were all returned to me, from their very start in 1931 to his death in 1959. I find them now topical and so informative of our lives that I shall quote some of them as they reflect our doings when I was absent from London. In between letters, we spent many an hour drinking tea in the 'Cave', as he called his basement kitchen – never forgotten visits of perfect understanding and blessed friendship.

Escape to
the Middle East

Fuir, là-bas fuir
Je sens que les oiseaux sont ivres
D'etre parmi l'écume inconnue et les cieux.

MALLARMÉ

The sequence of time lost all meaning for me. With no will to survive, I was devoured with anxiety about my sons. I went for long dreary walks at night, trying to kill the maggots in my brain – uselessly exhausting myself. I could not escape the nightmare of my present, nor the anguish of the future. Julian wisely lived at his club, supported by his own need to be right, at whatever cost. We were both trapped in our contradictory dilemma, having argued ourselves to checkmate. In the midst of our entanglements, a glaring absurdity defied all reason.

My friends became concerned about my condition. I could no longer bear the situation, neither could I function as a mother; my torments took me over. Why did I fall apart in so disastrous, so abject a manner? At the time I knew only the nightmare I was in, not alive but drowning, conscious only of despair. And what of my sons, more precious than anything else in the world? What lay in the future for them if I could not protect them? That way madness lies. And I was closer to it than I knew.

Finally, Violet Hammersley took things in hand. She was an old friend of Julian's since his undergraduate days when he had tutored her three stepchildren during a memorable holiday in Scotland. She had remained much attached to him and accepted me warmly as his wife. It was she who suggested my going right away, as far as I could go, until I came to my senses. In fact, go to Baghdad.

Hubert Young had been at Eton with Julian and, when he married his lovely wife Rose, we all met again between his diplomatic posts abroad. They were now in Baghdad and agreed to put me up and to put up with me. Plans were made, with the help and warm understanding of Julian's father and his second wife, Rosalind, for Francis to go for a term to Frensham Heights School and for Anthony to continue at Abinger Hill.

Aldous and Maria, who then lived at Sanary, saw me off at Marseilles on a white and gold ship where I found my name listed as Mr J. Huxley. Why not steal a man's wardrobe and be born to a new life? I felt disembodied, '*Frei lebt wer sterben kann*'* – lost on the eternally anonymous sea, improbably launching out. At Marseilles Aldous gave me a copy of his latest book *Brave New World*. His books usually brought me a mixture of apprehension and relish, for his brilliant and yet cruel characterisation was often hard to take. This book, however, was on a different plane: it created a society artificially nurtured and 'imprinted', which dehumanised human beings, offering a quick escape from grief and the whole gamut of emotions with a nice variety of protective devices – 'One cubic centimeter cures ten gloomy sentiments'; 'A gramme is better than a damn'; 'There is always soma, delicious soma . . . ' He presented the first possibility of 'babies in bottles', treated as soon as 'born' according to the role which the ruling class devised for them.

My response must have pleased him; he had seen me in the depths of obsessive despair which he so often tried to mitigate. His message had gone home – I did not want that oblivion of emotions however painful.

*   *   *

* Baroness Blixen ('free lives who can die').

'*La mer, la mer, toujours recommencée . . .*'* eternally anonymous, uncommitted. Improbably, I took the crumbs of new encounters, sensing the cool treasures of blue waters of barges filled with luminous oranges, the outlines of an antique land marked with history – answering the need to escape from my dreary self.

After cutting all links with home it became possible to consider the incidents of my life – to find their significance; gradually they could be detached from the flood of emotional pressures and evaluated, as if they did not concern the *me* who was experiencing the surgical operation. At the back of my mind, the self-observer was watching, with an awareness free from the poisons of a sick mind. Thus floating away from the epicentre of the crisis, a subtle detachment became possible, gradually blunting the edge of pain and, which was much more important, rebuilding my reason.

I started keeping a diary (an old habit) making it strictly factual and exteriorised. It was, as it were, an exercise in exorcism, for indeed, these last months had been a voyage of 'lidless eyes in hell', to regions haunted by ghosts; a strange malady of the spirit, out of all proportion to the cause.

Landing at Beirut, I explored Byblos, Baalbek, Damascus. Then drove into a sandstorm just like a thick London fog, on Nairn Transport's great bus, driven across Mesopotamia by a chauffeur with St Vitus's dance. At Ruchbah, we stopped for refuelling: Arabs were camping in tents walled in with petrol tins and very friendly. Then all through the night, the silent desert like silver under the bright moon, I slept on top of the mail bags. On towards Baghdad, through endless streams of people, camels, donkeys and sheep grazing invisible grass. The Euphrates rolled by through a stony impervious waste, with here and there a palm-tree plantation, all greys and greens.

Dear Rose at the bus-stop was waiting to bring me to their

* Paul Valéry: 'Cimetière marin'.

large house at the edge of Baghdad. She and Hubert were the kindest and most generous hosts and I remember my six weeks with them with deepest gratitude, for no one in that warm loving house could have been more gentle and understanding of what I believed to be my secret.

Rosemary Olivier, Rose's niece, came with me to Mosul – a dear companion; by train to Kirkuk, then a mining town and the terminus of the railway, on by rusty taxi through high stony waste. We stopped to allow the straggling Iraqi army to pass by: a strange mixture of every gene – Assyrians with pendulous nose and big rolling eyes, Armenians, Parthians, Kurds with fine profiles and intelligent features, Mongols and Tartars, and even the occasional Greek, possibly a descendant of Alexander's great army. On and on they passed, on their little frisky horses. There was a war on, Sheik Ahmed in his mountain fastness refused to give in, having suddenly announced that he was Jesus Christ. For a few months his fame swelled, until some of his subjects showed signs of unrest. So he dropped the idea of Jesus Christ and became simply God. As such he had supreme power over all sects. The army clambered towards secret passes between rugged hills to restore the order of things.

We struggled too, making our tracks as we went, stopped by the Tigris, which we crossed on a sort of double tin-ferry. Troops, horses and guns had to go first – then a large family guided by an enormous grandfather all in black, his middle protected by ten metres of coiled cotton cloth, into which an impressive dagger was stuck. Handsome fellows under great turbans, with black fierce eyes and the proud hooked nose – an ancient heroic race.

We travelled on to Nineveh under its sandy shroud, some 2300 feet high, covering the dusty magnificence of Sennacherib. American archaeologists were digging up Khorsabad, waking the ghost of Sargon, father of Sennacherib. The winged bulls have lost their spell, fragmented on benches – so has the palace of the King of Kings.

We hoped better from Sheik-Adi, the seventh fallen angel, worshipped as Satan in a crude dark shrine lit by kerosened wicks. This devil's names must never be said – his threshold must be carefully straddled – smoke blackened the dark walls. There was a tank of crystal-clear water where little black and yellow salamanders sported, lovingly tended by priests. We attended an Assyrian wedding, in Mosul, where the poor little doped child-bride sat through three days of celebration while the tribe drank lemonade and danced the ritual everlasting dance

On our way back to Baghdad, we stopped at Erbela, the oldest continuously inhabited city of the world, so they say. This was Darius' first base after his decisive defeat by Alexander at Gaugamala. The vast plain asleep for centuries after the thunder of war chariots, Erbela is now a giant dried mud-heap, sitting on fabulous relics of a past too sacred to be disturbed. My days, thus fed with vestiges of vanished glories, passed lightly away. My nights were otherwise obsessed.

Back in Baghdad I met Freya Stark, a great friend of the Youngs. She was there to polish her Arabic, preparing for perilous journeys with quiet determination. To support herself in Baghdad she wrote for a local newspaper. The Youngs had adopted her, enjoying her wry sense of humour, cool ironical surveys of the city and foreign community, and her single-minded courage. She was, one could say, unique: her charm entirely natural, her looks depending more on character than beauty, with a defiant sparkle in her eye; perhaps more than anything, I was struck with the quality radiating from her, that of being at peace with herself. And so she has been ever since those far-off days; we have kept in touch with each other, through decades of our varied experiences.

The highlight of my stay with Hubert and Rose was their taking Freya and me to Kuwait, flying down the river in the huge Imperial Airways plane, past the noble arch of Ctesiphon and over interesting patterns of the ancient buried city, then down to the mouth of the Euphrates, thickly covered with reeds cut by canals used by the Marsh Arabs. Flocks of pelicans and flamingoes flew up as we approached, and we came down safely near Basrah. We arrived at sundown, to stay with the Political Agent, Colonel Dixon, and his tall handsome wife.

Kuwait was a large fortified city, with mud-brick walls all round it, four gates with bastions, heavy door and sentries on guard; within, more mud-bricks and blind walls, heavy nail-studded doors, a city watching with no eyes. On the sea front, a serried line of dhows with carved high poops and long curved prows, vessels of ancient trim, towered into the sky. On the lagoon others were floating, their big bellies resting on blue water. They were the famous pearling fleet refitting for their departure in the middle of May, their sails spread out on quays, giant white wings swarming with men at work, repairing and strengthening. Many sailed away for four long months on the Erythrean Sea, diving into the depths, dying in their prime with lungs exploding; they gathered fabulous pearls, cream pearls, pink pearls, perfect and imperfect pearls from the vast oyster beds, slaves of the shipowners, mortgaged for yet another deadly season. Yet the lovely orient pearls now lie doomed in the tomb-like safes of the owners, out-bidden by the Japanese cultured pearls.

Colonel Dixon took us all along to Araf Jan, a Bedouin encampment thirty-nine miles away in the middle of the desert. The Bedouin came out to meet us, women in black veils, their eyes shining in the slits of their burgas, graceful and dignified. One carried her baby, an ugly little thing with blue paint on its unformed face. The mother walked about with a huge iron tent-nail in her hand to keep off the evil eye.

The large tent of black woven goat hair was hospitably opened. A beautiful camel-saddle marked the place of honour; others, less handsome, framed the tent at the back. Bright coloured rugs, saddle-bags and gaudy strappings with gay tassels filled the shaded space. Squatting round the vast platters, we plunged our right hands into rice fried in ghee, towered with chicken and mutton, using our thumbs to shape a small portion into a ball to push into our mouths. This was not done without mishaps: face covered with grease, half the thumbful dropped on to the rug we sat on. We ate a sumptuous meal, finishing with dates sticking together, the most delicious I have ever tasted. A sand rub for greasy hands, a spray of precious water, a rest in the shady cool.

The women then sang a song, repeated by the chorus – the song of the white man riding alone on his white stallion. Little girls danced, hopping on toes, then twirling round with hair flying like a wheel, first on one side then on the other: a long impromptu, unfinished dance, a dance of joyous grace.

This was no legendary Arabia, but a world of ancient lineage, still rooted in its traditions, its cultural manifestations, its sexually divided society holding women in partial bondage, repositories of meaningful rituals. Walter de la Mare's poem rang in my ears:

> Far are the shades of Arabia
> Where the Princes ride at noon
> Neath the verdurous glades and thickets
> Under the ghost of a moon

But there were no verdurous glades and thickets round the great black tent; the sun was setting, the aroma of night-scented stock filled the cooler air, asphodels, lovely grasses, long twisted petals in tight rosettes grew surprisingly on dry sand, coming to new life with evening. Everything was softly enchanted, under stars of fabulous brilliance: piercing in so dark a sky – did the early Arabic astrologers not see the moons of Jupiter long before Copernicus and Galileo, with their Allah – given sight unspoilt by artificial lights?

A large fire was lit, we bathed economically and ate another feast while outside the flocks gathered for the night. Mrs Dixon in her robe of dark and bright reds walked like a biblical figure among the crouching camels, the bleating sheep and tethered lambs. * She stroked the white silky wool, the long soft ears: furry, milky, animal smells, the smoke of the fire, the night enfolded its peace over all – a peace of grave fulfilment.

One of the women told fortunes, throwing upon the ground a handful of pebbles and broken shells, bits of pottery and date stones. She spoke with a deep voice while following a secret pattern with her finger. Someone translated the prophecies, which were curiously valid: mine was the only dark one. I knew well enough.

*   *   *

Then on to Babylon, with its rampant Beasts in bright tiles on tall brick walls, encircling the jumble of the palaces. Then to Kish where I spent hours in the ruins of King Sargon's city with the enchanting old Mr Watelin, an archaeologist, who believed in fairy tales and precise data. He presented me with a terracotta dish and base from one thousand eight hundred years BC – more symbolic than beautiful, cherished ever since because this purely accidental encounter of a few hours was singularly blessed. The ruins of the great battlements of the palace of a long-dead king became alive for an instant – marking my precarious reality with their timelessness.

Looking back on it now, each step had its importance in liberating me from my obsession. Specially so was that sheltered and healing stay with Hubert and Rose. It gave me 'the approach to the meaning' which T. S. Eliot wrote about in his poem, the understanding I had so totally lacked before of an unknown Julian. Within its imponderable dimensions, I found a growing point, an 'importance' in the living of my life, such as it might be, and the will to face it. How extravagantly, how absurdly long, it had taken me.

As I had always intended, I returned to London in late

* She and Colonel Dixon were much loved and trusted by the Bedouin, and when he died she chose to remain with them; now in her old age, she is still there. She was made a DBE some years ago.

March for the boys' holidays. We flew by the old Imperial Airways, then a sea-plane line, designed to land both on sea and land. We came down on the glassy waters of Lake Tiberias, the two side-floats biting water like celestial plough-shares, throwing up their crystal arches. And so, at last, to London.

I I

Solution

*Nous ne serons jamais une seule momie
Sous l'antique désert et les palmiers heureux.*
MALLARMÉ

While I was away in Iraq, out of reach, wheels were turning their different ways. Sandra and her sister Lily had come to Europe, visiting France and England; on their way through Paris, Lily had found a husband. The marriage lure was waving, Sandra's audacity dazzled everyone, and Julian was under her spell deeper than he knew. He was carried away to a fiery world of dreams unimaginable, unless blinded by passion. When Sandra left London for New York, it was with the understanding that he would join her shortly, and they would build a new life together. I was conveniently out of the way, somewhere in the desert.

Meanwhile, the desert had worked its spell on me. *Inshalla* descended from the myriad stars imperturbably shining over my head, quelling my rebellion and restoring my sense of balance. With this new power given me, I found strength to face whatever was ahead, to live in my own reality. I felt a great sense of deliverance, with the urge to survive that deplorable waste of emotional tangle; I was returning to my sons, to my true self – for the Easter holidays.

The house at Hillway was empty save for a faithful servant who looked after Julian when needed. It was midnight when, utterly unexpecting, he found me standing on the landing, more like a ghost than a living creature. Neither of us knew anything of our separate voyages of the last weeks: we met within the silent conspiracy of home, the protective familiarity of old habit, like phantoms of our past. For one moment of pure joy, we stood together, outside time and reality, a moment burnt for ever in both our memories. Few words were said: I felt a power held us in this fateful moment. Then, silently, we resumed our formal roles, each retiring our separate ways, to the inescapable present and its torrent of emotional compulsions. The next day, he was gone.

Soon after, the boys came home for their holidays. I had planned a second visit to Port Blanc in Brittany, the enchanting village where the dear Chevrillons had a place. *'L'homme propose, et Dieu dispose.'* Instead of sand and sea and rocks, I was imprisoned in a sick room, suffering a painful bout of suspected stones in the kidneys. An operation left me almost inert, and the boys had a miserable time bullied by a stern governess with no sense of fun.

That Julian, at the same time, was enduring parallel storms was altogether out of my ken. How he arrived at his own self-realisation was something I had no way of knowing. All the action was happening on the other side of the Atlantic, and in any case, I had opted out of all resistance to the capricious will of the gods. Could it be that Julian's daimon, disarmed now by my withdrawal from the conflict, had given up his urge to assert his own choice? Stranger things have happened in the labyrinth of human impulses.

> 'Tis not by holding in the hand
> That one can hope to understand . . . *

He sailed for England within three months. Crossing the Atlantic took seven days. He spent most of the time in his cabin suffering from a violent attack of sciatica – and God knows what torments. Yet his instinct was sound. What had begun as a *grande passion* of almost legendary scope could not have survived the fettered bonds of marriage. It could only have ended in disaster.

* *The Captive Shrew*, Julian Huxley.

He went to stay with Aldous and Maria; letters poured in, pressing for a decision I was far too unwell to make. I only knew that, for the sake of all of us, and especially for the boys, I deeply wanted him to come back. But this was too abrupt, too sudden a volte-face, anyway for me, to be lived through without a time of adjustment.

A note came from H. G. Wells:

Friday night, 26 July 1932

Dearest Juliette,

Thank you for a charming and wise letter.

Julian my dear has been (and still is) an ass, but also he is really a first class man who must not be devastated. You are able to help him over a bad time or smash him up and I don't doubt now which you will do.

Rest assured my dear of my very warm affection.

Yours ever, H.G.

This was pressure of a new kind. Bewildered as I was, I wrote back rather tartly: 'Don't be an ambassador.' To which he replied: 'All right, I won't be an ambassador. But let him get back to *work*.'

Work. Like most of his clan, Julian was addicted to work. As his grandfather wrote to a friend: 'I am sure that the habit of incessant work into which we all drift is as bad in its way as dram-drinking. In time you cannot be comfortable without its stimulus.'*

And was Julian himself not exclusively married to work? It was, in fact, not entirely and only to me that he had been unfaithful, but to that tyrant, *work*. Work had also been Julian's as well as Aldous's supreme defence from perilous emotional ventures. Yet both had succumbed to the claims of passion, Aldous with Nancy Cunard, Julian with Sandra. Their baptism of fire had been costly, but could one deny that it was needed?

Shakespeare comments:

* *Life and Letters of T.H.H. II* by Leonard Huxley, Macmillan, 1900.

> The expense of spirit in a waste of shame
> Is lust in action; and till action, lust,
> Is perjured, murderous, bloody, full of blame,
> Savage, extreme, rude, cruel, not to trust . . .

Marriages crack but some survive; the storm passes. So it did for us. Much had been uprooted, leaving the ground bare and the trees stripped, ready perhaps for new growth, for different ideas and ways of living. We had come to the place where a choice had to be made.

Some weeks later we took the boys to the seaside for the rest of their holiday, and our reunion. We never spoke of what I called 'the fugue'. We never returned to the scene of that storm.

*   *   *

Reunited after those years of torment, we found ourselves changed – not only ourselves, but the basis of our lives. It was far from easy; we had to readjust, to ignore the past, to accept each other with perceptive sensibility and dignity. It took its time of learning, of fumbling in the dark; throwing our bread upon the waters . . .

> . . . Redeem,
> The time. Redeem
> The unread vision in the higher dream
> While jewelled unicorns draw by the gilded hearse.

wrote T. S. Eliot in 'Ash-Wednesday'.

It would have been much more difficult but for the boys who mercifully had been kept in ignorance of our crisis. They were growing into schoolboys now, full of eager vitality and promise. Francis joined Anthony at Abinger Hill, and we always took them with us on holidays. It was essential that they grew within the security of a stable home, as it was also for our two selves, returning after our critical journeys. We were walking on thin ice, still with the shadow of insecurity about us. I was often ill with dismal maladies and Julian was still entangled with an exacting Sandra.

We had to live with the means available, and make the best of it. In the burning adventure with Sandra, Julian had reached both the highest and the lowest point. He had gone, with trumpet and drum, to another planet right out of my reach. I never wished to hear of the wild journey he plunged into, led by what the French call '*le démon du midi*'. Instinctively I knew it would do me no good. I could guess that it had been a sustained romantic experience, from which he could only recover by moments of another kind of romance: withal he was searching for his renewal, and was at a loss, in strange perplexity. We had truly lost that romantic flame which, in our early days, coloured our lives and saw us through our deficiencies; it was, perhaps, among others the main casualty of 'the fugue'. I learnt to accept the inevitable. We had found within ourselves a weakness which could only be filled from outside sources.

And yet, within its shortcomings, our relationship was alive and true; if we did not, in Naomi Mitchison's words, 'belong to each other', we knew ourselves to be bound together by a deep bond, again best described by Julian in a letter from Blickling Hall, where he had gone for a conference:

. . . This lovely place has settled my soul, with its beauty and with the feeling of being with a group of interesting people, doing something useful – and I have been thinking a lot about us, you and me. It's no good talking, we have to live out our togetherness: the bond between us is so strong and deep that it makes anything else unthinkable and unlivable. You are my wife, I am your husband, we care deeply for each other, we want to make a go of things jointly. It is a very true and very big love, which has survived very much, which is alive, which has shed its larval skin of romantic immaturity without losing its deep core. I have had my lesson; I know myself and you; and I only say what you already know, that I have no thought or dream of wishing for any other woman as my life companion.

This is what I feel, and you feel the same from your end, I know, and yet we manage not only to hurt, but what is in a sense worse, to paralyse or inhibit each other at intervals. That seems to me *the problem* between us. We cannot afford to do this. For my part I know I can't.

Clearly we had to learn many things on this new launching.

That he needed me was undeniable. And just as he needed me, so did I need him, and could not imagine life without his vital concern, his intellectual challenge, the ventures whose accomplishment seemed beyond my capacity yet which he so confidently trusted me with. At this stage of our relationship, both of us had different sorts of wounds to recover from, resulting from the utterly different experiences of the last years. We could not help each other in recovery – in fact, as he writes in the last paragraph of his letter, we only managed to hurt each other more. His somewhat brutal decision against 'leading a smaller life' was really based on a sound instinct and wise balancing act. We both needed outside help, the venture into a different kind of love, which he proposed for himself and equally for me. He continued his explorations, and made no secret of his *amitiés amoureuses*.

It was about that time that Jason came into my life, and I was indeed fortunate in my 'other kind of love'. What I inevitably missed in Julian, Jason gave me in abundance – a devotion which made no complex demands, a constant understanding and tenderness: 'I think of you with a tenderness you have only found in me, which you have created, and which I can give only to you,' he wrote. It was a liberal exchange, a blessed sharing of new joys, of lazy beaches, silent woods and poetry; a happiness which for a few years nourished me and kept me sane, for it filled the vacant space and healed the wounded heart. I left off my Calvinist shirt and made friends with myself.

He taught me so many things: to be free of myself and my clutter of guilt, and to get over my fear of bulls, for we made love on a summer day beside a herd of cows guarded by two large bulls, browsing in the high grass.

This implausible equation was a saving grace for all of us. For myself it was more than that, infinitely more. Sustained by this spring of love, I discovered a new self and understanding, and found in our free allegiance a deep love of life which these years of storm and pain had destroyed. We both knew it could not last and blessed each day as it came. Some unknown poet wrote these lines, it seems expressly for me:

> I thank thee, Love, that thou hast overthrown
> The tyranny of Self; I would not now
> Even in desire, possess thee mine alone
> In land-locked anchorage; nay, rather go
> Where white-winged ships are set for barren shores
> Though freighted all, these lovely argosies
> And laden with a wealth of rarest stones . . .

Jason did, in fact, disappear at sea during the war. And I sometimes wonder now whether he really ever existed, except intact in my liberated heart. For only in a dream world can one escape within so bright a freedom from human bondage – touch the flame of deep happiness without being burnt by it. By this dispensation, a blessing was laid upon us: I learnt the evil of possessiveness and the vanity of attempting its rule.

We were not original in the way we solved our problem; I have told it here because it is the only way I can make sense of my salvation. And so we reached our understanding – respecting each other's emotional outlets, loyal to each other but not, in matrimonial terms, faithful; hiding nothing from each other, yet respecting each other's exploration. It was, of course, what Julian had wanted since our trip to Africa, and probably before, since the days of H. G. Wells, Odette and Lou Pidou. Julian had pleaded for our mutual freedom within the compact of renewed trust in each other. Looking back on this strange evolution, I cannot but agree that to both of us were given the rewards of his passionate hunger for more life.

To me it brought the joys of new growth, within the limits of my capacities.

*   *   *

Back at his desk, Julian was working hard at the book he had been planning for some time. With the collaboration of Gavin de Beer, he was disentangling *Principles of Experimental Embriology*. He was full of zest: though a 'freelance' with no regular income or hours, he found plenty – if not too much – to do, and he had to earn our living. Ebullient, devouring and writing books, absorbing and enhancing life by the full extension of his being, he was the vital centre of parties, telling his funny stories with gusto, creating gaiety and laughter by his contagious exuberance. Carried away by his overriding vitality, he was perhaps insensitive to other people's more serious moods; forgiven too easily perhaps, considering the spoilt child he had been and always remained; but he was also light-hearted and generous, without vanity or malice, always ready to give a helping hand and swift to protest against injustice or narrow-mindedness.

There were, in fact, so many Julians within the tall carelessly dressed wanderer bent on his various ploys, escaping from one activity by diving into yet another. 'So many fingers in so many pies', I once said to him at Oxford. 'What a pity you haven't got a few more fingers!'

In early days, his restlessness could have been described as his search for the right niche, a testing of his powers against the wind. But, in truth, he had no single habitation for his many-sided gifts and curiosities. He was, in very fact, obeying a deep compulsion urged by the complexities of his personality in seeking similar complexities in emotional encounters and intellectual, scientific and poetical explorations.

One needs only to look at the list of his publications to realise the different facets of his work; as well as their important common factor, in itself remarkable, of pioneering across new frontiers.

When his grandfather T. H. Huxley visited America in 1876 he became fascinated by the purposeful, concentrated power of tug-boats guiding their bulky charges to their appointed place in harbour. Considering the matter in deep thought, he then remarked: 'If I were not a man I think I should like to be a tug-boat.' In a manner of speaking Julian was a tug-boat to many unspoken, undefined ideas which, by his determined dedication, influenced our times. I am thinking of his popularisation of science, begun by T. H. Huxley at his Working Men's Lectures, but brought to a much wider public by Julian's popular articles till then taboo to fellow scientists; also, of course, his wide-ranging collective contribution to Unesco (of which more later) where every move was an innovation, a step across boundaries, and where he was able to promote the IUCN (International Union for the Conservation of Nature), followed by the World Wildlife Fund and the Charles Darwin Foundation for the Galapagos Isles. The Brains Trust, where his uncommon breadth of knowledge and versatility, sparked off by an instantaneously obedient memory, became a by-word and created for him an unusually wide reputation.

Julian wrote to a young woman friend: 'One side of me finds Juliette the ideal partner, and another finds satisfaction only in work. In reality I am a pluralist in my philosophy, having given up the quest for unity.' That he had given up the quest for unity was, of course, inevitable, taking his persona into consideration. No circle, however perfect, ever could cage the whirlwind. The obvious consequence was to make him suspect to the scientific forum – to deny him the emblems of distinction he should have had, and to make him often aggressive and petulant. He, who could not suffer fools gladly, could not tolerate not being *right*.

And here we come to that untranslatable French word, *amour-propre*, which is subtler than conceit: neither self-love (the flat translation) nor pandering to one's foibles. It is the deepest image a man has of himself, of his capacities and finally of his dues. Julian's *amour-propre* had been built up by his loving parents since birth. He was grandson of T. H. Huxley and of Thomas Arnold of Rugby – with all the genetical entailments. A wound to that image, however inflicted, could be dangerous and create, for its alleviation, an excessive defensiveness.

I wonder now at the power which animated his voracious spirit and the strange dichotomy between the man whose mind combined the skills of a computer with an added creative energy, and the other man, the romantic youth, who never quite grew up.

*   *   *

It was about this time that I discovered a dormant talent for sculpture. That particular story began in 1933, linked with what, for want of a better word, one calls destiny. We all went for a holiday in Ireland, at Baltimore, and visited the surviving author of *Some Experiences of an Irish RM*. Miss Somerville lived with her kinsman, Admiral Townshend, rooted in old Irish lore, with stories such as the beast, half pig and half dog, who walked round the mountain with shorter legs on the inside than on the outside. The Elizabethan, Francis Bacon, believed this of badgers, and that it was nature's thinking. They could only go round in one direction, ' – a nuisance when hurried'. Miss Somerville also believed in a prophetic sea-monster which announced war and had been seen recently (1933), and also, very firmly, in the delectable world of fairies.

When we confessed that we had left no offerings at the springs sheltered by bushes, hung with bits of ribbon, stubs of pencils, buttons and blossoms as humble thanks for the blessings of pure water, she was horrified. She warned us that even though fairies did not usually cross water, our disrespect would bring some bad luck for sure.

And so it did. Anthony, then aged twelve, riding with a band of children on rusty bikes out of the drive at the house of friends in Micheldever, was knocked down by a passing car and left unconscious by the wayside. Francis ran back to call me, white and shaken: 'Anthony is dead, come quick.' I ran out and, horrified, found him with arms behind his limp body like a puppet whose strings were broken. But when suddenly he sat up and screamed twice, a great relief flooded through me. The doctor diagnosed concussion. The anguish of the morning was lifted; we were assured there would be no consequences of what could have been a terrible accident. The child must miss school for a term, 'not using his brain'.

To occupy Anthony during those weeks, we called in Alan Best, the young sculptor and naturalist from Pembrokeshire whose story Julian tells in his *Memories*. Modelling clay was brought into the house, tools to work it and tuition given. I watched with fascination as shapes emerged, deftly modelled into recognisable things. And one weekend, the teacher gone but the clay available, I seized upon a docile guest as a sitter. To my surprise I reproduced the long unusual features with striking likeness. In fact, it was a momentous shock to all the household – the model, Julian, Anthony and myself and our faithful maid, Alice.

The Irish fairies relented; Anthony went on with his modelling and soon recovered completely. He was able next term to return to school. But the impetus given me by this event, by the combination of deep anxiety and redemption, became for many years an important part of my private world. It was, truly, a most unexpected gift. The deep joy of discovery led me to new perceptions of works of art, to natural forms in their beauty, enriching my life. It seemed to be the crowning of my falling in love with Jason, who led me through new discoveries into fulfilment.

My apprenticeship at the Central School under John Skeaping was almost like a recollection. I soon left modelling for sculpture and now it was my chisel which sought the shape locked within the block of wood, each chip bringing it nearer to release. It was a rare and perfect joy.

12

The Zoo

Under its title 'The Zoo Cage' in *Memories* Julian told the story of his nomination as Zoo Secretary, to succeed Sir Peter Chalmers-Mitchell, an admirable director whose skill and subtlety created Whipsnade, and put the Zoo 'on the map'. It was for Julian a totally new experience, which he took up with alacrity and zest. It seemed to be all he could wish for. It ended badly, and even the memory of his definite contribution to the Zoo is now curiously blotted out of the records.

He was full of ideas, inspired by his official visits to continental zoos, and his own knowledge of animal behaviour and needs. The trouble was that he, who had so brilliantly unravelled the meaning of the courtship of the crested grebe and analysed their complicated ritual, he, whose patience had taught him to recognise the birds singing in a wood, spending hours watching their behaviour, had never applied any watching whatever to human beings. He had never asked himself what made them tick, made them interested or annoyed, touchy or flattered, whereas Peter Chalmers-Mitchell was a master of the art, and practised it with fine judgement in all his dealings with the group of prominent personalities round the Council table. He had created his Zoo by manipulating individuals – whether bankers, industrialists or diplomats, guiding them through the labyrinth of his mind to accept policies they would never have dreamt of tolerating themselves. Julian's approach to the Council was far from Sir Peter's. He was direct and enthusiastic, often more than a little brash. The velvet gloves were off – the President was baffled.

Julian was planning a Zoo which was to enlarge its influence into a world of untapped opportunities: a studio for art students to draw animals from life; a film unit to show wild life where it was wild; a weekly paper with reports of Zoo doings; a Children's Zoo, with friendly animals they could make contact with; and as much research as possible on the precious material available. Then there were buildings which needed rethinking – and more inspired designs such as had been promoted by Sir Peter, namely the lovely Penguin pool by Lubetkin.

He was impatient and lacked tact. It was, of course, unpleasant to be curbed in cherished plans. The Executive Council – chosen friends of Sir Peter's – had the final authority, and clung to it. In his *Memories*, he describes them as 'altogether a curious assemblage, largely of wealthy amateurs, self-propagating and autocratic'. Without tact authority is bruised, and simple problems become thorny. Of much of this I was unaware; Julian did not choose to discuss it with me, besides it was, for the first years, far from being a cause of discord. It was more a subterranean rumble which could be undetectable in social relations.

There was so much else to absorb my full attention: the Zoo flat had to be redecorated and I was allowed to do it. It was a spacious apartment on top of the offices and Julian's own study, splendidly convenient for all sorts of parties and for living. But I missed a garden.

We became familiar with lions roaring at night, trapped in their narrow cages and challenging their lost horizon. It was terrible to see them pacing to and fro, behind their bars, their eyes glazed with inward hunger. They are much better housed today, on a green hillock with tall trees, and lounge around just as they do in Africa, with fewer flies to flick away. We adopted a small lion cub rejected by its mother – fed it on bottles of milk and it was tame as a dog. Jimmy often joined my tea-parties, and helped to entertain the guests. Then its teeth went wrong – growing into the roots – and Jimmy had to be put away. I wondered if its mother had known it was not viable, and pushed it away from her nipples? I was also given a bush-baby, Moholi galago. Enchanting agile leaper, it climbed to the top of curtains and flew back on to one's head, never missing; it fed on mealworms which came from Germany, holding one in each little hand-like paw, and nibbling at them as if they were sausages.

Julian, being on duty at Whipsnade at weekends, had a small flat over the restaurant there. Soon he was lent a vacant field with a grand view over Ivinghoe Beacon where first we camped, then out of simple resources created for ourselves and our guests a happy anchorage far from official duties. Two hay huts became dormitories for us and our guests, replacing the haystack we first slept on; lovely picnics brought from the restaurant saved all the housekeeping chores; and at night we built large fires from fallen branches, sitting around and singing a vast repertory of old and new songs.

Two Iceland ponies were acquired for the boys, and during their absence at school we all took turns riding round the deserted park after closing time. Thor and Odin were gallant trotters and flew round the tiger and lion pits whose occupants prowled menacingly behind their high fences; antelopes and deer pricked their ears, alert and curious; giraffes launched their balanced amble keeping pace with the riders; the wolves' red eyes shone between the pine trees of their paddock; and sleeping birds woke up to blink at our passage.

I remember those days glowing with simple joys, close to nature and rich in happy friendship. I even planted a garden, fertilised by manure from zoo animals. The first crop was choked by carrots, cabbage, maize, tomatoes, etc., seeded by the opulent remnants of elephants' coarse digestion.

Julian did his turn of duty, planning new ponds for hippos and ducks and, near the restaurant, for flamingoes with their knitting-needle legs, delighting the lunchers. We visited new arrivals: white-tailed gnus galloping across their domain with their tails flashing like flags; the baby giraffe unfolding its clumsy legs and tottering beside its solicitous mother; the sad

widowed elk; the king penguins proudly wearing the magnificent evening suits fashioned by what evolutionary tailors . . .
They all got to know us, nosing their tameness through
enclosing wires. And on Monday morning we rushed back to
London, having tasted the rare felicity of communing with
our wild friends.

It was after one of those intoxicating new spring weekends
when we returned to the Zoo flat that Alice, our faithful
housekeeper, met me with a serious face. The message had
come from Millie, Ottoline's maid: Lady Ottoline had died
the day before at the nursing home in Tunbridge Wells. It was
April 21, 1938. She was sixty-seven years old. A light went
out of my life.

I had first seen her twenty-three years before in that
waiting-room at Oxford station, a girl not quite twenty, to be
interviewed for the post of governess-companion to her ten-
year-old daughter. Garsington had then become my home for
two years, and Lady Ottoline the strongest influence in what
was to be a whole new world. I still treasure her letters to me,
written in her significant handwriting, sepia-coloured on the
vellum paper she always favoured; a handwriting which expressed her search for beauty even in ordinary pursuits and
which, in well-spaced lines, gave out its unique quality.
Re-reading them now, they bring back vividly the moments
spent with her, her wish to share, her concern to help in
troubles. She was generous to many, involved deeply with
human beings.

Virginia Woolf wrote to her in April 1917, 'you have
become one of the romantic myths of my life, and when I hear
of other people seeing you, I don't believe them', and later,
'my images, after leaving you, were all of the sea – mermaid
Queens, shells, the bones of the shipwrecked . . . It was a
great pleasure and reassurement to find that my memory had
not been mythical or romantic enough'.

Courageous in her convictions and in her actions, she also
had the ultimate courage to forgive her detractors, to rise

above their malice without becoming bitter herself. Her doors, to whoever knocked, were never closed.

I see her getting into her carriage helped up by the devoted Millie and being handed her very large brocade bag containing cigarettes and peppermints, and as many of her precious books of poetry as could be added to the load. She was off on a picnic with Gertler or Lytton or Bertie; but she had to bring the talismans of her search: to reassure, to define the moment of illumination in a clear line of poetic vision.

Augustus John's portrait of Ottoline as a *monstre sacré* with that questioning, daring smile is misleading. A more accurate impression can be gained from a typically impulsive but perceptive letter written to me by Stephen Tennant, who knew her well:

> *Wilsford Manor, Salisbury, Wilts.*
> *October* 1972.

Ottoline Morrell was one of the outstanding women of her day. Although dazzling and brilliant, there was nothing vulgar or flamboyant about her – or trite. In appearance she was rather startling – she used too white a face powder and this, with her dark-red purple hair, gave her a slightly Borgia and bizarre, a Maria de Medici, look.

She had a genius for drawing out men of letters – talent of all kinds fascinated her. But she was extremely discerning in her knowledge of the quality of each talent, and its measure of greatness: just how considerable a talent she could discern at once. She was a woman who had a great deal in reserve; she had no vanity or conceit, and even her greatest friends felt that she was mysterious. On certain people she made an ambiguous, uneasy impression; not always a pleasant one. She was never catty or spiteful – her blind patrician way of ignoring the cheap or vulgar was characteristic of her. She loved the Grand Gesture in art . . . The meditative element in her character was most attractive and set her apart. Fastidious, patient with fools, she deeply treasured the Rare, the transcendental poetic mind. She was, of course, a Bas Bleu, brilliantly equipped to meet the great man on his own terms, or to nourish the gifts of the young who showed promise.

There was much of the philosopher in her: the sage, the Sybilline oracle. She brooded constantly on the great mystery of human life.

She wanted a better truth than most people want, and often got it. I have always revered the truth seeker in her. She was very complex, subtle; she was the Artist; original in many of her intellectual exercises; *very* intelligent indeed.

The aristocratic sensibility was very evident – she was very patrician – all that a duke's sister should be: shrewd. There was nothing of the foolish lion-hunter in her. Of course she was a Renaissance princess, lock, stock and barrel. With a mystical streak in her.

I think she was not 'Bonne comme du pain'. She liked to be mysterious, and her deep interest in human nature sometimes led her beyond the boundaries of discretion – but I know she only wanted to help people to be happy: she wanted to guide them, and sometimes her zeal was misinterpreted . . . I think she was apt to make a great favourite of one friend, and her other dear ones felt a little peeved, and left out in the cold . . . Of course few people realised how finely perceptive she was. Shelley said: 'The Cold World will never know', and this applies to Ottoline.

That is the Lady Ottoline I recognise far more than the many hostile descriptions left by others among her contemporaries.

*   *   *

We spent our summer holiday, August 1938, partly at Neuchâtel with my mother, and then motored over the St Bernard into the Tessin where our old friends Rosy and Franz Moser had a house and a steep terraced garden on the slopes above Lake Maggiore. It was a favourite resting place for us, and a fine ground of exploration for the boys, who hunted for scorpions and stick insects, aloes and cacti.

Suddenly we woke up to rumours of war. Hitler was screaming defiance and Britain was alarmed – so much so that we felt we must return at once, sending Anthony by train to rejoin his school, Dauntsey, taking Francis with us, and stopping on the way to say goodbye to my mother at Neuchâtel. We were not to meet again until August 1945. Driving back at a good pace, we had a severe accident just outside Abbeville, swerving sharply to avoid a straying

donkey-cart laden with careless children, and hitting a tree –
not head-on but miraculously sideways, and so we escaped
what could only have been a fatal crash. I remember sitting by
Julian in front of the violently checked car, Francis at the back
among piles of luggage, thinking quite calmly that we must all
be dead: 'and all that for a donkey . . . !' As Julian writes in
Memories, 'Silences occur at such moments, when shock in-
hibits the vital processes. We all remembered this silence, this
apprehension of death.' Francis, just fifteen, shaken but un-
hurt, was a tower of strength, and helped me to look after
Julian who mercifully was but slightly hurt. I had a small
concussion from hitting my forehead on the mirror. The
children on the donkey-cart were untouched, and so we left
the car, taking our luggage for a quiet night in a hotel.

*   *   *

1938 saw the return of blinkered Chamberlain, flown to
Munich for the appeasement of Hitler, waving a Peace Treaty.
'Peace in our Time', he called it. The Time lasted a year,
during which it seemed all plans were like a walk on the edge
of a knife, the future clouded by doubts. The Second World
War broke out over almost complete disarray.

Anthony, not quite eighteen, went to Trinity College Cam-
bridge, where he read English on a war degree of two years.
Francis, at Gordonstoun, was evacuated with the school to
Wales, the War Office deeming it safer there with an exiled
German, Kurt Hahn, as headmaster, than Elgin, so near the
Scottish coast. We stayed in London, at the Zoo flat, with
blessed escapes to Whipsnade. Our petrol ration, stretched by
free-wheeling down slopes, just permitted these weekly trips.
Whipsnade meant returning to a sort of normality after strain
and tension, constant anxiety and absence of hope.

Julian had offered to work for half his salary for the dura-
tion: the London Zoo had but few regular visitors and several
large animals, elephants, giraffes, hippos, had been sent out to
Whipsnade. Though facilities were still available they were on

a very small budget; but Julian was keen to plan various improvements for 'after the war'. Meanwhile he attended to the running of the place, restless, suffering not only the dark hours of the war but feeling the cruel waste of time and effort, and having deep doubts about what the future – if there was a future – would bring. Air-raids began fierce and crazy. In my journal for September 11, 1940, I noted:

Since last Saturday air-raids have been raging over London. We got back from Whipsnade on Monday morning to hear of the ghastly time they had had, and had a taste that night and every night since. The docks are burning, The East End is being demolished, Buckingham Palace has had a fire bomb; Regent Street and Piccadilly are railed off, two museums are burnt, several stations hit, fires, fires burning in many places; it is so incredible that I almost feel I am dreaming, that it could *never* happen. But the Primrose Hill guns are barking loudly, and as we looked out of the front door we saw the angry flashes lighting the trees. We are sitting in the basement; the boys are playing chess, Julian reading; next door, people from the Zoo are chatting. We left everything upstairs, and God knows what we'll see again. The horror is unremitting like a Juggernaut approaching, grinding, destroying.

The previous Saturday we had watched from Whipsnade the London sky-line reddening under the bombs, and the fire devouring the docks. I remember the next day wandering miserably round the grounds and returning to my plot of garden as to a last hope, the hope of the good earth nourishing the seeds I planted, holding in its depths the roots of future growth. I always found appeasement and reassurance in the green world of nature.

In London I took to bicycling to whatever job I was then doing; carrying my bike over dunes of broken glass; serving lunches at the National Gallery Concerts, the canteen superbly run by our old friend Irene Gater; later working with the WVS in a small unit under a dear old lady, Mrs L., whose job was to prepare houses for bombed-out people. Some of these houses were in Mayfair, luxuriously lovely but empty of all necessities. We 'borrowed' linen and blankets from bombed houses until a horrified delegate from Headquarters discovered and put a stop to our doings, which she called 'looting'. Mrs L. sweetly replied that we would obey at once, as anyway there was nothing left to take.

After Dunkirk, because I spoke French, I was roped in by May Spears, 'Madame la Générale' (Lady Spears was the wife of General Louis Spears) to help in the White City canteen where the rescued French soldiers and sailors had been parked. The French, picked up from the beaches with our Expeditionary Forces, were not allowed to leave the Stadium without permission, had nothing to do but play cards, drink the coffee we offered and listen to Vichy Radio. They were completely demoralised and their officers never attempted to contact them. A few could speak some English, but mostly they were ignorant, helpless and desperate. As they only wore the uniforms they were rescued in, they began to get very unkempt and dirty. We arranged that the Red Cross should fit them up with what they needed, a very popular move indeed; so popular that they soon bought themselves cheap suitcases and, returning again and again to the Red Cross in their dirty rags, obtained yet another pair of grey trousers and sports jacket, shorts, etc. The practice was discovered and stopped. They looked like stage boys in their English sports clothes instead of the sailors' striped vests or khaki-bags tied with a string round their middles.

Lost and pathetic, they were bewildered by the delays in sending them back to France and were never told that the British had no ships with which to do so. I looked hopelessly at these lonely men surging round the canteen, aimless, dirty, cold now that the weather was changing, listening to the Vichy radio news with cynical jeers.

My journal August 1, 1940
Jean-Pierre Giraudoux, son of Jean Giraudoux, the author, arrived looking very ill, his shirt fastened with safety pins. He has left all in

France, escaped from a camp where his regiment, disarmed, was awaiting demobilization and the wishes of Hitler; he hitch-hiked to Portugal, friends paid his fare to London and he is joining de Gaulle and the budding Free French army, then called the Legion. I asked him to get me an introduction to the General which he did. The Legion had their H.Q. in a bunch of small offices on the Embankment, the General sitting at a deal table. I told him of the Frenchmen at the White City, and asked for some liaison between these lost men and his planned resurgence of the French Army – someone to talk to them and give them a chance to fight for France and the Allies. 'Madame', he replied, 'je suis sous les ordres de Monsieur Churchill de n'approcher aucun des Français évacués de Dunquerque. A Aintree on m'a tout simplement défendu d'entrer'. The British troops were given orders to destroy all war material belonging to the French. All the men, willing or not, were sent back to Vichy France on the 16th September. They would have been returned earlier had any available ships been provided. There were about 8000 of them given six shillings a week with passes from 2 to 9 p.m. and the devil take them if they grumble.

No wonder that de Gaulle – not by birth an easy character – was exasperated.

Re-reading the journal of those 1940–41 weeks and months – perhaps the most painful of the war with constant bombings and oppressive fears which, even unspoken, spread from person to person – I find here and there fascinating bits of living *malgré tout* – of being conscious of something outside our precarious future.

Met Dorothy Thompson – a big strong woman, fat round face, small features, bad clothes, firm and definite action: a sort of dynamic Juno. She said she felt our experience was very hard to transmit, and that she goes back to U.S.A. to ask for more young writers to come over and write it up. Churchill at Potomac with Roosevelt – a well-guarded secret. We go to Connel Ferry (Argyllshire) on Friday next.

August, 1941

Connel. Anthony, Francis and I came up on Friday night: downpours of rain. Mactalla (lent us by Rosalind) exactly the same as 23 years ago, the loch, the little white house opposite. Much rain. Rowed round the islands, while the sun was out, blue and white Loch Etive shining and beautiful. The boys collect beasts for their aquarium, which is of great interest.

August 20

Set off in the boat and rowed across the bay to Benderloch. Squalls of rain and patches of sunny weather polishing the water. We went round the wreck – a 10,000 ton ship which sank after bombing last November, full of blood – horses sent to safety in U.S. Oozing oil and curious air bubbles. At low tide, one could see its deck and upright funnels, now furry with sea-weed and encrusted with barnacles. Water grimly black over this phantom ship of death. We leave silently.

August 21

Julian arrives this morning, great excitement, bringing two large cases of food – most welcome. He looks tired. Set off in boat, round Dunstaffnage, romantic, on its promontory with many fallen trees. Came back with just turning tide, and now the sun has set in lovely polychrome glory. The hills change colour from blue to purple, the water shines like molten gold, points of land black and trenchant. A plume of smoke floats up – some convoy departing?

August 22

Anthony left this morning. He is starting his new job at Stanmore, Operational Research at R.A.F. Fighter Command.

August 23

Francis goes back to Gordonstoun, transferred to Wales. Julian better with new treatment – eleven minutes in a cold bath and eleven drops of arsenic three times daily. I work at National Gallery Canteen 12–3, serving lunches to hundreds. Russia still holds out, though losses must be hideous. Germany still manages to pour out armies and machines like a plague of locusts.

October 9

Another diversion: Dinner party in Zoo flat: Boris Anrep, Desmond MacCarthy, Victor Speight, Theodora Benson and Sibyl Colefax (recovering from her broken back but still in plaster, shrunk, haggard-looking but indomitable; still admirably doing her self-appointed job of entertaining, knowing everyone worth a dinner and retaining affection and gratitude). Mixed talk – little about the war. Anthony (Huxley) with us, hating the party and bristling.

An almost indecipherable and undated letter from Sibyl to Julian: 'Can you come on 22nd June to lunch here H. G. Wells, you and the King of Siam, Victor Cazalet who insists on bringing the King together with H.G., apparently hero of this small orient dwarf's life. It is so like a joke. Please come and help – there is literally no-one else'. Canteen as before – abrutissant. News of Russia critical. If Russia falls are we not doomed?

October 15

News of Russia very bad – Germans claim to be within 65 miles of Moscow. Anxiety spreads, newspaper editions multiply.

Youth Congress on Saturday. We sat in a box at the Albert Hall next to the Maiskys (Soviet Ambassador in London), who get the only real ovation. Any mention of Russia brings down the roof. Show very moving and successful, particularly the Finale, small groups of ARP, munition workers, fire-fighters, women's corps, etc – slowly marching through the Hall to the platform, then various flag-bearers from all allied countries join them and two youths, a boy and a girl, read out a Declaration of Youth. They had a Youth Rally in Neuchâtel too, says a letter from my mother. As she put it: 'Sous le regard de Dieu'.

Julian all this time was getting more and more restless – unwell, tetchy, secretive, attending PEP meetings, the Royal Society (he had been elected Fellow in 1938) and spending many late evenings accumulating the formidable material for his book on evolution. His downstairs study mantelpiece was covered with towering piles of reprints on every aspect of biology and manuscript pages on odd scraps of paper pinned together for typing. Some of the chapters had been rewritten several times already.

November 20

. . . Julian in bed with a temperature and a disease which is not flu but looks like it. A funny party round his bed with John Gunther, American world journalist, looking enormous, speaking eloquently. The Congress has rejected the vote for arming merchant ships sent out here; even went so far as saying that Churchill's magnificent gesture in speech last week, to declare war on Japan the moment she attacks USA, might have been unwise. Thinks the only hope of the USA entering the war is to be attacked.

Julian then offered to go to the States and give lectures on war aims as discussed by PEP, to see influential people – anything which might help the cause. He finally arranged a tour of lectures as a start, sponsored by the Rockefeller Association while he looked round for more active support. I was against his going, which seemed at the time futile. The Zoo Council gave a reluctant and qualified 'permission' for six weeks at most, adding ominously that 'it was on his own head'. This of course made Julian all the more anxious to go.

He went to see Attlee and Eden who were both interested in the Reconstruction problems for *after* the war: they gave him a sort of *laissez-passer*, but no definite line to follow. He started packing (though his visa had not yet come through), told Anthony, spoke to Francis after great telephonic spasms in a few hurried words. One minute deeply depressed with the difficulties in his way – then exultant when some small cog fell into place. He saw the voyage as a mission worth risking everything for. I saw it very differently.

November 20

He did go, Anthony and I took him to Euston – and there he went into the night. Of course I cried and they were rather ashamed of me.

Euston, dark and dank; people scuttling with luggage; Julian already projected into his adventure to pastures new, with hardly a look at Anthony and me. How vividly I remember it, and the heavy weight of premonition and anxiety. He was catching a transport leaving from a northern port in the deep secrecy which now shrouded every sailing as the German submarines were swarming the seas like hungry sharks. The whole thing was fateful as a Greek play. I was deeply hurt, for all of us, and especially for Francis, who in four days' time was to play Hamlet at Gordonstoun. Julian was betraying the boy's expectation that his father would be there, watching a performance which Hahn, the headmaster, had been in the habit of preparing every two years for the school. And the boy chosen to play Hamlet was deemed honoured, through his personal character and merit. It was, in truth, the high test.

On Saturday November 24 I went to Wales and that night Francis acted his Hamlet. It ended about eleven. We came out together, the night was clear and one brilliant star fell as we looked up. Francis was rather dazed, still half in his part, yet now in his school uniform looking so boyish, transformed from the complicated and tragic figure he had just so deeply lived and expressed. We sat on my bed a little while, talking of Hamlet, until, tired out, we went off to bed.

I went home on the Monday. A letter from the coast was waiting for me from Julian. 'I don't think you understand even yet, how much I rely on you in all sorts of ways, how much less I should be without you . . . ' What did I want then? That he should say: 'I love you. I miss you. I hated leaving you . . . '

★   ★   ★

A cable on December 5, 1941 announced Julian's safe arrival – a great relief. Very soon after, he gave a press conference where he was trapped into saying in answer to the question: did he hope that America would come into the fighting? 'Yes, under certain conditions'. If only he had said something like 'You may have trouble with Japan' or some vague generalities like 'The future depends on too many things . . . ' but his 'yes' was like a red rag to a herd of bulls. People in England well knew of the isolationism of the USA who, though they were manifestly interested and profiting by our war efforts and inventions, certainly were not in the least anxious to be drawn into the war. However, only three days after the storm of opprobrium had fallen on Julian's head for raising the possibility of America at war, Pearl Harbour shattered all hopes of their avoiding it. Overnight the nation became violently bellicose and furious to have been taken in by the Japanese mission in Washington, only a week before their well prepared bombing of the US Fleet. America was now marshall-ing all its power for war.

Julian's six weeks' leave had expired and I was daily expect-ing news of his return. But somehow he repeatedly failed to get safe transport, and repeatedly cabled delays. Meanwhile moves were afoot at the Zoo, threatening his job.

February 20, 1942

Francis Hemming wrote to tell me that the Council had decided to suppress Julian's job 'in order to save expenses'. Just as I expected: I am not surprised therefore; the shock is mitigated by the expectation of it – but is nevertheless very unpleasant. I wonder as I pass to and fro in the Zoo hall how many of these clerks and staff know, and feel they watch me suspiciously. 'Il faut garder son panache'.

Of course they all know. But no-one says a word. Lord Onslow, President of the Council, will publicly announce the Council's decision in March at the General Meeting. And that evening, the Meeting having made the decision, Lord Onslow sends for me. He is busy putting on his coat and too embarrassed for courtesy. So he just mumbles that the post of Secretary of the Zoo has been suppressed. I turn on my heels and cable Julian 'Come back and fight it out.'

I wonder what he thinks. I still feel that his Reconstruction programme will not give him any sort of satisfaction; that he will continue to be tormented by a deep sense of frustration. But then he may also find the *real* job for himself, co-ordinating ideas of recon-struction within a wide pattern of living needs. He would do this well, and be fulfilled in it, but it must be a *real* job, and not a fragmentary report here and there. He will also definitely be much happier without the millstone of a suspicious Council round his neck, if only he can accept this not as a defeat. Nevertheless, I am deeply troubled. It becomes impossible to sleep or to escape from a multitude of thoughts, including anger with Julian for having gone, after all the warnings, to the U.S.A.

As soon as the media announced the news, letters arrived from friends and supporters of Julian. Francis Hemming, the noted entomologist as well as a very able civil servant, valiant-ly supported and advised me; so did Cyril Diver, Max Nichol-son, James Fisher, Lord Horder, Gavin de Beer, Tom

Longstaff, Gestetner and many others. I was deeply moved and grateful; and why, I wondered, did these friends in official positions risk trouble on behalf of a fight against the Establishment? Gavin de Beer phoned to offer any help he could give, 'because', he said, 'I owe so much to Julian who taught me all I know and inspired me all through my work. I am only too happy to help him now in this trouble.'

Julian cabled that his return was again delayed: but he was going to fight the decision, and I must prepare the ground. No time was lost: we formed an 'Informal Committee' and Gestetner offered to pay for all printing expenses. I went to see Lord Horder, who generously agreed to stand as President for a new Council elected by the Informal Committee, the supporters of Julian. It was a long-drawn battle, every day filled with problems, anxiety and dismay. Still Julian cabled delays. Very few of his letters came through, generally beside the point, as obviously he had not faced the naked truth of his position. When he finally managed to board a Portuguese ship and fly back from Lisbon it was on the eve of the April Council, and the Fellows were to vote – for or against. The grim old Council won by three to two. Julian had nothing left but to resign.

It was, as he writes in his *Memories*, 'a bitter pill to swallow'. Having tasted this same pill for over five months, I had but little swallowing to do: we had to face the fact, and look for a house as soon as possible. The Council, however, granted us permission to stay on at the Zoo flat until the next dwelling was suitably prepared. We chose a house in Pond Street which was in a derelict condition but otherwise just what we needed (the fourth No. 31 I had lived in). We moved in on a cold rainy day in January 1943 after improvements to the house, according to the sparse standards of the time.

Julian had been clearing out his study at the Zoo and was hard at work finishing his book on evolution, published in 1942, just before we moved. It was a remarkable achievement, and he often said he thought it the best thing he ever did. A second edition was produced in 1964 and a third and last in 1974.

The clear success of his *Evolution*, the work of four years in the small hours of the night, helped Julian to swallow his bitter pill. But I feared that, in the end, he would have to pay for his defeat: it was therefore with immense relief that I heard of the offer to him, in 1943, to join the Colonial Commission on Higher Education in West Africa.

13

Time of Darkness

Julian set off for Africa early the following year. I recorded the occasion in my journal:

15 January, 1944

Harold Channon, one of the members of the Eliot Commission to West Africa, arrived last night attired in tropical suit and boy-scout-on-his-adventure spirit. Tries to mitigate the thinness of his trousers with Francis' or Julian's long pants, but neither suits as he is too fat. So I finally advised pyjama legs under his trousers, and sent him off to bed with sleeping draught and cough mixture at 10 p.m. Called this morning at 5.30 by 'phone – and by 6.0 they were both plunging into the fog with their rucksacks and an air of going to Epping for the day. Julian posts his glove instead of letters on way to the station.

Once more good-bye. Once more left alone in the house with his voice. Feeling unreal and barely conscious. He said to me last night: 'Isn't it lovely we are so happy together – and love each other so well'. Yes, it is true some of these months have been truly happy – I will think now of this quiet happiness we have had . . . which grew and fulfilled itself in daily life . . .

And with all the vicissitudes of our 25 years we are firmly and happily bound together without tyranny or jealousy – with a love that grows unobtrusively into daily life. It grows – like the Edelweiss on a precipice perhaps – but it does grow. And such as it is it remains the most precious thing in my life.

While Julian was exploring the fascinations of West Africa, our first grandchild, Susan, was born in London. Anthony wired me the news as I was on the Isle of Wight, helping Violet Hammersley get over a nervous breakdown. I rushed back as soon as I could, in spite of Violet's pleas, and saw this tiny person, with a neat compact little face, an adorable enchanting baby filling our hearts with new life. Anthony, grave with his fresh responsibilities, Anne his wife calm and trustful – both so young.

Meanwhile the war had returned to London:

February 23, 1944

The big raids have started again. VIs are loose over London. Today my solar plexus has been horribly active and unpleasant. Down town the same picture, morale very low.

February 28

I don't remember being so worried during last blitz of '41. I have this fear in me, sharpened of course by loneliness . . . I discover that Anne has also lost her nerve in their upstairs flat, collect the family to stay here for a few days. Bad raid last night, we put the cradle under the kitchen table, the safest place in the house . . .

March 4

Jimmy Crowther offers me a job: preparing house in Burlington Street to be the home of the Society for Visiting Scientists, under the British Council. Now in the hands of builders, then, for me to furnish and finally decorate. Gladly accept. It is an anchor, much better than running away to Elspeth and Gervas in the country [Gervas was Julian's first cousin, married to the writer Elspeth Huxley] . . . as I was planning to do, being so scared.

Lovely sun today. I have a captive chestnut bud downstairs, pale green velvet groping for light and life. Start job tomorrow.

March 13

My job is quite fun, hunting for furniture and getting Ministry of Works to allow coupons for curtain materials. Go to various wholesale houses, in one of which I am told that the US Forces have bought every remaining yard of white satin in the country for dead GIs' coffins . . . Demetrio Capetanakis, died yesterday – a friend of Anthony's at Cambridge, young Greek poet – leukemia. Poor boy.

March 19

Our silver wedding. I send Julian a cable:

> Can wisdom be put in a silver rod
> Or love in a golden bowl

> (*Book of Thel*, Blake)

He was baffled and surprised, having forgotten.

While in Africa he had caught a bad fever, probably malaria, was quite ill and was given massive doses of mepacrine, then the favourite remedy for malaria. When he arrived home, still very shaky, his yellow face shocked me into calling our doctor, Leo Rau. His liver was badly affected, but even more seriously, he was in a deeply depressed mood.

I had dreaded a nervous breakdown since the Zoo conflict – and there it was, seriously complicated by hepatitis. Did the Greeks not believe that the 'soul' resided in the liver? This was my second experience of seeing Julian through a period of total disablement. The first had been in 1919, when I had taken him to Dr Vittoz in Lausanne. But then he had been physically mobile, and the depression was far less acute: this time, I realised very soon, we were in great trouble; far beyond the treatment of Dr Vittoz which had cured Julian then.

The illness lasted the best part of the year with a long convalescence; and it was the first time that the consultants, Russell Brain and Lord Horder and the clinic doctor, a red-faced pugnacious man, tried to cure Julian using electric shock treatment. When this new cure was suggested, I refused to sign a paper defining the risks to patients, such as dislocation of limbs and vertebrae, which could occur under the violent shock, and absolving the doctor who applied this treatment from legal or medical responsibility. Above all I was horribly frightened of what these shocks could do to a brain – any brain, but particularly Julian's. However, the doctor confronted me during my visit to Julian at Harrow and made a violent scene in front of the patient, threatening to throw Julian out of his clinic if I did not agree to the ECT.

I was then advised by Dr Russell Brain and Lord Horder that my signature was but a formality, for, although the shocks induced convulsions, these were mitigated by holding the patient down; they also held out great hopes of a cure. It was a nightmare, but with great anxiety I did at last sign.

Actually, I must admit that in the end Julian was cured, but I am still doubtful that he would not, in any case, have emerged out of his depression by some other treatment. Julian was to suffer three further breakdowns, and was treated again with ECT; the method has improved in that the patients are now injected with curare to paralyse the convulsions. There has recently been an attack on this inexplicable method of treating nervous breakdowns, but it is now agreed that it has had highly successful results. The latest trend, however, is to discard it in favour of tranquillisers. These are also dangerous with addiction and side-effects. Psychoanalysis is a very slow process of unravelling the tangled roots of the ego, and can be merciless. Its success must also depend on the insight and compassion of the physician.

So Julian was exposed to what I always consider as a dangerous treatment – and as he wrote in his *Memories*:

I shall never forget the doctor's eyes peering into mine as he fixed the electrodes on my skull, nor the horrible moment of threshing about before I fell into unconsciousness. However, the treatment did me good, though to this day nobody understands why electro-shocks should help in depressions: probably they wipe out memory-traces of the predisposing incidents. In any case they do affect memory – it takes a month before it is fully restored.

Of course I was never allowed to be present during this operation. I could only imagine it in all its horror, and suffer accordingly. He was just about fifty-five years old – 'in the prime of life' – and was to die at eighty-seven in 1975. During those remaining years and after his death I was to ponder much on the fragility of the human spirit, the constant need to mend it and the hit or miss methods that are all we have to help us at the present. My involvement with Julian's depressions was total.

One question remains: how much did Julian, the firstborn grandchild of T. H. Huxley, possibly owe this tendency to nervous breakdowns to the mixed genes of his two very different grandfathers? On his mother's side, the religiously ambivalent Thomas Arnold, son of Arnold of Rugby: on his father's side, T. H. Huxley, agnostic, fighter, fiercely over-working scientist, often prey to serious illnesses, including a deep-rooted melancholy. This state of mind often darkened the lives of his wife and family. 'Grandmoo', as Henrietta Huxley was always called, wrote to John Tyndale (always addressed as 'Brother John') on Good Friday 1873: 'Hal is very cast down "melancholy mad" as he himself describes it. But last night, having pent up all my anxiety about him for two long years I, who had never shed a tear all that time, sobbed for an hour.' (From an unpublished letter.)

When such a spell occurred T.H.H. shut himself up in his study – 'A man must consume his own smoke' – and fought the devils single-handed. How much, one wonders, did Julian inherit of this dark strain from his idolised Gran-Pater? Little is known of the nature of T.H.H.'s melancholy, said to be due to constant overwork, except that he cured himself during his long visits to Switzerland. Maloja in the Engadine was a favourite place. There he used what physical energy he had to climb – gradually working up to ten and fifteen miles every other day and up to 2000 feet. He writes in 1888 to Herbert Spencer:

In fact, as long as I take rather sharp exercise in sunshine I feel quite well, and I could walk as well as any time these ten years . . .

My wife sends her kindest regards. She is much better than when we left, which is lucky for me, as I have no mind, and could not make it up if I had any. The only vigour I have is in my legs, and that only when the sun shines.★

In fact, this last paragraph could have been written by Julian. The parallel of T.H.H.'s 'I have no mind and could not make it up if I had any' strikes one forcibly. This was so absolutely the condition of Julian's breakdowns, his total reliance on outside help, mostly mine, as T.H.H. relied so fully on his wife Henrietta, that one inevitably finds a link of genes. Yet people have nervous breakdowns without a family

★ *Life and Letters of T.H.H. II* by Leonard Huxley.

precedent, and it is now accepted as a legitimate illness, needing medical help and research. There is still a long way to go.

But this was late spring 1944. The V2s were savaging London, both physically and psychologically much worse than the V1s; like the Duchess in *Alice in Wonderland*, who felt the prick of her brooch before the pin touched her skin, these horrible inventions exploded destructively a few seconds before one heard the roar of their approach. The very air was full of expectations of disaster.

Julian was in the Harrow clinic, still under treatment. My regular visits left me overtired, empty and hopeless. Then, on June 6, the long-awaited, deeply kept secret invasion of Normandy was set off: D-Day.

Francis, who had by then joined the Navy and was serving as Assistant Navigating Officer on HMS *Ramillies*, saw that half-dawn on the ship's radar, a twenty-mile stretch of sea, with the vast armada of battleships, destroyers, carriers, frigates – any craft able to carry troops or materials – each in its appointed lane, silently steaming towards the Normandy coast; and above, the sky swarming with planes, bombers, gliders, parachute-droppers, fighters.

What I do not think history will ever relate is the strange event which may, perhaps, have saved *Ramillies*. The 36,000 ton cruiser, built during the First World War, had travelled the Seven Seas between active service. On landing in New Zealand, the then Captain and crew had established a firm friendship with a Maori tribe. The Captain was presented on a formal occasion with a black and white reed skirt, knee-length, which the Chief requested him to wear 'whenever great danger threatened. The skirt will always protect the great ship'. The skirt was traditionally kept in the current Captain's cabin and every sailor knew about it and, in the way of sailors all over the world, implicitly believed its magic. Now, if ever, the moment had come. German torpedoes from shore, bombs from defence batteries round Brest, every

expected resistance, fiercely defending the coast. *Ramillies'*
immense size was an easy target. Captain Middleton emerged
from his cabin wearing the magic skirt. The ship was un-
scathed except for a small scratch from a shell. I still wonder at
the sartorial courage of a Captain of the Old School, scrupu-
lous to maintain the full dignity of his rank, walking the bridge
in a grass skirt for the morale of his crew.

      *   *   *

So the days passed, burdened with anxiety on all sides,
endured perforce. On September 20 I noted in my journal:
'Outlook still fearful. Myself in a state of utter misery and lack
of direction. I feel almost as sick as Julian but not inside a
Nursing Home.' The end of the long tunnel came at last. Julian
came home and the kind, warm-hearted Elmhirsts lent us a set
of rooms in the great courtyard of Dartington Hall, within its
enclosed peace. It was indeed a peace dearly needed, for Julian
was still lost with no appetite for living, no urge to deliver
himself from that dismal entropy. We stayed there a month,
then a fortnight at Northallerton with dear Philippa Pease who
put herself out to amuse and interest this listless man. Francis,
transferred now to HMS *Vengeance*, an aircraft carrier, came for
a blessed visit, before departing for the East, on a mysterious
mission fraught with apprehension. The Navy was in fact
preparing for an intended invasion of Japan.

    Julian at last got himself back on his feet. The cycle of
depression came full circle, as appears to be the general rule – if
only one could have faith and hibernate until recovery . . . He
went to stay with James Fisher and together they went bird-
watching, the ultimate panacea. This left me free to go back to
my job at the SVS.

    It was during that fortnight that a cable from the USSR
Academy of Sciences arrived, inviting Julian to attend their
Bicentenary (1945) celebrations. I urged him to go, knowing
that such a voyage would restore his full self-confidence. He
writes about the experience in *Memories*, describing listening

to Lysenko, the notorious pseudo-scientist, who was responsible for misleading Soviet science for many years. He heard him make the famous remark: 'We know in our own persons that digestion is not always complete. What happens then? We belch. So-called Mendelian segregation is nature's belching.'

Lysenko exasperated Western scientists; but more tragically he was the cause of many brilliant Soviet scientists' exile and death in Siberia. They disappeared without a trace, in spite of the Royal Society's efforts to help them. Jack Haldane broke his allegiance to Communism because of the Lysenko-inspired persecution of research not in line with his insane deviation from scientific truth. Having been able to study and deplore the Lysenko system at first hand, Julian in 1949 published *Soviet Genetics and World Science, Lysenko and the Meaning of Heredity*. He was to have another chance of challenging the hallowed heresy in 1953, when in Karachi he attended an 'impressive gathering of scientists, not only Indians and Pakistanis, but myself and Nushdin from the USSR, a disciple of Lysenko and Michurin, in their false doctrines of heredity'.

A special debate was arranged between Julian and Nushdin and Julian had the satisfaction of demolishing the Lysenko champion. Not long after this episode, Lysenko was dethroned, and one heard that he finished his days in a mental hospital: he had subverted the course of science in the USSR for many years by victimising and destroying his opponents.

But to return to the Academy of Sciences celebrations: they marked the complete recovery of Julian, who came home fully restored and ready for new ventures. The nightmare was over – to my immense relief.

*   *   *

Meanwhile work at the SVS became more and more interesting. France, liberated, welcomed back to their laboratories many of its scientists who had been able to escape to the

United States. Some passed through London on their way home and stayed at the house in Burlington Street, where modest accommodation was arranged for them. By then the furnishing and servicing of the Society was done, and I stayed on with the curious title of 'hostess'. Gatherings were arranged in the large drawing-room between our scientists and the visitors, presided over by our President Professor Donnan; it was my job to introduce the guests. I also lunched with such French scientists as spoke only French.

I remember particularly the days after the Liberation, the elation, the warmth of our encounters and the freedom with which people talked of their experiences. There was Professor S., seized from his physics chair by the Nazis, and brought to Penemunde to be used in the final trimmings of the V1 and V2. He and two or three of his colleagues managed to sabotage some ten per cent of these devastating weapons – with constant risk of their detection. I knew the enormous difference this ten per cent made to our morale during those horrible times.

Julien Cain arrived on a short visit. He survived his deportation from his post as Director of the Bibliothèque Nationale in Paris because the prisoner in charge of registration of new arrivals at the concentration camp recognised him as his former professor. He made no sign (nor did Julien Cain) but systematically excluded him from the lists calling prisoners to hard labour. Cain kept alive on the meagre diet provided, while most of the others died of exhaustion and hunger.

The SVS survived a few more years, most efficiently run by Miss Esther Simpson, until the rent of that lovely Queen Anne house more than doubled and the Society had to seek other accommodation in the Royal Institution. The house was pulled down and a garage built in its place. It was a brave venture and met a need, still extant, of providing hospitality for voyaging scientists.

*   *   *

And then – unbelievably – after all that trauma the war came to an end. Curiously, little remains in my memory of those days of clinging to the radio for news of peace treaties, of immense relief. Maybe emotions were exhausted.

As soon as it became possible, we flew to Neuchâtel to visit my mother: Julian was to lecture for the British Council in Berne, Neuchâtel, Lausanne and Geneva. It was almost a shock to see a country unscarred by war, incarnating all that one remembered as peace, while summer ended in opulent beauty and richness. My mother was shining with happiness, she climbed up and down mountains with us, cooked delicious meals and shared our feelings of delight in this small paradise. Forgotten were the black years of waiting for letters, for news of our safety between bombings, of sparse rations and cold winters with fuel shortage. It was for all of us like returning to life.

Back in London Julian was busy with the Committee on National Parks for England and Wales; he went to New York for a great rally against nuclear weapons at Madison Square Gardens and became an assiduous observer of the Preparatory Commission of what was then called UNECO, soon to become Unesco after he and Joseph Needham had led a delegation pleading for science to be a part of the project. This, in the strangest way, was the prelude to the most intensive years of his life, first as Secretary of the Preparatory Commission in London, then as First Director-General of Unesco in Paris.

14

Unesco and Paris

It was Senator Fulbright and Clement Attlee who wrote the banner of Unesco in letters of fire: 'Wars begin in the minds of men, and it is in the minds of men that Peace must be pursued.'

And Peace, ineffable hope of Mankind, was the intended child of Unesco, born after the horrors of two World Wars. Its godfather was the old League of Nations Institute for Intellectual Co-operation, and the newly created United Nations its midwife. As it had no actual parents, the greatest intellectuals then available were assembled as The Preparatory Commission, to equip this miracle child with the necessary genes to accomplish its purpose. Their many distinguished names can be found in all the books on Unesco. This was November 1945 in London, still scarred from its ordeal of fires and bombs.

Julian was not a member of this Olympian group, but an assiduous follower of its discussions, fascinated by its vast potential. Sir Alfred Zimmern, himself a remarkable classicist and member of the League of Nations, was then its Secretary. Julian was in the USSR participating in the Bicentenary of the Russian Academy of Sciences when Sir Alfred was taken ill and had to undergo a serious operation.

On Julian's return in early spring of 1945 he collided with his old friend Sir John Maud (later Lord Redcliffe-Maud) on the steps of the Athenaeum, and was invited, then and there, to take the place of Sir Alfred, who would take too long to recover from his illness in the urgent days of the creation of Unesco. That evening he returned home in a state of shock; the shock was catching, we both had a racking night. He had promised 'to think it over' – but in as short a time as possible. This was a tormenting process. So far mostly generalities had been aired at the conferences. From day to day, meeting to meeting, speaker to speaker, new choices arose, utopian projects and winding quests. Not unlike a Pirandello idea in search of a destiny, or so, anyway, it appeared to me – from my distance and non-involvement.

Still undecided, he met the Minister of Education, Ellen Wilkinson, that fireball of forthright vitality and dedication, next night at dinner, when she put his mind at rest about his chief anxiety, namely a distaste and disability for administration. There must be, she assured him, a fully fledged administrator under the Secretary. Julian's function would be, essentially, to co-ordinate the projects.

And if, in truth, he had no experience of such a job, he had, deeply and consistently, given much thought to the needs of a post-war world. Not for nothing had he been a founder-member of PEP (Political and Economic Planning), actively pursuing its intensive researches.

Finally he was induced to accept the post. We both felt:

that the momentous decision had been virtually forced upon us; but I had given my consent and it was up to me to carry on . . . Though I felt like one of those early Christians who were kidnapped and compelled to become bishops . . . The first time I entered the portals in Carlos Place in my new capacity, I was very nervous, as if I were both a headmaster and a new boy entering school for the first time.*

I was reassured, but still apprehensive . . . Moreover I felt entirely incapable of being of any use. This thing was bigger, almost more improbable, than my imagination could contain. Julian's familiar daimon here showed an almost visible hand in the proceedings. He sprouted psychedelic wings which enabled him to accept his new position and responsibilities.

It was a strange time – a sort of no-man's land, marked with the experimental character of its inception. One could not

* *Memories II*, Allen & Unwin, 1973.

escape being disturbed by this. Preparations were in the air for moving the London Secretariat to Paris, to be the seat of Unesco, and for the final nomination of the First Director-General who would have full charge of the fledgling, until it grew into the magical Bird of Peace.

Sir Alfred Zimmern recovered and claimed his right. The Council thought of solving his demand by giving him the role of Adviser to the Acting Secretary. Neither he nor Julian was happy about this, and rightly so. There was no common ground between Zimmern and Huxley, no possible agreement on advice not requested. Lady Zimmern saw Julian as the cuckoo in the nest she had feathered for her husband, and was determined to oust him. Julian thus had a foretaste of competitive intrigues attendant on large and complex organisations, while he himself was totally unpractised in the exercise.

Finally the Preparatory Commission moved to Paris in September 1945 – lock, stock and barrel – in a special train met by a *garde d'honneur* at the Gare du Nord, white gloves and red carpet. I was presented with a large bouquet, which a hiss from Lady Zimmern, walking just behind us, nearly made me drop.

The staff dispersed to lodgings, the machinery rooted itself in the Hotel Majestic; much too big, too plush, too expensive, but the only place the French Government could offer. Julian's office had been last occupied by the Nazi General Stupnagel and was unaltered: pink du Barry brocade in panels on walls, gilded scrolls, upholstered doors. His secretary's room next door and each chief of section had a similar grand set-up – a change after London's Carlos Place where they had one room for their whole section and one telephone. Life was very expensive, but we all lunched together at the Canteen of the Majestic.

Paris was lovely in the autumn sunlight – crystal clear, luminous, enchanting, with no reminder of the war to our fresh eyes, awaking like the Sleeping Beauty after its psychological trauma. I felt better from the moment of arrival. We lunched with Leon Blum, President of the French Delegation, and his wife. He was wonderfully judicious, aware, experienced and friendly. Madame Blum told me that in 1941–42 she used to bicycle thirty kilometres every day, bringing him a little load of wood with which to heat himself. The prison where he was kept was a half-demolished castle with no windows. It was used for high-ranking prisoners.

Winter set in early with biting winds. Paris was still under strict rationing of fuel and many commodities. There was no central heating in private houses, though the Hotel Majestic basked in tropical warmth. Julian had the highest salary he ever touched, a car and chauffeur at his disposition, yet we never suffered such discomfort. By then we had found a flat at the Avenue Alphand, close to Unesco. One room only could be heated and there we also slept. To use the telephone in the hall one had to bundle oneself up into blankets; we could not keep a cook as the servant's room was in the frozen attic, so every night – when not dining out – we went to a nearby restaurant and fed on frozen oysters and hot soup, picking up on our way the traditional *baguette de pain* for breakfast. This was made for us by lovable little Nellie who came daily to look after us. She had been all through the Nazi occupation and bore up much better than we did – or rather I did. For I was quite miserable at the Avenue Alphand flat, and desperately looking round for a more suitable one. Julian seemed unaware, disappearing into the portals of the Hotel Majestic for the day.

From my journal:

Dinner at the B's with Pierre-Jean Jouve, exquisite poet, Monsieur Secretan, Swiss Under-Sec. for Foreign Affairs concerned with UN, and Jean Thomas, Julian's Assistant Secretary. The B's have managed to get the flat of my dreams, the flat I desire, the flat I *need*. Every moment of that evening was an agony of jealousy and annoyance. They even found two servants there, china, silver and glass – the perfect setting. B. added to my annoyance by revealing that he had made absolutely no effort to try and find *us* a flat in spite of his solemn promise to do so.

   That night I woke up at five a.m. tormented by my dislike of this flat and of living as we are. This slum-life, discomfort, untidiness, mess, mismanagement, compared to the B's life. Julian offered me a glass of water which somehow I couldn't find in the dark and which, somehow, accidentally spilt right over me, over my warm sheets and everything. I blazed with fury, leapt out of bed, tore off my wet pyjamas, then the sheets, all in the freezing cold whilst Julian, huddled in a corner was waiting for the storm to pass. Finally, he refused to go to his room and accused *me* of spilling the water – which was one way of continuing the fight. So we had a good fierce argument till I remembered I had nothing on. I found a nightie, made a nest of blankets and retired in dignified silence. Curiously it calmed my passion of jealousy against the B's, but made me very determined to get out of here at all costs.

   The whole secretariat suffered from that first hard winter and the result of so complete a change of environment. Colds, 'flu, tummy troubles – we all had all of them, yet work had to go on. Very hard work it was too. As I wrote to Kot, on November 21, 1946:

The big conference is on, so far so good. Julian made his opening report yesterday, which I hear nothing but good of. It was *good*. He was clear and honest about the difficulties, clash of nationalities and ideologies – nor did he gild any ginger bread. The delegates are busy now choosing a candidate for the top man, putting forward their orators and talking round the subject. They will have to get a lot off their chests before real work begins, but it is profoundly interesting even now. The Americans are putting pressure through their embassies on every country they can . . . Julian has lots of friends – has proved his worth, but I look with not much hope at the political set-up. The tension anyway is too great, one feels engulfed as in a great machine, trepidating and nerve-racking: mine at breaking point, Julian just bearing up but with constant migraine.

   Bless you, I must go. I look awful, I feel awful, but I send all my love.

                                                                    J.

Eventually Julian was appointed Director-General. But here again fate intervened with a merciful if unplanned dispensation: Sir Alfred Zimmern had gone round the Paris embassies, spreading rumours that Julian was a dangerous Communist, put into the heart of the machine to do the will of the Party. Julian had been twice to the USSR, in 1931, and then in 1945 for the Anniversary of the Academy of Sciences. He was the most apolitical animal, but under the McCarthy blight two visits to Russia were enough to brand a man for life.

The American delegates to the Council were suspicious on that score; the very mention of USSR made their hair bristle; but even more serious was Julian's avowed philosophy of humanism, derived from his belief of the psycho-social evolutionary man, emerging from the purely biological process. 'The earth was not created: it evolved. So did all the animals that inhabit it, including our human selves, mind and soul as well as body – so did religion.'[*] And, more immediately, written in the small pamphlet before he took office as Director-General of Unesco, entitled, *UNESCO: Its purpose and its Philosophy* 1946:

> From acceptance of certain principles or philosophies, Unesco is obviously debarred. Thus, while fully recognising the contribution made to thought by many of their thinkers, it cannot base its outlook on one of the competing theologies of the world as against the others, whether Islam, Roman Catholicism, Protestant Christianity, Buddhism, Unitarianism, Judaism or Hinduism.

They finally agreed to elect Julian, but limiting the years of office to two years instead of the statutory five. Zimmern little knew that his plot would prove a blessing in disguise, for more than two years of such labour would have killed any man. Zimmern was sent on a distant mission, neither consoled nor mollified, and Julian was left to do his job.

Julian put all he had into the building-up of the organisation.

---

[*] *The Humanist Frame*, edited by Julian Huxley, Allen & Unwin, 1961.

Everything, it seemed, had to be learned by trial and error, with no pilot to guide the contraption through unpredictable currents, no precedent to follow, no magic to invoke.

As he wrote in his *Memories*: 'I had to call on capacities I hardly knew I possessed – powers of co-ordination, and conciliation, essential in a community of such diverse interests; quick understanding and resilience; initiative, even against opposition; and above all faith that what I was aiming at was right, or at least in the right direction.' I quote from Richard Hoggart's book.*

It is easy to list those characteristics of Julian Huxley which made him unsuitable as a D-.G.; for example, administration bored him, and the Executive Board bored him extremely. But in some important ways he was an excellent choice for a first D-.G. He had foresight, over thirty years ago he recognised the emerging importance of environmental and population questions, and even saw forward to the likely costs of mass tourism. He was inventive: one still comes across activities set off by good ideas of his, whether to do with non-governmental organisations or cultural initiatives or much else. He had great courage; he argued directly that respect for human dignity and for the individual should be more important for Unesco than the idea of the State. Reading his early speeches one is struck by how many fundamental matters he got right, whether about emerging major issues or about the best way to tackle a potentially vast programme on a tiny budget. Sooner than anyone else he was talking about the need to concentrate the programme. He was less perceptive in proposing that the Organisation propound a sort of World philosophy, a new Humanism, that could never have been adopted. But in general he kept up the flow of good ideas throughout the two years of his tenure, and his speech to his last General Conference is still not only useful but exciting reading. He gave Unesco an intellectual head of steam and a restless sense of enquiry at its start.

This could serve as a link across the complex sum of his

* *An Idea And Its Servants*: Unesco from within, Chatto & Windus, 1978.

achievements, seen nearly forty years later. Subsequent events prove that many of Julian's guide-lines were followed and that even his manifesto, 'Unesco, Its Purpose and Philosophy', written before he took office, is now recognised as a part-basis for the organisation. At the time of its publication (Paris, December 6, 1946) the General Conference voted that 'it should be published as in the form of a separate signed document, as a statement of his personal attitude'. This document carries much of Julian's ideals for a future society and could be the subject of a special study. It is not within my scope to analyse it.

Among the problems was the urgent need to consider the population explosion,* a problem which had concerned Aldous and Julian since the early twenties. He tried three times to organise a conference on this thorny subject, but was defeated by the Vatican. Another subject for concern over many years had been the need to protect nature wherever man became dominant. This was an urgent claim which, before the war, had not been ignored, but which had failed to get off the ground as a powerful movement. Julian knew that with the backing of Unesco the International Union for Conservation of Nature, created as an affiliated agency, could and would succeed at least in attracting the attention of the great powers, and influence them to intervene in the conflict of man and nature. To save what was left of this vulnerable heritage had become imperative.

A conference on Nature Conservation with the Executive Board and many renowned conservationists was held at Fontainebleau in the late summer of 1948. I well remember the three days of discussions before Julian and the conservationists succeeded in convincing the Executive Board, whose principal objection was that nature as such was no concern of Unesco. The final victory was one of the great moments of

---

* Standing now at 4,721,887,000, to double over fifty years due mostly to improvements in public health measures. U.S. – 1983 Census Bureau.

Julian's life; IUCN became an agency affiliated to Unesco, and has ever since done a great deal to preserve both nature and natural resources *for* man – and not only protection of nature *from* man. It is now known all over the world for its timely, dedicated work.

Later, in 1960 and 61, Julian was also the promoter of what is now known as the World Wildlife Fund. The inception of this Agency followed a series of articles he wrote for the *Observer* after travelling from the Cape to Ethiopia, observing the depredations caused by a growing population and hunters and poachers, out for the fun of killing or for gain. It was set up to protect endangered species of animals and plants, and their survival, precarious though it is, is due mainly to its efforts. Julian's contribution to this venture was considerable, best summed up perhaps in this letter from John Owen, then Director of National Parks in Tanzania, at the time of Julian's death:

Julian Huxley was one of the world's great men, a fount of new ideas and a creative force in many areas of scientific and social endeavour. The variety and scope of his achievements are set out in Professor John Baker's excellent Memoir for the Royal Society, vol. 26, 1976.

But strangely enough, Baker makes no mention of the seminal role he played in wildlife conservation in Africa – particularly in East Africa – in the early days, nor of the far-reaching influence he exerted after the war to get the international community involved in this field . . . To the people working in the national parks and the game departments, during the crucial post-independence years of the sixties, he personified more than anyone else the world outside that had so dramatically come to our rescue. Not only that, but his wonderful zest and enthusiasm gave us fresh confidence and hope for the future.

I feel that during the testing time at Unesco Julian reached the summit of his achievements. He made full use of the experience and knowledge of all he had gathered during his life with interest in so many subjects. As he wrote in a letter: 'I want so badly to go on growing, to achieve what is latent in me, to distil my brains in real lasting work, to feel I am living at the highest pitch I am capable of'. And indeed he did, thus at last denying what Jerrard Tickell once said of him: 'So busy trying to be a Huxley that he couldn't be himself.'

*   *   *

One of my frequent worries was sartorial: French society women play an important role in the ruling classes of Paris, and they dress for their parts. It is essential to be in the fashion of the day, whatever the cost. This meant an effort for me; I found myself suddenly faced with the levitical necessity of 'wearing the right clothes'. I sat on gilt chairs at crowded fashion shows, surprised at the power of this histrionic function. The parade of models displaying the designs was in itself a piece of acting endowing the garments with magical potentials. The ritual, set in luxurious decor of crystal, mirrors and perfume, with solicitous *vendeuses* bending over rich women past their youth but not their income, had its beguilement, but became an ordeal I resented. Julian never took the slightest notice of my struggles and their results.

Re-reading now the journals I kept, more or less regularly, of our doings, I find myself wandering like a lost sheep among strange pastures: presidents and ministers, ambassadors and intellectuals, great names and famous ones straight out of *Le Bottin* (the French Debrett) looming in on the Director-General of Unesco and his wife. That first year especially – how did we survive it? Only, I suspect, by our disarming ignorance of French Society and its complexities, by our being so very obviously outsiders. They say there is a providence which protects drunks and idiots – maybe we were taken under the same umbrella. Julian, in any case, never felt out of place in any group of people – his French was good enough – though not perfect like Aldous's, and he had not a trace of innate timidity. My own special asset was being bilingual.

Julien Cain, whom I had met at the Society for Visiting Scientists when he was just out of a German concentration camp, was back at his Bibliothèque Nationale, a favourite member of the Unesco Executive Board. He and his wife became marvellous friends, Lucienne enchantingly unpredictable and surrounded by a fertile disorder; he exquisite, so cultured and *fin*, always helpful to us in the literary world of Paris as well as in diplomatic circles. I remember him firmly advising Julian to respect the code and make his official calls on ambassadors. This excellent advice was rejected on the strength that Unesco was outside diplomacy. The fact that the D.–G. held what was called 'ambassadorial rank' did not deter him, and in the end it probably cost him the Légion d'Honneur.

We did, however, have to invite back the ambassadors who had 'dined' us, and I am afraid that there too we committed the crime of not placing them according to that most sacrosanct protocol. The Unesco member in charge of this ritual must have been absent-minded on this score. It did not take me long to discover how important the placing of guests was to their ego, and what a gaffe we had committed by yielding to Julian's refusal to sit at the middle of the table – the host's and hostess's privileged place, instead of the end of the table as in Britain. It was Princesse Marthe Bibesco who told the sad story of the young aristocrat who had married beneath her rank: '*Deux ans d'amour et vingt ans de bout de table*' (which meant minor guests). What havoc we created!

Yet, wherever he sat, end or middle of the table, Julian could and often did silence the twenty or so guests to hear his 'funny story', of which he had a grand repertoire, or by initiating an absorbing discussion. I remember hearing at my far end of the table the words 'female circumcision' put in a question to his right-hand neighbour, Princesse Marie Bonaparte. (She was married to Prince George of Greece, had translated Freud into French and studied anthropology.) The whole party fell silent while the two discussed the pros and cons of the subject.

★　　　★　　　★

Marjorie Wells wrote that Kot had had another serious break-down, and was in a clinic in Virginia Water. He asked for letters, and I sent him snippets of our life and gossip going round Paris to amuse him:

. . . An American and Russian soldier discuss the differences in democracy in their respective countries. Says the American: 'Any day I like I can go to President Truman and say to him: "Mr. President, I don't like your foreign policy at all: I think you are an ass". He will shake hands with me just the same.' Says the Russian: 'Why, I can do just the same – go to Stalin and say: "Comrade Stalin, I don't like President Truman's policy at all – and I think he is an ass!" and Comrade Stalin will shake *me* by the hand just the same.'

February 23, 1947

Dearest Kot,

Still looking desperately round for a suitable flat: meanwhile we had at the Hotel Majestic twenty to dinner last night; where? in the 'Louis' salon, trimmed and bedizened in every possible way to look less like a soulless waiting room. The table pretty with flowers, borrowed silver and stumpy glasses (civilization needs good tools, and there's your capitalism . . .) Armchairs gathered from all round the building, assembled in huddles, and after dinner, an air of debauch and disorder added to tooth-glasses and bottles clustered on guéridons . . . acutely embarrassing to the hostess, ignored by the host.

However, in spite of these handicaps it was a good dinner, a good party and certainly a happy feeling of good fellowship. The US Ambassador and Mrs. Caffrey, himself on my right – talked of going to Germany, Dachau, in the vanguard. Visiting the camp of corpses was bearable, but not the hospital of dying bodies who clutched at him with desperation and hunger for life. He couldn't keep a diary because it would be too hot and might get pinched. Everything could get pinched. He knew, because he could always obtain documents somehow.

Doré, on my left – the Belgian Ambassador – talked of friendship and love – regretting the short-lived flame of love . . . Princesse

Bibesco on J's left had many long chats (too long) at the cost of the Ambassador's wife who anyway only spoke Chinese.

February 27

An 'At home' to Madame de Ségur (always confused with the author of Les Malheurs de Sophie). Retired Ambassadors, high ranking diplomats, ladies with big names, too easily forgotten. Mme de Ségur, grande dame, wearing several strings of large pearls and a neckband of smaller ones (Madame Claudel admiring them she replied 'Oh, des restes . . .') most welcoming and kind. Talked to a smart woman who began by saying we should never have fought this war; should have made peace with Hitler; never allowed the Russians in Europe . . . Another said we must keep Franco in Spain to defend France from Communism . . . Lady Diana Cooper looking ravishing appeared for a brief moment, lovely in fox hat trimmed with a galon on one side, slightly military and gallant. We all kept on our coats, and gathered round the small stove . . . I felt how immensely fortunate it was that Britain had never been invaded – nor ever ran the danger of collaboration.

Between flats we stayed with Mimi Gielgud on the Boulevard de Lannes close to the Bois de Boulogne. Mimi was an enchanting sprite with a gift for embroidering her eventful past in audacious English. Her saga began with a young diplomat galloping a broken heart through wild forests of Carinthia – and suddenly in a sunny glade surprising a beautiful nymph bathing in a 'poodle'. He follows her to her parent's mud-hut and demands her in marriage – which being granted, he carries her back to couturiers in Paris before presenting her to disapproving parents. Mimi was the fruit of this unsuitable union, seeing her father but seldom and her grandparents hardly ever – with a beautiful mother who could speak no French and was covered with diamonds and Worth gowns, until her husband, Mimi's father, died and she was left in penury. It was Mimi who sold off her treasures bit by bit to keep the wolf from the door. A sad fairy-story, told with the relish of survival. Mimi had had two husbands, and the second was Lewis Gielgud, Aldous's faithful school-friend. Thus

were we acquainted, and as Mimi opened her heart and doors
to many, so she took us in when we were homeless: she
brightened our lives with her unfailing devotion and patience,
and included us in her wide circle of friends.

At one of her evenings we met Josephine Baker, who was
convalescing at Mimi's after a serious operation. She lay on the
sofa in a white dressing-gown, her hair in a turban out of
which peeped little white mice with red eyes, Mimi's pets.
They were quite tame and playing a game of hide and seek
among Josephine's brown curls. (Later we heard that 'communist brown mice' from next door had fought and killed the
pretty white mice.) Mimi died some twenty years ago, much
mourned by a grateful circle among whom were ambassadors
and actors, lion-tamers and princes, millionaires and paupers,
shipwrecked lovers and honeymooners. From her great heart
we all received the bounty of loyal love. I was often in need of
her help and reassurance.

Julian's Paris days were hectically busy, and he came home
tired and absorbed, asked me what I had done, and stayed not
for an answer. I had, in fact, done a few interesting things,
such as starting a club for the wives of the increasing staff of
Unesco to discuss the help that could be given to uprooted
families arriving in Paris from foreign lands, who often knew
no French. They needed advice and friendly aid. This job was
later taken over by a reception office, which proved very
necessary. A doctor's surgery was also installed at Unesco
after our persistent demands.

But in those pioneer days it was all a voyage of discovery,
and the early 'settlers' were indeed facing adventures; many of
them had been enrolled when their governments joined the
Organisation and might be North or South Americans, Hai-
tian, Polish, Australian, African, Scandinavian, etc. At first
the 'foreigners' forming the staff in Paris were invariably
enthusiastic about all the projects which promised great
things for the world. 'What can I do for Unesco?' was the
spirit which moved them. Alas, in days to come, it was

more often 'What can Unesco do for me?'

These days were full of contagious excitement and one felt it in the air, giving a buoyancy to hard work, energy to the next day. Julian himself was sustained by this indescribable faith in Unesco.

*   *   *

But the tension could not be borne without escape from Paris. On weekends we took over the car, by then a long-snouted Dodge which called forth '*Oh là-là!*' from villagers: we kept that name for it.

We went to Fontainebleau, picnicking in the grand forest with as many of the staff as we could get in the car; to Normandy and Lionheart's Château Gaillard, perched high above the Seine. To Louveciennes, where the Cains had a peaceful house and garden. Sometimes for a few days to Tours and Jo Davidson's Bécheron, a lovable old grey manor house round a wide courtyard, and he a lovely man with a twinkle in his eye and an exceptional gift for friendship. He lives vividly in my memory: white haired and bearded, full of fire, faith and fight, with an incredible memory, bursting into old songs, poems, brilliant imitations of Arnold Bennett and his funny walk and stammer, of H. G. Wells, of Roosevelt and many others, radiating life and warmth. He was a sculptor who could model a likeness in a few hours, and had 'done' most of the famous people in his time. He took a few sittings of Julian and turned out a puckish head with the long pointed eyebrows Julian was so proud of. The bronze bust was later acquired by the staff of Unesco and put in a place where the superstitious can tweek the eyebrows in a ritual pact-with-luck as they pass.

I dropped into the studio while Jo was modelling Julian and he spoke of D. H. Lawrence, in that last spring of his life: Jo was staying with H. G. Wells, who sent him to do a portrait of Lawrence – which he did and 'it was not a bad head: but who could ever fix that face . . . Lawrence was waiting for Aldous and Maria – talked only of that, waiting to die when they had come . . . '

The days we spent at Bécheron were free and joyful; Julian was so much better; wrote not a word, relaxed, enjoyed, slept, read and sketched; kind, warm, gentle, almost tender . . . We both felt renewed going back to our diverse tasks. Never a dull moment – but also the aftermath: seeking in vain the centre of gravity, the link to hold together, the gift to respond with imagination and to cope with urgent decisions with the recurrent unexpected. As I wrote to Kot: 'Life is like being vapourised, turned into foam, losing all substance. There is only time for the crest of the waves . . . ' I fell into a tailspin.

Julian escaped for an hour after lunch to a bench in the Bois de Boulogne, binoculated for the lively bird-life around. He was seen at meetings busily making notes. No one suspected the lists of birds that found their way between recommendations for a new expert on education, for a protest to some distant government who had failed to pay their dues, for demands for a higher budget. The ducks and rare migrants of the Bois de Boulogne had the full attention of the Director-General or almost: with a receptive tentacle groping around, he could catch the gist of the matter in hand and instantly respond.

Every year a large conference abroad, invited by a member of Unesco, was busily organised: in 1947 it was Mexico. Julian was deputed to rally as many governments in South America as possible beforehand, and we gave a large luncheon party at Unesco to all the Ambassadors of South America where Julian was going the next week. I wrote to Kot:

It was a terrific meal, with ham jellies, anchovy eggs, tomatoes, asparagus, cucumber salad, roast beef and young potatoes, three kinds of cheese and strawberries, liqueurs, ices and coffee. Quite disgusting. Paris is not starving anyway. I didn't order the menu – but even if I had it would probably have been the same because one has to feed Ambassadors as they are used to be fed . . . Julian made a little speech but I didn't listen because I was wondering why he must stuff his pockets with so many note-books and wallets and bulges so that he looks like a successful poacher, in his best suit . . .

To my regret I was left behind when Julian flew off with his two Spanish-speaking assistants, Jimenez and Arenales, and returned after five hectic weeks, in a plaster corset, during a heat wave. He had flown successfully to Washington, Mexico, Guatemala, Panama, Bogota, Ecuador, Lima, Santiago, Buenos Aires and Rio. There he was taken on a special sight-seeing trip to the ancient city of Petropolis not far away. The car crashed into a lorry, turned over, damaging all the occupants in a miraculously minor way. Julian got his collarbone fractured and a bruised rib. After a few days in hospital he arrived back in Paris having flown twenty-seven hours. At the airport I was shocked by his great fatigue and helplessness. Luckily he was out of plaster after ten days, but suffered from delayed shock and a temperature, which kept him in bed.

By then we had found a flat on the Avenue Foch – the loveliest Avenue in Paris, wide and planted with superb trees: we floated above the Chinese Heaven trees in full flower, a white froth of small blossoms delicately scented, under our balcony. I wrote frequently to Kot:

> *Avenue Foch*
> *27 July '47*

I wonder if you have the same terrific heat wave that we painfully and grumblingly endure here. Unesco is having its big Council Meeting. The poor delegates sit under the glittering candelabra of the Ball Room at the Hotel Majestic, without even as much as one electric fan, going through an agenda bristling with controversies and harassed by the shortness of time. Julian has, I am glad to say, sufficiently recovered to be able to attend, although he needs a complete escape which we hope to get next week.

But you see, we are dauntless in our efforts. Last night, we, that is the three heads of Unesco (Julian, Jean Thomas and Walter Laves, assistant D-Gs) threw a party, if you please, under the same candelabra. It was in honour of Professor Gilbert Murray, to whom a group of friends presented a bust sculpted by your compatriot Memlikoff. The bust was given to Unesco in memory of the godfathership of Gilbert Murray as former President of the Intellectual Cooperation, now swallowed up by Unesco.

Well, the old man came, in spite of the heat; ate a vegetarian dinner with us in company with Sir John Maud, then adjourned to hear his praise in many speeches, and finally to make one himself. His was delightful: he said there had been too many compliments and that, when he was younger he would have blushed. But he was now an old man and he might say they didn't bother him so much now, in fact he rather liked them. He offered a vote of thanks to his bust, a rather grim affair, for looking like a man who could say 'no'. Himself he had often been accused of being too soft and gentle, but, he said 'Look at my bust. *He* is strong and can say NO. In fact, one could almost say he has a Molotov complex'.

Jack Priestley is in Paris, heading a group of Theatre experts, doing things about an International Theatre what not. He is staying at the George V, the most expensive hotel in Paris, and horrifically enjoys quoting the exorbitant prices of a bean or a melon. He was sitting, when we left exhausted, a perspiring happy Yorkshire man, with five girls and a bottle of whisky.

You know, Kot, being here in the midst of such a lot of 'foreigners' I begin to agree absolutely with your opinion about the British. [Both Kot and I were of course uprooted foreigners.] They are really the Only People. One can trust them, one can believe them, one can laugh with them and at them, and above all, one can understand them. They are simple and rather innocent. They believe in the Good and the Truth. And then they *work* – oh how they work . . . If only Unesco could be entirely British . . . Just what you said; just what you *always* said. *We* are the salt of the earth. Thank God for that.

Avenue Foch
1 August 1947

Our heat wave is still in full swing. Paris has never known anything like it. There is only one place to be in, water. Meanwhile we are having another meeting, and able to study a remarkable variety of braces and shirts. Last night Julian gave a cocktail party for the theatre experts and some press, and a few very distinguished guests. Something happened, no-one quite knows how, but the party began to be like an alert on board a ship. Chairs were pushed about and left in heaps among the mass. The buffet was stormed and only the very strong got to the edge where fierce cocktails were served. Then the glasses ran out; then the ice, then the iced coffee.

And all the time more and more people pressed on . . . About 30 press boys had been asked, about 150 arrived – all thirsty for strong liquor. I don't know why we survived – and our distinguished guests . . . This was one of our painful moments.

Jack Priestley came to lunch to-day. He was bitter about the party from a personal angle. He complained that every time he asked for a drink I gave him a playwright. Then that he couldn't drink the stuff anyway. Then that the George V had no water from 1 – 10 p.m. So when he returned for a wash he had to store some water in a champagne bottle and pour it out in a tooth-glass out of which he washes. Ah, but wait; five hundred francs a day will be taken off when the day comes. And the George V will know one doesn't dally with a Yorkshire man who wants to wash . . .

Towards the end of that year I accompanied Julian to the conference in Mexico, stopping off in New York on the way. I wrote to Kot describing our travels:

New York
1 Nov. 1947

Landed on the 23rd of October, and beautifully received by members of Unesco, who brought us to a hotel where the beds were the only place one could put anything on . . We saw a lot of Aldous and Maria and Stark Young and several lovely people. Then we stayed the week-end at Westbury (the family house of the Straights, Dorothy who married Leonard Elmhirst at Dartington), with Binnie Straight; Michael is away in Palestine. Endless fun, with people in and out of the house – fine autumn weather, beautiful and serene, the park perfect in autumn colours. Aldous came to lunch and Henri Laugier (French Assistant-Secretary General of Security Council at U.N.O.) and Dolivet, a fanatic Frenchman with sinister eyes who edits the U.N. Journal and wants to save the world from war which he thinks approaches. At dinner that Sunday they just talked the grimmest black prophecies and facts . . . Much more than in France do people here talk grimly – critical of all nations, themselves included – critical mostly of mankind, driving to its disasters. But nevertheless papers go on shouting the same silly slogans, furious waste of food continues, and shops are full of tempting things. Food very good and costly, though not as high as in France.

Aldous is now well, but Maria says how careful he has to be: rests two hours daily, goes to bed at ten, sees few people, etc. He is writing a novel of the future – not a *Brave New World* but a destroyed one [*Ape and Essence*] . . . Frieda Lawrence still going stong at Taos, Brett paints fearful pictures according to Aldous and sells them. Marian Dorn still decorates and drinks heavily. Ted McKnight Kauffer suffers her but cannot escape – we saw them.

Maria is really wonderful: devotes all her life and thoughts to Aldous who would be entirely lost without her. Moura Budberg also here in New York. She feels very lonely and missed H.G. [who had just died] desperately, she told Maria.

Hotel Luma, Mexico
13 Nov. 1947

It was lovely getting your encouraging letter – many thanks for it. Had a great trip to Mexico, about a week ago and never a minute to think since. Conference going as they go – with complicated currents, criticisms galore, budget battles, words, words, too many words. The great hall of the brand new education building full to the brim, grand mixture of international intellectuals, the best being J. Maritain, head of the French delegation – truly a wonderful man. People very friendly, welcoming Unesco with any sort of thing: receptions, cocktails, dinners, grand theatre parties – much food and drink. Julian carrying on so far, but over-worked and over-entertained. I am well till evening, when I only want to sleep. Not easy.

Met the Mexican writer Covarrubias, who produced the best account of the Conquest by Bernal Diaz and illustrated it perfectly. Also Diego Rivera – a great figure who makes his own laws, artist and archaeologist, with a formidable collection of pre-Conquest artefacts. He gave me some fascinating pottery figures. [He left the whole of his private collection to the Museum of Arts in Mexico City.] Also Orozco, a savagely patriotic painter of genius.

Have seen but little of the country so far but plan expeditions to Cuernavaca, where Cortez built a palace facing the great volcano Popocatepetl. Also to Pueblo, and the city of Aztec temples.

Hotel Luma, Mexico
23 Nov. 1947

We are mixing life at all stages – ancient and modern, pyramids and museums, modern architecture with a vengeance, hotels, shops, cars and the bumpiest roads, beneath worn tawny hills with meandering tracks that climb to nowhere. Parties with sequined, high-heeled purple-mouthed flashy ladies, and the staid Unesco people eating caviar canapes and drinking the hottest cocktails. Nights are never silent, hooting cars and ascending elevators.

But we did escape into the old hills, last week-end went off with a large party in a plane to Oaxaca (pronounced Whohaca) down south, where a great religious centre attracted the ancient Mexicans. The flight was wonderful, very clear over this seemingly immense country at the foot of the three great volcanoes, Ichtyziwatle, Popocatepetl and Orizaba. There they stood into the sky with their white snow-caps, and the hills crinkled into solid frozen waves for miles and miles of uninhabited land. The beauty of the landscape was positive and superb . . .

Interrupted a thousand times – tremendous receptions of five hundred people churning around, buffets laden with every possible delicacy, more people and more noise. It would have been better to have one a week instead of three a day. One is caught in the machine and there is no escape.

Julian is bearing up, but getting very tired. Sundays alone save him, and we love our short escapes, even if they too are apt to be exhausting. What an undertaking to move this tremendous show so far away from its desks . . . on the whole a good thing for the host country, and for some of the open-minded delegates. But for many just a damn nuisance.

I am sodden with handshaking and trying to remember people's names and not to worry about things that go wrong.

The Conference ended, battered participants returned to their jobs.

My next letter to Kot was almost a *Guide Bleu* of Mexico; one could not be in that country without being exposed to and absorbing much of its fabulous history, assiduously extracted from Prescott and Bernal Diaz, and mordantly refreshed by patriotic painters and writers. Modern Mexicans have done much to restore the balance between Aztec, Mayana, Toltecs and Zapotecs cultures on one side and blatant propaganda of the Spanish Conquest on the other. We were taken by a colleague of Julian's, Emilio Arenales, to Guatemala: Arenales was a wonderful guide to the treasures of his country.

Soon we flew back to Merida, then Haiti for three days, Washington and New York and back to Paris. Julian enjoyed this, but began to feel restless: much to do awaited him at his desk.

Back in Paris my letters to Kot continued:

Avenue Foch, Paris
7 Feb. 1948

Our news is – well – good but not exciting. Julian is more than ever absorbed, we see each other at the week-end but hardly ever alone. Curious life, built of so many odd pieces joining artificially. Interesting always, but in an imposed fashion which destroys all initiative in me. Having never had a lot anyway, I now depend more on the accidents of the day than on planning the day. And there are many accidents, as you may guess. I wake up with a sense of urgency – for I don't know what – which cannot be satisfied.

Unesco is fixing to go to Beirut after next Conference – so Julian plans many journeys to stimulate the near-by countries, in May, flying to Iran, Iraq, Arabia, Greece and Turkey. Meanwhile Paris is struggling with all the difficulties imaginable.

Aldous writes a long letter about the dwindling resources of the world and reckless extravagance of nations. He is obsessed by it all. Francis is going to lead an expedition of young scientists to Gambia, to study the hippo problem: they climb out of the river at night and devour the rice planted alongside.

Occasionally Kot wrote back and his letters were always welcome, marked by his own strong and idiosyncratic opinions:

Acacia Road, London
February 1948

Juliette, my dear,

I'd rather have de Gaulle as the head of a French Government than any socialist. France is rotten to the core, and only a strong man will be able to put the French nation on to the right way of behaving and living. It will probably take a number of years to recondition the humans in Europe (and in America); and the simplest and most efficient way is to do it drastically, if necessary, by a de Gaulle – than to let the world drift waiting for 'democratic miracles'. The humans everywhere must be conditioned (in Pavlov's sense) anew, and conditioning the masses must be a painful and laborious process. But it must be done, and I think it will be done after a few more great troubles and worries. Even the English, the most decent, the best human beings on earth (surrounded by seething millions and millions of bloody foreigners) must somehow be conditioned again.

Well, I'd better stop. You must come to London in the spring, and we shall have long talks about all sorts of things.

And here is another:

22 February 1948

There's no news here, except the newspaper news, and all quite unpleasant. My sole prayer in night and day is for American bombs to fall on the Kremlin, after which there will be peace and good will on earth . . .

With love, ever your
Kot

I wrote back:

chez Mimi, Bld de Lannes
24 February 1948

. . . We have, I believe, found our next flat, right upon the Seine, but not in the Cité which I greatly coveted. Still, the river flows swift and grand at our feet, even if factory chimneys frame the horizon. We hope to move in on March 1st – next Monday.

We are deep in snow – 8 to 9 inches after a violent cold spell which nearly took one's breath away. Now everything looks enchanting, the Lake in the Bois de Boulogne frozen under a virgin crust of snow – the ducks at one end and the pleasure boats snowed under at the other. Julian strides daily in the Bois before breakfast and counts his birds, blackbirds, chaffinches and hawfinches, and even, the other day, a kingfisher. Then he disappears behind his desk at Unesco, his hair gets more windswept and his telephone manners more abrupt, and we don't see him again until evening, when he rolls up under a rug and goes to sleep anywhere.

Yesterday was a blessed day of peace – we walked together in the white Bois, snow on eyelash and eyebrow, watching the bright-cheeked girls, throwing snowballs at passing cars. Home to Mimi's cosy tea – and guess who was there? Alice B. Toklas, complete with poodle Basket and very definite moustache. She is the 'widow' of Gertrude Stein, as of course you know. A nice, plain, intelligent kindly woman. She was wearing a lovely brooch of pale yellow brilliant stones with ring to match, and, as Mimi remarked afterwards, it gave her a distinct 'Pansy' look. The dog Basket is a heraldic white animal immensely beautiful and dignified. Mimi has a ridiculous tiny 'Papillon' growing fat with age and with eunuchifaction, who was wildly jealous, growled, sneered and yapped to Basket's disdainful and regal sniff of contempt. Alice B. Toklas has all the Picassos and Picabias now, and she is going to show them. [She never did, alas!]

Quai Louis Bleriot
24 March 1948

The sun streams into my window, and I can just see from my bed the last span of the Pont de Grenelle. If I get up, the Seine is there, flowing so slow it might be a lake threaded under bridges. At night, the wide space of water is tinselled with lights and the sky immense above.

Julian rushed off to Geneva last night, to be at the U.N. Meeting on Free Flow of Information. No-one went hopefully, because the Russians will boycott it. He returns tonight in the small hours. Poor J is being so overworked, he has no private life left – unless he tears it out of the early morning and goes for a walk, looking at birds and fishermen for 10 minutes a day. Quelle galère! However, Francis arrives to-morrow for a week and we shall go off to Bourges, the heart of France, and look at things. Thank you for your letter, dearest Kot. What a dream, to liberate Russia . . . We are all, they as well as us, so blinded by fear that we don't know anymore where to turn for hope. Two years ago we had so much more hope . . .

Last Sunday we went to the forest of Compiegne, picked masses of wild daffodils – saw the green foam of young leaves expand under the spring sun – basked with joy and delight in peace, a lovely whole day's peace . . .

Last Friday dined at the Turkish Ambassadors – a large party with the Prime Minister Robert Schumann, sitting on my right . . . He looks just like his caricature, and is a charming and simple man with slight Alsatian accent. After the first difficult moments of 'setting off' we got on so well. I told him how frightened I had been when I saw the table plan and my name next to his. 'Ah, Madame!' he replied 'You can't have been as frightened as I was . . .' So we both enjoyed our dinner enormously. He talked of the avariciousness of the French and how difficult it was to break their selfishness. He is very honest – perhaps too honest for a French politician – but so far has held his government together in spite of his unpopular methods . . .

Julian's two years with Unesco were coming to an end and we were preparing to leave Paris. My feelings were mixed, as I told Kot:

> *38 Quai Louis Bleriot*
> *3 November 1948*

The summer has been a sort of bad dream. Enfin all things come to an end, even Unesco, as far as we are concerned, after the Conference. If we go to Beirut, which as yet is slightly doubtful as troubles keep on arising there, and it seems the maddest adventure into which the Executive Council has landed us. If we go, we may stay in Italy over Xmas and return to London in early spring. It will be good to be back in our own little place, to have done the job and finished with it. So little remains in the heart when all the astonished bitterness is gone . . . I am too naïve for this crazy arena – too unworldly. Thank God for the few like you.

We are in the thick of saying goodbyes – we say it with a dinner last night for 20, to-night and to-morrow cocktails for 50 each and Friday a dance for the Unesco Secretariat.

I am sad at leaving Paris, the loveliest town in the world. And now the leaves are turning, falling one by one in the wide Avenues, like so many hands waving good-bye.

> *Hotel St George, Beirut*
> *22 November 1948*

Incredible it is, but we are all here; conference in full swing after a few initial difficulties and complications. There is now a terrific buzzing of lobbying and underhand manoeuvres concerning the election of the next D.–G. Why anyone should want the job I don't know . . .

Julian is working hard, but happy in the thought that it is soon to end for him. Planning a good holiday afterwards, a real release. For me, you know I always 'shrinked' from this job.

*   *   *

In due time, the Conference elected their new Director-General, Dr Torres Bodet, a highly cultured Mexican, Julian's favourite candidate. Free now from all official duties, we indulged in an orgy of sight-seeing, hiring a car to take us all the way to Aleppo, through a country which many travellers explored and with good reason. Julian wrote about it in his *Memories*, delighting, as was his wont, in seeing a wall-creeper flashing his red underwing on its way up the face of the huge outer wall of the Hittite fortress of Aleppo. We landed back in my home town, Neuchâtel, from where Julian flew to Paris to discuss many things with the new D-G, who says: 'C'est passionant, mais c'est très dur.' And Julian gives sighs of deep relief that he is no longer at the top. We then went off to Naples, hoping to sit in the sun to settle our rumbling brains, without the burden of Unesco in the solar plexus.

In Naples, our hopes of sun demolished by icy-cold grey skies, we found unheated houses, depressing food – and our dear friends, the Dohrns, ill with prevailing flu – ourselves deflated, deprived of the constant demands and incentives of Unesco, for which energy and response had almost instinctively been available; now, to our dismay, impoverished and dismantled in our secret selves. Hoping for a renewal of old memories, we drove to Amalfi, once a treasured discovery, and found nothing but our two selves. And so to Sorrento and Positano, climbing the cleft of the rocky hill on which no Phoenix nested: Paestum slept on in fossilised sacredness. We needed more than the sun to warm our spirit and bones. We held each other's hand under the smelly horse blanket solicitously lent by the coachman. Now, without the illusory aura of Julian's D-G status, not really appreciated while it lasted, we suddenly became aware of its withdrawal. Cinderella's coach had reverted to the pumpkin. For both of us it was the end of a rich chapter. There was comfort in our shared feelings. Suddenly I remembered the hump of the road above Valangin which seemed to me, as a small child, to lead over a precipice into fearful nothingness.

The horse plodded on under a cold grey sky.

NOTE I have firmly abstained from describing any of the official labours of Unesco in these pages. Several books have, most professionally and critically, analysed the subject in every detail.

15

Aldous

Faithless the cloud and fugitive;
An empty heaven not burns, nor wets;
At peace, the barren land regrets
Those agonies that made it live.

ALDOUS HUXLEY, *Arabia infelix*

Many years have gone since that return from Unesco; more than thirty years packed with small and great events. Julian's second volume of *Memories* recalls the important ones, and leaves me little to add. As I read it again, ghosts from the past rise up and I walk through a forest of memories.

Poignant are all the encounters with death: parents in the fullness of their days, dear friends, great men and women whose images remain vivid and fertile – silent visions. Everyone of us has looked into the eye of mortality, and endured its wound.

We that did nothing study but the way
To love each other, with which the day
Rose with delight for us, and with them set,
Must learn the hateful art, how to forget.

'The Surrender', BISHOP HENRY KING

Not to forget: but to accept.

The most shining of those ghosts is Aldous – calling me across the landing, on his visits to us at Pond Street: the unhurried, evenly tuned, pearl-like voice which captured, even in the three syllables of my name, the whole essence of the man. Listening to Aldous (recorded live from the Lecture Hall at Santa Barbara) is to hear a man borne along by an inner flow of energy, managing it as beautifully as one of Plato's Charioteers and, at the same time, in the strangest way, conveying in his voice an unforgettable tranquillity.

Aldous had chosen, because of the clearness of the light, to live in California, which separated us all. After the war we met more often; in New York, on our Unesco voyages, and in Paris. Letters covered distances, typical Huxley displays of intellectual adventures. But it was after we returned from Unesco that Aldous spent at least three weeks with us every year in Hampstead.

At first these visits left me disturbed and disconnected. I was suspended between these two singular creatures, brothers steeped in their heredity, in the exclusiveness of their predestination. It seemed that the common ground between them could only be that of learned discussions of intellectual matters: fascinating to listen to, but leaving no room for the small coin of everyday topics, of affectionate exchanges. It was a competition of sharply informed minds, equal in quality and scholarliness and range; covering the latest scientific news, not unfamiliar to Aldous whose polymathic interests were as keen as Julian's, but if anything more based in esoteric explorations. In fact, his fascination with and acceptance of the questionable, unprovable extensions of a variety of ideas was, at times, surprising. Yet, and more important, one could not but be conscious of a higher reach in Aldous's visions, and Julian was ever conscious of it, thus dividing his allegiance to his younger brother with a tendency to compare himself detrimentally to him.

There was another clear difference between them: whereas Aldous and Maria were not only prepared but keen to try almost anything coming their way to improve their often failing health, their perceptions, their spiritual development and understanding, Julian's approach was critically prudent and discerning. He was concerned by Aldous's relish for experimental therapies, whatever they might be, and resisted their promises. In early youth, before his sight failed him,

Aldous had wanted to be a doctor – like Uncle Harry, and throughout his life was deeply interested in medical problems. He became a writer *malgré tout*.

Aldous's readiness to experiment with every kind of new idea was prompted by his need to fulfil the universal urge to self-transcendence: 'To find, instead of smoke and drink, a drug which would (harmlessly) change the quality of consciousness; stress the sacramental vision of reality.' As he wrote in the closing pages of his book, *The Doors of Perception*:

But the man who comes back through the Door in the Wall will never be quite the same as the man who went out. He will be wiser but less cocksure, happier but less self-satisfied, humbler in acknowledging his ignorance yet better equipped to understand the relationship of words to things, of systematic reasoning to the unfathomable Mystery which it tries, forever vainly, to comprehend.

Perhaps the sixty-odd pages of *The Doors of Perception* reveal more of the seeking, questing Aldous than all his books put together: hovering on the point of conquering the enigma – the unfathomable Mystery – which haunted him all his life. He never ceased from his explorations. 'His battle', in the words of Flaubert, 'was an assault upon the frontiers'. He was so convinced of the importance to himself of Mescalin, and then LSD, that he did not hesitate to publish his findings. Would he think differently now, with the plague of hard drugs destroying so many less-sure-footed explorers of that dimension?

In one of his very last letters to me, late 1963, he was still wondering at the extraordinariness of existence:

. . . do you feel, as I do, that the older one gets, the more unutterably mysterious, unlikely and totally implausible one's own life and the universe at large steadily become? For practical purposes, one tries to make a little scientific technical sense of it all; for non-practical purposes – aesthetic and 'spiritual' – one cultivates Wordsworth's 'wise passiveness' and opens oneself up receptively to the *mysterium tremendum et fascinans* within and without . . .

He knew there was no answer – not for the living – yet in all his

life one can trace the enigma, throughout his books, remembering it in the conversations which created their unique
quality wherever he was, and in his *Letters* generous of his
private truths. What can one call it, this tap-root which
nourished him from childhood to death, drawing forth a
juvenescence, a childlike freshness of questing? How vividly
one remembers his exclamation, inhaled as a draught: '*Extraordinary!*'

For ever luminous in the darkening past shine the words
that Aldous had once said to me: 'Don't stand in your own
light.'

He himself, it must be remembered, had suffered enough
calamities stretching from his youth to the later years in
America, to darken any personality. When I first met him at
Garsington, it was obvious that he was searching, insecure.
His dearly loved and lovable mother died of cancer when she
was forty-seven, Aldous fourteen. It was to him the irrepar-
able loss, a betrayal of his faith in life. He never got over it.
Two years later, a scholar at Eton, blindness descended on him
through the carelessness of the matron, who allowed an attack
of keratitis punctata to be treated as an ordinary stye. He lost
one eye completely, and the other was only partly saved by the
accidental visit of his Uncle Harry (brother to Leonard), a
great doctor, who took him immediately to the best specialist
in London. Aldous was entirely blind for two years, believing
it was for life. All this he told me one summer night many
years ago as we were sitting on the roof at Garsington, under a
full moon – as if it was not of himself he spoke, but of some
boy he had known, and the curious things which happened to
people. He learnt Braille, read and prepared entry papers to
Balliol with a tutor. He got into college and finished with a
brilliant first. He enjoyed music and learnt to play the piano
with one hand on the Braille notes and one on the keys.

His father had remarried, but no one, however devoted,
could hope to replace the wonderful mother he had lost. On
top of all this, his brother Trevenen, nearly five years older

than himself, a warm, protective influence, took his own life, just as the First World War began. Trev was reputedly the most gentle, compassionate and gifted of the three brothers. His death affected Aldous deeply. In a letter to his cousin Gervas in 1914, he wrote: 'It is just the highest and the best in Trev – his ideals – which have driven him to his death . . . He had the courage to face life with ideals, and the ideals were too much for him.' And then much later (October 1951) in another letter, to his son Matthew, whose own son had just been born: 'I have been thinking about names and asking myself why we shouldn't think of my brother Trev. "Trevenen" has the defect of being a bit out of the ordinary, but the merit of being euphonious and of commemorating a very rare being, whom we all loved.'

The death of Trev so many years before still meant much to him; Maria's untimely death in 1955 devastated him. A bush fire then destroyed the new home he had made with his second wife Laura. With it burnt a lifetime's collection of letters, manuscripts, books, and most tragically, the irreplacable journal kept by Maria – an unimaginable disaster. In one moment his past was destroyed utterly and the future stripped like vacant land. Yet, in the end, it must be seen that although he had to endure many calamities, he achieved a profound serenity of acceptance. Whatever anguish he felt, he faced these disasters with never a word of self-pity. In this finality, he was remarkably in tune with his grandfather T.H.H. who wrote in 1854:

My intention . . . was by no means to express any satisfaction at the worms being as badly off as ourselves, but to show that pain being everywhere is inevitable, and therefore like all other inevitable things to be borne . . .

I doubt, or at least I have no confidence in, the doctrine of ultimate happiness, and I am more inclined to look the opposite possibility fully in the face, and if that also be inevitable, make up my mind to bear it also. You will tell me there are better consolations than Stoicism: that may be, but I do not possess them, and I have found my 'grin and bear it' philosophy stands me in such good stead in my course through oceans of disgust and chagrin, that I should be loth to give it up.*

These very words could have been said by the grandson T.H.H. barely knew, but whose philosophy of life had a basis.

*　　　　*　　　　*

It was inevitable that as the wives and companions of these two brothers, Aldous and Julian, with their exclusive and individual intellectual gifts, Maria and I should often feel outwitted, subject to their innate laws. It was both rewarding and difficult – Maria wrote to Jeanne, her sister (how lucky she was to have sisters to share her problems with):

April 1952

. . . I have come to another aspect of all this, Aldous . . . you do know for how many years we've loved Aldous and know his goodness and sweetness and honesty – but you also know how tiring, in spite of all this, he was to live with – sad to live with. Well now, he is transformed, transfigured.† What I mean to say is that this change has been working in an intangible way and for a very very long time but that the result has suddenly exploded – and I say *exploded*. Aldous no longer looks the same, his attitude is not the same, his moral and intellectual attitude, his attitude to people, the clouds, to the telephone ringing (and that is going very far) – no, let's go further and say that he even decides his own decision . . . but he also *offers* his services, whereas up to now he has always been content to offer a little money rather than to pay with his person, or rather with his soul. At last he has reached the point of putting into constant daily practice everything he wants to practise, and even this without realizing it . . . He goes to doctor's meetings, he went to defend a friend of Matthew's in court; he telephones Mrs. Corbett to ask how she is – he eats Marie's dinners with pleasure, and even orders them . . .

---

* *Life and Letters of T.H.H.* I by Leonard Huxley.
† This had been achieved by a course of hypnosis, described by Sybille Bedford in Chapter 2, volume 2 of her biography of Aldous.

His search for this road, we know, did not come only out of his philosophical interests; he helped himself by psychological experiments, by spiritual exercises . . . what we shall never know is where the virtuous circle begins and ends. My illness, which might have muddled and blackened everything, had been both the starting point and the arrival of this development . . . Aldous's illness, already, was a great step in the good direction or let us say, an enlightenment. And it encouraged me a good deal. We need not fear anything . . .

Maria's letter mentions two illnesses, hers and Aldous's, which triggered off this metamorphosis of Aldous. Both the illnesses were serious: Aldous nearly lost his remaining eyesight, attacked by very painful iritis, and Maria, always reticent about herself, was operated on for a cancerous growth about which absolutely no one was allowed to know. Above all not Aldous.

But Aldous did not want to know.

That it was not an easy life pierces through the lines of Maria's letters. 'It doesn't do to have one's way; I found that out long ago.' Sybille Bedford's biography, remarkable chronicle of two remarkable people, gives readers an insight to their lives, illuminated by Maria's transcendent letters to her sisters: a Maria whom neither Ottoline nor I ever knew at Garsington, refined and enriched beyond compare by the enduring love and fortitude of her creative life with Aldous. And this also revives the grief at the loss of Maria's journal, started before the last war with the express purpose of leaving a record of Aldous's life 'pour raconter la vie d'Aldous' – a double loss because Maria possessed the delicate, intuitive perceptions and attention which could so uniquely reflect the complex nature of Aldous.

Maria – exquisitely feminine, fastidious as the Princess and the Pea, with rare beauty and jewel-like eyes; bemused by her teenage 'refugee' life at Garsington; then sophisticated by her experiences in Italy with her reunited family, releasing her gaiety, her social gifts and deepening the intuition of her own truths.

Years later, neat and small, she could get into Matthew's jeans size 10 and, thus equipped, tackle the housework, the gardening, the constant heavy driving (knowing also what made the engine of the car go wrong) and the cooking; that done, type out pages and pages of Aldous's script, never critical of his work; and read to him by the hour; she read in monotone while Aldous, trained by his blindness to use his memory, listened quietly.

After Aldous's visit to us in August 1954, when he reported casually that Maria had had a 'small' relapse but was now recovered, we heard no further news of her health. Then suddenly in February 1955: 'Maria is very ill, seemingly without hope. Her cancer has suddenly exploded . . . she is coming back from hospital with a nurse she is attached to, and I will do my best to help alleviate her pains (by means of hypnosis – she is luckily a good subject). Think of her with all your love, and think of me too.' Soon after came Matthew's cable announcing her death.

Tragic and terrible was the bereavement – which Aldous talked of as 'being amputated'. He had truly lost his right arm, for she was, in every possible way, his true companion and sharer of his very life. How to live, now, this immense long everyday life alone?

The record of Maria's last days is published in Sybille Bedford's biography – also in Laura's (Aldous's second wife) *This Timeless Moment*, and best of all described by Aldous in *Island*. It is the heartbreaking document of a journey into death, illuminated by unearthly love.

Just a few months after Maria's death we met Aldous in New York. In the midst of this party with old friends Aldous told me that Eileen Garret, a great friend and also a remarkably honest medium, reported that Maria had 'been through' to her. Her message for Aldous was of deep acceptance of his guiding her in her last days. She heard all he said as she lay dying, especially about 'Eccot' and the 'Todi'. Eileen could not make out what it was and feared it was nonsense, but

Aldous knew at once. 'Eccot' was Meister Eckhart, the great mystic of the Middle Ages, and 'Todi' was the Tibetan Book of the Dead which Aldous and Maria had been reading together, and from which Aldous had learnt the way to help the dying, to loosen the chains of living. She also told Eileen that she had been over 'to the other side' several times, and came back to the sound of his voice (this is the case with many dying souls). Maria, said Eileen, was the happiest *spirit*, because of the help he had given her, because he was with her to the very end, taking away all fear.

'What can we believe?' I asked Aldous.

'I do not know; I cannot know.'

I walked back with him to his hotel; his strides too long for my step, hobbled by a narrow skirt, I could only keep up with difficulty; nor could I follow his exploration into that unfathomable world of after death which Eileen Garret seemed so familiar with. Perhaps he too was lost: 'I do not know . . . I cannot know . . .' Without looking back, he disappeared through the glass doors of his hotel.

*   *   *

More than a year later Aldous married the violinist Laura Archera. It was a great solace to us all, his loneliness had been unbearable. For seven years he found a new way of loving and living a full life. He resumed his yearly visits to us, while Laura went on to Turin to stay with her own family. Julian's possessiveness relaxed. Aldous enjoyed seeing his English friends and fellow members of the Huxley tribe.

I used to take him to museums and art galleries for which he had an insatiable appetite.* One never knew how much he could actually see for his uncanny instinct led him straight to one particular picture; on one occasion an etching by Rembrandt – the dark mass of watchers with a shaft of light on a

---

* At Sanary in the 1930s he had enjoyed painting and shown in his gouaches perception and skill. It made him deeply happy but the strain on his eyes was too great and this joy had to be abandoned.

group eagerly discussing. He drew out his small monocular and, as if talking to himself, explored the perception of the artist and its translation into form. It seemed to me, watching, that Aldous had, by his own intuition, sensed and shared the artist's visionary truth.

We also went to see films, and among them the most strange of our experiences was Tatzieff's record of volcanoes. A disturbing intimacy with Mother Earth daringly filmed from the very edge of an explosion, the violent outburst of red-hot rocks, a fast-moving coil of boiling lava. Aldous preferred to sit right under the screen rising almost vertically from his shaded eyes. I could not imagine how the scene registered in his sight, having myself to sit further back. We saw it twice, absolutely spellbound.

In *Memories*, Volume II, Julian tells of our weekend visits in 1963 with Aldous, to the Nichols at Lawford Hall, in Constable country, to K. and Jane Clark at Saltwood Castle and to Dartington, where the Elmhirsts were, as always, angelic and concerned; August weather was richly coloured and Leonard took us on exploring drives to the moors. From my diary I retrace the days:

17 August, 1963

We listen to Leonard telling about early tin-washing which 'perhaps' the Myceneans collected from Cornwall to replenish their shortages. There is a pool where a tame seal obeys commands, scratches his nose, claps his flippers and plays with a ball. Aldous watches, silent. The wind is blowing close to the ground, bending tall grasses into pale waves. Clouds throw their moving shadows over them. I mention this to Aldous, who quickly takes his monocular to see for himself. 'How could one describe the sunlight on the seal-pond' asks Aldous, 'as it shatters into wavelets? How difficult to describe nature.' He saw the flecks of light, his mind seeking the words – I only looked at the seal.

18 August

Last night Aldous was telling of his idea for his next book, a revalu-

ation of history which he would hold together by recounting the
tale, told by the Florentine of the 15th century, Vanzetti, about the
priest who was castrated by order of a Sienese potentate (whom he
had disobeyed) and who got back his severed balls so he could continue to officiate as priest, wearing them in a small bag about his
person. Aldous loves this story, and I remember his telling it to me
last year, in a grave penetrating voice, as we were riding home
together in the number 24 bus. The rest of the passengers listened
spellbound as the velvet voice pursued the episodes all up Fleet Road.

*   *   *

If it happened that Aldous's silences were soothing, understanding, sharing, they were also sometimes disturbing. Some
people tire one by talking too much, Aldous by talking too
little; by his detachment, by what could have been his distress
– or his defence. Who can tell? The palms of his hands cupping
his eyes, I have often seen him sitting motionless, in deep
meditation. One could only retreat, on tip-toes.

At the time his mind was playing with a vaguely formed
idea, which he tentatively outlined to Humphrey Osmond,
who had become a close confidant of his thoughts: 'I always
have the feeling, when I read history or see the greatest works
of art, that if we knew the right way to set about it, we could
do things far more strange and lovely than even the strangest
and loveliest in past history.' The theme and vision of this idea
was with him for many years, no doubt like many creative
artists the world over; we know from Laura's book that he
tried to explain it to her on his death-bed.

On his last visit but one, in 1962, we were lunching together
at the Tate Gallery when he surprised me by suddenly asking:
what could he write now – he needed a new subject? I came up
with the obvious answer: 'Why not write your life?' His
searching eye had a look of despair: 'How could I? All the
records were burnt in the fire!' – the heart-breaking reality of
that utter depredation. Aldous, a year or so before, beginning
to think of writing his memoirs, had asked Suzanne, Maria's

sister, to return Maria's letters to her. They had just arrived, and were still in their boxes when the fire devoured everything. 'It is odd to be starting from scratch at my age – with literally nothing in the way of possessions, books, mementoes, letters, diaries. I am evidently intended to learn a little in advance of the final denudation, that you can't take it with you'.*

At the Tate that day he had a look of despair, but as usual not a trace of self-pity. I remembered the moon looking down at us on the roof of Garsington, when he spoke of his mother's death, of his attack of blindness, of his brother Trev's tragic death. We were both very young then – in the presence of such sorrows I could find no word – nor could I, so many years after, sitting at lunch under the Rex Whistler frescoes. It was as if he had created a wall round himself, making words one could say meaningless and importunate.

'You are getting terribly remote,' I said to Aldous on August 22 as we were driving him to the airport. 'I feel remote,' he answered. 'I have nothing in common with the young now – they are only interested in sexual problems.' I remembered Jacques Caban's review of the French edition of Aldous's *Isle*: 'It is less the alienation of the social condition, which Huxley denounces: it is he himself who has not resigned himself to the frailty of the flesh. Like Swift, *frénétiquement* he attacks those two eternal monsters, Pain and Death . . . Could it be that Huxley so deeply loves this abominable worst of all worlds – where we live "cahin-caha" – and which he, too, cannot bear to leave? . . .'

We left him in the crowded, noisy waiting-room, already gone really, stooping over his brief-case to extract *The Times* after saying goodbye – so grey, so ghost-like, so truly remote from us all.

---

* Letter to Robert Hutchins – May 15 1961. Grover Smith's *Collected Letters of A.L.H.* (Chatto & Windus, 1969).

'I bring you sorrow; and the end of sorrow . . .' Did not Aldous have more than his share of sorrow? In his profound humility, his utter absence of resentment, his acceptance of grief as the common design of life, he reached a heroic quality. He died on November 22, 1963, aged sixty-nine, the day of John Kennedy's assassination.

Epilogue

Oh Saisons, Oh Châteaux,
Quelle âme est sans défauts?

RIMBAUD

This is the end of my tale: a tale strung together with memories, anchored here and there by my journal or a letter which brings back the time and occasion when it was written – sometimes etching the shadow behind the sculpture, the dark thread in the tapestry. This should not be left out nor unduly stretched: it belongs to both of us. Here, for instance, writes Leonard Elmhirst after a weekend Julian and I spent together at Dartington: a perceptive letter which I treasure, for it helped to guide me through. It is curious to remember now that particular occasion: the long train journey to Devon, Julian in a tormenting mood, wilful and destructive.

Had I not known, from the beginning, that it would not be easy? That I did not have the mettle and experience to cope with his vagrant moods, his need to dominate? God had never said to me: 'I shall light a candle of understanding in thine heart, which shall not be put out'.* At Dartington, that weekend, my distress was obvious.

Dartington,
November 1959

My dear Juliette,
 . . . I have, since you were here, been wanting to write to you about my own experience of living alongside persons with a strong

_____
* *Esdras, Apocrypha.*

sense of world-unity and mission, and so driven and confused by their imaginative tensions: these sometimes eliminate, almost entirely, from their field of consciousness the needs, hungers and feelings of those who, often at close quarters, try to serve and love – worship even; and yet, just at these moments when, like a faithful dog, they need a pat or a gesture, either draw an absolute blank or worse. In my own experience, and I have lived at close quarters with two world-conscious people in my time 'they know not what they do' – wrapped up in the world of their own imagination, locked-up in their contemplation of the universe; they can seem at moments as if they wanted to bite the helping hand they most need and even commit murder on the most sensitive part of one's devoted care and respect for them. They don't really mean it, and can be absolutely devastated when they discover of just what heinous crime they have been guilty. . . But it has somehow to be borne. 'Why don't you laugh at me when I do that or say that or behave like that, next time?'

But, by gum, it was no laughing matter – one's world had come to an end. But they don't know that . . . In the world there simply are not more than a few of these far-reaching people at a time, and they are immensely precious – for me Julian is one. They need all we can give and be, to give of their best; and so, through bitterness we learn, if possible without becoming bitter in return.

My 'learning', as Leonard wrote, 'through bitterness but without growing bitter in return' took many years of our lives together. It was often a poor job, with nothing to boast about; only a sense that there was a next day and a new hope for halcyon times between the clouds. Blessed among these are our long voyages: our explorations in Africa were repeated several times, taking us deeper into perceptions of its character, its problems and its terrible vulnerability. Then there was India and its multiple faces, Java and Bali where one wanted to stay for ever; Borobodur brooding in its sacredness; Thailand and its Buddhist reality; Angkor devoured before our very eyes by the sheer power of nature; Persia before it became tormented Iran; Syria and Lebanon, with clearer eyes after our official stay with Unesco; and later, Israel with its indestructible charisma.

On these occasions, Julian seemed to find his true self; neither euphoric nor depressed nor self-absorbed, but the most endearing, intimately generous and inspiring of loving companions. Meticulously planned, enriched by guidance from books and friends, every step was a discovery, a creative awakening of the art of seeing. An art it certainly is, rousing dormant faculties of perceptions, life-enhancing beyond description; added to which the enchantments being shared in perfect communion of spirits enriched every moment. Why did we not put a rucksack on our backs, and wander for ever round the munificent world? . . . Alas, we all know the answer.

★   ★   ★

Back in London, we continued to live in the gentle house acquired in 1943. Our lives were filled with the discipline of hard work, social encounters, nourishing friendships and deep family ties. We always loved this house, full of the trappings and furnishings of a lifetime, fated as they are to outlive the memories they carry. As I sit here, in Julian's library, surrounded by the tools of our work and the many things we collected together, I am supported by the friendly connivance of true companions.

Julian did not substantially affect our sons' destinies — probably wisely; he was too involved in his own problems to be deeply affected by theirs. Both Anthony and Francis, after their war service and university years, chose their own ways. Anthony, by his own efforts and choice, acquired a renowned knowledge of botany and horticulture, his thirty-odd books on these subjects crowned by his *Green Inheritance*, the book of the World Wild Life Year. Francis chose first biology and then anthropology as his field, writing of the Amazon Indians, the Haitians and even Lewis Carroll. They are both attracted by the deviations of their subjects, Anthony by the fantastic world of plants, Francis by the understanding of human quirks — both of which are apparently limitless. Their lives remain my deepest loving concern and blessing, their doings quite properly beyond my reach.

In 1966 Julian fell into what was to be his last nervous breakdown: a long and difficult one which led him after months of helpless depression into a waste land. It was when he finally began to recover, that I put to him the idea of writing his memoirs. The first volume was published in 1970, and he had just been correcting the proofs of the second in 1973 when he suffered a stroke. He was eighty-five, the years were leaving their mark on him. Mercifully it was but a slight stroke from which he recovered in due time, but those last years were changed, filling our lives with the tyranny of helplessness he was a very sick man. The ungentle daimon of his childhood seemed to have reasserted its power, confusing the mature spirit, transposing time in a manner of wish-fulfilment. I heard him say to his doctor: 'My wife died a few months ago; my mother is now looking after me.' Should I, in fact, have been just that? Did I fail to be a mother to a wayward child who, perhaps, never quite 'grew up'? The beloved mother, Julia Arnold, had never died in the hearts of her four children. She had now returned to shield her son from the terrors of the approaching night. Julian died on February 14, 1975.

*   *   *

In Lewis Carroll's *Sylvie and Bruno*, the Earl says to Sylvie: 'We waste so much pleasure in life by not paying attention.' We waste even more: deep communion with minds who give our being its spiritual habitat, its understanding of that ever-lasting problem – human destiny.

Could I live my life again, I would set myself to learn the art of paying attention. And then I might here, in this chronicle of what one could call a privileged involvement, have reaped a better harvest. What if too much had been told in candid retrospect – or perhaps too much left unsaid? The voice was heard. The words were written. The wind blows all away. We

die a little with every paragraph. Our withered leaves await
their gathering.

> We see, we heare, we feele, we taste,
> We smell the change in every flower,
> We only wish that all could last,
> And be as new still as the houre.
>
>

The Vision of Delight.
BEN JONSON

Index